Tea Rooms Northwest

Featuring Tea Rooms,
Tea Events,
and Tea Time Recipes

Sharron and John deMontigny

J&S Publishing
Corvallis, Oregon USA

The Tea Cup Graphics in this publication
are the property of Pat's Web Graphics.
Other photos are from the private albums of
J&S Publishing and/or were provided by the
Tea Room proprietors.

Cover photo by Renaude
Cover design by Karen Freeman

Also by Sharron and John deMontigny:
Tea Time Journal
Tea Rooms Northwest

J&S Publishing
2397 N.W. Kings Blvd. # 148
Corvallis, Oregon 97330 USA
Telephone: 541-753-1502
E-Mail: *demontigny@proaxis.com*
Web Site: *www.teatimeadventures.com*

ISBN # 0-9741814-2-0

Printed in the United States of America
Cascade Printing Company
Corvallis, Oregon USA

J&S Publishing

TABLE OF CONTENTS

About the Cover Photo

The very special "Thistle" tea set, which is featured on the cover was a gift from Sharron's brother and sister-in-law, Mike and Lorri Robertson. They live in Alexandria, Virginia, where Sharron's Scottish heritage is celebrated, and where they purchased this lovely tea set. The soft green Irish linen tablecloth was brought from the "Emerald Isle" by Sharron's dear aunt, Alice McClory Hurley, in the 1950s, and the depression glass plate was from a set belonging to her grandmother, Rose McClory Ritzenthaler. The gloves were first worn by Sharron in 1962. Again, Sharron's mom, O'Day Tynan Robertson, graces the cover, as do the pearls that were a gift from John to Sharron.

About the Photographer

Born in Canada, Renaude learned the love of photography at the elbow of her father, Etienne Grenier, also an accomplished photographer. Renaude migrated to the United States in 1968, and after raising a family, took up the art of photography while living in Los Angeles, California. When she and her family moved to Oregon, she discovered the beauty of the Oregon back roads. Passionate about still life photography, Renaude and her sister regularly roam dusty lanes and byways for inspirational glimpses of scenic barns and pastures.

Promoting the Love of Tea

The past two years, since we published the first edition of *Tea Rooms Northwest*, have been quite an adventure for us. We could never have foreseen how much joy our tea travels would bring us. As we ventured from tea room to tea room, we met some of the nicest people in the tea business. It was also quite enjoyable meeting fellow patrons who were anxious to share their tea experiences with us. We had the opportunity to do numerous book signings, and saw in others the enthusiasm we feel for "this thing called tea." Along the way we made many new friendships that we will cherish as we continue this exciting journey.

Our main interest in publishing this book is to encourage you, the tea lover, to see and visit the many tea rooms in the Northwest. Our intent is to share some personal observations, not to either endorse or critique any of them. We are not experts, we just thoroughly enjoy visiting tea rooms.

Tea Rooms Northwest is your resource for finding tea rooms, learning specific information about them, and getting updated information. Remember that prices, hours, locations, etc., change. Unfortunately, tearooms occasionally close, but, happily, others open. Some tea rooms are not wheelchair accessible, but that is usually due to their historic designation. Check our website *teatimeadventures.com* for regularly updated information. Please feel free to call or email us for information and updates.
Phone: 541-753-1502
e-mail: demontigny@proaxis.com.

As you take this book in hand, think of it as something that will bring you many fun and memorable hours spent in pursuit of the wonderful tea rooms it shares with you.

Happy Tea Times!

Sharron

Acknowledgments

We would like to thank the many people who took the time to contact us during the past two years. It was with their help that we were able to keep abreast of the many changes in Northwest tea rooms. Because of them, there are many more new tea rooms listed in the second edition of *Tea Rooms Northwest*.

Sincere thanks go out to Ruth Elliott, Brenda Hamilton, Sue Walker and Alicia Jacob for their invaluable help with proof-reading our material. It was an arduous job and their efforts are most appreciated. Special thanks go to Karen Freeman who did the lay-out for our cover. Also, many thanks to Irene Gresick, who shared her publishing expertise with us.

Last, but certainly not least, we want to acknowledge all of the tea room proprietors who returned our questionnaire, took our many phone calls, responded to our e-mails, shared favorite recipes, welcomed us to their tea rooms and in every way helped us complete this labor of love. We hope that we are representing them in a manner that pleases and benefits them.

Thanks

About the Authors

John and Sharron reside in Corvallis, Oregon, a college town midway between the mountains and the ocean. Yes, they are avid Oregon State University Beaver fans!

John was born in Quebec, Canada, and moved to the states when he was five, settling first on the East Coast. He eventually moved with his family to California, where he was raised. After high school, he enlisted in the Air Force, where he served for twenty-five years. After retirement in 1991, John went to work for Hewlett Packard, where he is still employed.

Sharron was born and raised in San Francisco and is proud to call herself a "fourth generation San Franciscan." She met John during the summer of 1963 and they were married in 1968, at which time she became a military wife. While raising their three children in California and Oregon, she owned a catering business. Upon their move to Corvallis in 1990, she gave up the business and became a cook for the men of Tau Kappa Epsilon Fraternity, whom she calls her "other family."

John and Sharron are also the proud grandparents of four boys and four girls. Fortunately, they all live nearby and are able to visit each other often. They are also wonderful tea companions.

Disclaimers

We made a sincere effort to find and include *ALL* the tearooms in the Northwest. However, we know that some are missing from this book. If you are a tea room owner or if you have a favorite tea room that is not in this guide, please let us know. We have also added some tea rooms in Northern California, but we have only been able to contact a small number of them.

Our website *teatimeadventures.com* will update this guide on a regular basis. Additional tea rooms will be listed in the next edition of *Tea Rooms Northwest.*

Everything is subject to change! To the best of our knowledge, the information we have included in this guide was accurate at the time of publication. Tea rooms may change their *prices* (*), days and hours of operation, location and menu offerings. Unfortunately, they also close or discontinue offering tea. We highly recommend that you call ahead before venturing out and remember… many tea rooms *require* reservations!

(*) The prices quoted in the British Columbia section are in Canadian funds.

Dedications

As with our first edition of *Tea Rooms Northwest*, we dedicate this book to our wonderful family: Stephen and Jennifer deMontigny, Todd and Alicia Jacob and Eric and Deanna Reisdorf, with loving appreciation for all their support and assistance during the writing of this book. We also dedicate it to our grandchildren Brandon, Ashley, Jason, Christian, Jessica, Daphne, Hannah and Marcus, who have added joy to our lives in so many ways

We especially dedicate it to all the tea room owners who gave us the basis for this book. Without them, there would be no book.

Tea with the Grandkids

Marcus at
The Tea Party

Daphne at Althea's

Jessica at Mrs. B's

Brandon

Ashley at Mrs. B's

Jason at Tranquility
Tea Room

Hannah at a Sister
Act Tea

Christian at
The Charms of Tea

The Origin of Tea Time

In the early 1800s in England, dinner was usually served quite late at night. It is said that Anna, the Duchess of Bedford, started having hunger pangs while awaiting the evening meal, which was often served around 9:00 p.m. She requested that a tray of bread and butter, along with a pot of tea, be sent to her room. Soon, along with the tea and bread, dainty pastries with clotted cream and preserves were added. It then became the custom for her to invite some society ladies to join her and "tea time" came into being. Though intended to be an evening snack, it is now what many of us think of as afternoon tea, and it is served anywhere between 11 a.m. and 4 p.m. The other wording for afternoon tea was low tea, as it was served at a low table, much like our modern coffee table.

High tea was actually the evening meal of the common people, and it was served at the dinner table, or high table. Served around 6 p.m., High tea consisted of trays of meats, cheeses, fish or eggs along with bread and butter, cake and tea. Side dishes were often added to the meal. Today, many tea rooms serve a Ploughman's Plate, which is similar to the traditional high tea.

It seems that one was more suited to women and the other to men. One was a diversion and the other a meal for the working man!

Theme Teas

One of the most enjoyable ways to enjoy tea with friends is to hostess a theme tea. I am including some suggestions which are easy and fun ... and anyone can do them! For colored bread, order your bread from a bakery and request your desired color.

Seasonal decorations may be used to adorn your table, and napkins and tablecloths in the appropriate colors complete the theme. Individual favor which match the theme are always a nice touch.

Valentine Tea

Strawberry slush
Cherry scone
Lemon curd and Devonshire cream
Stuffed cherry tomato
Cranberry chicken salad on pink bread
Sun-dried tomato and basil on crostini
Open-faced cucumber on pink bread round
Heart-shaped cherry cookie
White chocolate brownie with pink frosting
Strawberry tart
Rose flavored tea

Fall Tea

Apricot scones
Devonshire cream and apricot jam
Warm fruit compote
Cucumber sandwiches on yellow bread
Turkey and golden raisin sandwich
Cheese and walnut sandwich
Maple shortbread
Pumpkin tart
Ginger spice cake
Yorkshire Gold Tea

Saint Patrick's Day Tea

Colcannon soup
Green salad with avocado and grapefruit
Irish soda bread
Open-faced corned beef on rye round
Cucumber/dill sandwich
Bacon/avocado sandwich
Irish whiskey cake
Pistachio tart
Shamrock cookie
Irish Breakfast Tea

Down-on-the-Farm Tea

Fresh fruit medley
Savory scone with butter
Roast beef with horseradish on whole wheat
Shredded carrot and pineapple on white bread
Egg salad ribbon sandwich
Chicken biscuit
Ham asparagus roll-up
Mini broccoli quiche
Bacon Ranch Pinwheel
Mini apple pie tart
Lemon Madeleine
Strawberry lemonade

Hawaiian Luau Tea

Sweet potato scones with Devonshire cream
Pineapple/cream cheese sandwich
Ham sandwich with apricot jam and cream cheese
Shrimp and celery finger sandwich
Chicken and chopped macadamia nut wrap
Pork pie on filo
Pineapple cookie
Coconut cake square
Banana tartlet
Iced Green Tea Paradise

Brewing Tips

Always start with cold water.
Heat your teapot with warm water.
Add one teaspoon of tea leaves per cup
(a heaping teaspoon for iced).
Do not over-boil the water.

Black Teas

Bring water just to a boil and remove from heat.
Add tea and steep for 5 minutes. If you like a
stronger, pungent cup of tea, add a bit more tea.
Steeping longer than 5 minutes may produce a
bitter tea. Add hot water if tea is too strong.

Green and Pouchong Teas

Bring water to a pre-boil and remove from heat.
Add tea and steep 3 minutes. Longer steeping
will cause tea to be bitter. Quality green teas can
be steeped more than once.

Oolong and White Teas

Bring water to a pre-boil. Add tea and steep 4-6
minutes. Oolongs can vary in steeping time, so
taste to test. They can be re-steeped several
times.

Tisanes (Herbals)

Bring water to a rolling boil. Add herbs, one
heaping teaspoon per cup (for iced herbals, add
one tablespoon). Steep 5-9 minutes. Herbs will
not get bitter if left longer.

What is a Tea Room?

A tea room is a place where you can go to escape the realities of daily life. It is not a restaurant, but a comfort and place to take refuge. It is a place where you feel pampered and special, a place where you can share your deepest feelings with your best friend.

Time stands still in a tea room, it is not a rushed event. You leisurely sit and talk. You are not there to eat or even to drink tea, but rather to relax and enjoy the moment of friendship.

Author unknown

Welcome

to

Oregon

A La Fontaine Tea Room

and Day Spa
1708 Springhill Drive N.W.
Albany, Oregon 97321
541-928-0747 / 800-531-4306
l.bardell@juno.com / www.alafontaine.com

From I-5, follow signs for downtown Albany, then for Hwy 20 / Corvallis. Cross the bridge, take a right and go approximately 1 mile (between Quarry and Ferguson Streets). Just past Quarry, watch for the Nebergal intersection.

More than a tea room, A La Fontaine offers a recipe for relaxation along with afternoon tea. The garden-style, turn of the century tea room, is done in yellow with black French toile accents. French doors open to a billowy, curtained, private, garden room which features a demitasse tea tasting bar. There are several outdoor settings which Linda and Andrea use during the summer - patio, veranda, lawn and garden.

The Full Afternoon Tea consists of scone or crumpet, crème fraichê, lemon curd, fruit, a variety of tea sandwiches, wrap or quiche, crackers and cheese and dessert for $24.99. This tea is offered to groups of four or more and for special events only. This would be a great location to hold a birthday, anniversary, shower or corporate meeting. The proprietors will work with food allergies and special diets and offer whole foods/organic whenever possible.

Doll collectors may want to gather for tea since another business, L.B. Designs, a doll sculpting studio and school, is located on the premises.

Linda and Andrea offer a spa menu that features everything from massages and facials to mineral soaks and a quiet room. A Spa Plate can be added to any spa session and it includes an arrangement of fruit, cheese and crackers, sandwich, vegetables, and dessert for $15.

Treat yourself to a special day at Touch of Class Day Spa.

MC/V/AE/DEB/DIS/Checks
Wheelchair Accessible
Parking Lot

Open Tuesday through Saturday. spa treatments are by appointment. Tea time is by reservation 2 weeks in advance. Cancellations required.

Proprietor's
*Autograph*_____*Date*_____

Afternoon Delight

Tea Room and Gift Shop
831 S.E. Cass Street
Roseburg, Oregon 97470
541-677-9010

From I-5, take exit 124 and go East toward downtown. At Rose Street turn right. Go one block to Cass Street and turn left. The tea room is in the middle of the block on the right.

What a treat to now have a tea room in the place we called home for 10 years!. Opened in 2002, Afternoon Delight surely lives up to its name. The soft background music, pale lavender walls and garden theme immediately welcome you. They invite one to "come in and sit a while," enjoying one of life's simple pleasures ... afternoon tea. Sharon Martel has carried out the garden theme with the use of floral table coverings and napkins, floral border surrounding the room, and greenery and flowers placed about the room.

As for the tea offerings, there are five to choose from, starting with a Sandwich or Dessert Tea for $4.95 to the High Tea for $12.95. High Tea includes 2 scones, 5 tea sandwiches and savories, meat pastry and 5 desserts. The Afternoon Tea, priced at $10.95, offers 1 scone, 5 tea sandwiches and savories and 5 tea desserts. For $8.95, the low-carb tea has a garden salad with tomatoes, cucumbers, egg and chicken served with low-carb dressing and a low-carb muffin. A garden salad or bowl of soup may be substituted for the chicken pastry on High Tea. A pot of Long Bottom Tea from Hillsboro, Oregon, is included with all the teas. Sharon offers a lunch special of cup of soup, 1/2 sandwich and pot of tea for $5.95. Some menu items are available à la carte.

Special teas are offered seasonally, and the tea room may be reserved after hours for showers, birthdays, anniversaries, business meetings, etc.

 After enjoying your respite from reality, take time to browse through the "delightful" gift area.

MC/V/DIS/Checks
Wheelchair Accessible
Lot and Street Parking

Hours of operation are Tuesday through Friday 11 - 4 and Saturday 11-3. The last tea is served 30 minutes before closing. One-day advance reservations are required for groups of 5 or more and are recommended for others. There is a $1.50 split-plate charge.

Proprietor's
Autograph_____Date_____

Afternoon Tea by Stephanie

508 S.E. 9th Avenue
Canby, Oregon 97013
503-266-7612
stephtea@juno.com

Owner Stephanie Allen is an instructor for tea and etiquette. Her presentations are at various locations in the Northwest.

Stephanie does presentations for women, "For the Love of Teacups" and "Silver, Enriching Our Lives", as well as, workshops for youth, which are age specific. One class which is offered is Etiquette for Youth for 8 to 12 year olds, which ends with a tea party. The "Dining With Style for Teens" includes a three-course dinner to practice their new skills. For the 4 to 7 year olds, there are Imaginary Tea Parties complete with tea sets, hats and gloves. These classes are taught at various locations including the Historic Deepwood Estate in Salem and Carnegie Center in Oregon City. Special dietary needs can be accommodated with advance notice.

Stephanie retails Simpson and Vale teas, along with her special tea accessories, at Deepwood Estate and Carnegie Center.

She is making plans to offer traditional teas in the near future.

MC/V/and Checks Accepted

For dates and times of workshops, or to schedule your own, contact Stephanie directly.

Proprietor's
*Autograph*_____*Date*_____

Albertina's

Albertina Kerr Center
424 N.E. 22nd Avenue
Portland, Oregon 97232
503-231-3909 / 503-231-0216
www.albertinakerr.org

*They are located near Lloyd Center and Oregon Convention Center close to
the intersection of Sandy Boulevard and 20th.*

The house that has become The Shops at Albertina Kerr has a long and
interesting history. Located on land that was donated by Alexander Kerr,
founder of the Kerr Jar Manufacturing Co., it became a care center for
children in 1921. The nursery closed in 1967 then re-opened in 1981 as the
Old Kerr Nursery, housing the present volunteer-staffed Shops at Albertina
Kerr. Some of the current programs which benefit from the shops include
foster care for children with special needs, early intervention programs,
psychiatric residential services, group home and supportive-living services
for people with developmental disabilities and more. The businesses which
comprise The Shops at Albertina Kerr include a gift shop, antiques shop,
thrift shop and Albertina's, which offers luncheons and catering.

Though primarily a luncheon restaurant, Albertina's is described as
having a "tea room" atmosphere. Once a year that atmosphere becomes a
reality when a Valentine's Tea is offered on a Saturday afternoon in
February. A sample menu consists of ribbon tea sandwiches, chive and egg
pinwheels, chicken-almond fingers, lemon tartlets, fudge party bars,
chocolate-dipped strawberries, sugared grapes and tea or coffee. Sherry and
wine may be purchased at an additional cost.

This would be a wonderful opportunity to take tea in a very special
setting while helping out this very worthwhile organization. Mark your
calendar now so you don't forget about this very special event!

The property is available to rent for special events and there is an in-
house caterer.

MC/V/Checks
Wheelchair Accessible
Lot and Street Parking

*Luncheon seatings are 11:30 and 1, Monday through Friday. Reservations
are recommended. They offer an annual Valentine's Tea.*

Proprietor's
*Autograph*_____*Date*_____

Althea's Tea Room

184 S.E. Oak Street
Dallas, Oregon 97338
503-831-4777
pme16@msn.com

Heading west from Salem on Hwy 22, follow signs to Dallas. Once in Dallas, at the second signal keep to the left onto Main Street. Continue to Oak Street and turn left. The tea room is on the left-hand side at the end of the block.

Now celebrating her second year in business, Patricia, along with her daughter Frances, continues to offer a warm and friendly place to take afternoon tea. I am sure her mother, for whom the tea room is named, is beaming with pride.

Situated in an older building in the downtown area, Althea's offers three rooms for your "tea sipping" pleasure. All of the rooms feature large lace-covered windows, tables decked out in pink rose-patterned cloths with coordinating napkins, and white "doilies" at each place setting. Customers select their cup and saucer from one of the antique cabinets which are situated in the two main rooms. The tea pots are wrapped in pretty cozies and the tea sets are presented on tiered servers.

There are three tea sets to choose from. The first is Dena's Tea, which consists of tea sandwiches, fresh fruit, assorted sweets and a delicious scone with clotted cream, lemon curd and strawberry jam for $9.95. The other two selections are Hanna's Tea, which is scones and tea for $4.95 and Bethany's Tea, which is tea sandwiches, cheese selection, seasonal fruit, savories, assorted sweets, scones with all the trimmings and a pot of tea for $12.95.

Lunch items are available and may include soup or quiche of the day, sandwiches, or Fran's Pear Salad. Specialty desserts are featured as well as coffee, lemonade and iced tea. Theme and holiday teas are offered through

out the year. Groups are welcome with advance arrangements. There is a selection of gifts available for purchase.

MC/V/Checks
Wheelchair Accessible
Free Street Parking

The tea room is open 11-4, Tuesday through Saturday. Lunch is served 11- 2. The last seating for tea is 3 p.m. Tea reservations are required 24-hours in advance for more that 4 people and are recommended for all others. Tea and scones are served all day.

Proprietor's
Autograph_____Date_____

24

Amelia's Antiques

and Bakery
370 River Road
Eugene, Oregon 97404
541-688-3900
kathleenhall2000@yahoo.com
thetreasureseekers.com

From I-5, take Beltline west to the Santa Clara exit and go left onto River Road. The tea room is approximately 5 miles down on the right. You can also take Hwy 126 west to 6th Avenue. Turn right on Chambers and the tea room is one block down on the left, after the over-pass. The nearest cross street is Briarcliff.

This tea room is located in a period home which is listed on the historic register, and these charming homes are some of my favorite places to take afternoon tea. One can easily imagine the lady of the house serving tea here in 1899, shortly after the house was built. The owners, Kathi and Tami, offer tea in the "country casual" downstairs room or the lovely "pink room", which overlooks the garden from the second floor. Weather permitting, tea is also offered in the garden under the lilacs. The tea tables are covered with vintage linens and napkins, and the tables and table service are also vintage.

Anytime treats are: 2 scones with Devonshire cream and jam for $3.25 or a dessert for $3.95. Tea or coffee is an additional $1 per person. High Tea, which is priced at $17.50 per person, includes scones, finger sandwiches, soup, fruit, tea desserts and bottomless tea.

Lunch is offered daily from 11-3 and the choices are soup, sandwich, quiche, fruit cup with whipped cream or fruit plate with whipped cream. The prices range from $2.75 to $5.95. Vegetarian is offered daily.

Kathi calls their tea room comfortable and cozy, and she says they treat everyone like family. That's a wonderful environment in which to enjoy a leisurely afternoon tea.

MC/V/DEB/Checks
Not Wheelchair Accessible
Lot Parking

The shop is open Monday through Saturday from 10 to 5. Tea is offered from 10 to 4. The last tea is served at 4. Reservations for groups of 8 or more may be made up to the day of the scheduled tea. Reservations are also required for theme teas.

Proprietor's
*Autograph*_____*Date*_____

25

An Olde World Charm

Tea House and Garden
31277 S.E. Highway 26
Boring, Oregon 97009
anoldeworldcharm@aol.com

Take I-205 to Estacada. Go through Damascus into Boring. Cross the Hwy 26 overpass and look for "Ashleys" at Old Swiss Village on the right. From I-84 E, take exit 16, follow through Gresham towards Mt. Hood to exit 212.

Paula Johnson is thoroughly enjoying her new venture as tea shop owner, a title she acquired in 2004. She has taken a charming A-framed building and turned it into what she calls, "Old American with a British flair!" Each room has a special name - Grande Dining Tea Room and Sisters Garden Tea Room. The tables and chairs in both rooms are eclectic, as are the cups and saucers, teapots, dishes and linens.

Paula aims to please and has numerous tea sets from which to choose. They vary in price from $8 for the Poets Ryme offering soup and scone to The Imperial Tea which includes soup, assorted tea sandwiches, chicken, cranberry scone, fruit, tea desserts, scone and a chocolate course for $20. Other Tea Luncheon choices are a Countess Tea with assorted tea sandwiches, fruit and tea desserts for $8, and the following teas which are all $12: Lady Lucy's Tea with Albacore salad, scone, fruit, tea desserts and a chocolate course, the Heiresses Tea has assorted tea sandwiches, chicken, cranberry and a chocolate course; and the Kingmaker Tea offering soup, chicken cranberry scone, fruit and tea desserts. The Boston Tea party includes assorted sandwiches, fruit, tea desserts and a choice of coffee, cocoa or cider for $14.

Finally the Royal Tea Dining offers assorted tea sandwiches, scone, fruit, tea desserts and a chocolate course for $18.

Numerous items may be added to your order for a nominal charge. For small appetites you may choose the Fair Dame - tea sandwiches and tea desserts for $8 or the Brave Knight - a scone for $6. Every tea includes jam and cream as well as a pot of Culinary Tea.

Paula offers take-out orders, catering is available and private parties, (adult's and children's) can be arranged. Special dietary needs can be accommodated.

MC/V/DEB/Checks   Wheelchair Accessible   Ample Lot Parking

Open Monday through Thursday 11-6, Friday & Saturday 11-8 and Sunday 1-6. Last tea is at 4:30 except for Sunday, which is 7:30. Reservations are required, preferably 3 days ahead. There is a. 48-hour cancellation policy.

Proprietor's
Autograph_____Date_____

The Anzac Tea Parlour

218 W. 4th Street
The Dalles, Oregon 97058
541-296-5877
eagy@gorge.net / www.anzacteaparlour.com

Take I-84 eastbound to exit 84. Continue to Liberty Street, turn right. Turn right again on 4th Street. The tea parlor is on the left. I-84 westbound, take downtown exit, continue to Liberty. Turn left, go 2 blocks and turn right on 4th Street. The tea parlor is on the left near St. Peter's Landmark Church.

Opened in 2004 by Bev Eagy, this tea room's name stands for Australian New Zealand Army Corps. Located in the historic 1864 home of Northwest cattle king Ben Snipes, the ambiance is an Australian tea parlour in an historic setting. Bev lived in Australia for 20 years and says she has brought a taste of Australia to the beautiful Columbia River Gorge.

A bit if interesting information … Aussies call cookies "biscuits." The famous ANZAC biscuits are crisp cookies made for the ANZAC soldiers during WWI.

The tea offerings are numerous and interesting. Two tea settings are available for $4.50 - Crumpets and Tea or The Anzac Sampler, which offers chicken almond and cucumber sandwiches, sun-dried tomato quiche, petite Anzac biscuit and a scone. There are four different tea settings for $7.95. One of them is the "Good On Ya" Healthy Tea includes fruit and veggie plate with Aussie Ranch dip, Viva's healthy crackers and cheese, and a scone with sugar-free Devonshire cream and jam. "The Australian Romance" High Tea, which is offered for $15, includes almond chicken and cucumber sandwiches, sun-dried tomato quiche, petite ANZAC biscuit, seasonal chocolate dipped strawberry, Australian cream scone, Marionberry scone and a fresh-baked dessert. A fresh-baked dessert choice is available each day. All that with a bottomless pot of tea! The house tea is 2T (Australian).

There is a take-away menu, and catering is available. The gift hutch, which offers their house tea, is a must stop.

Checks/Cash
Wheelchair Accessible
Free Street Parking

Hours of operation are Tuesday through Saturday 11-4.

Proprietor's
Autograph_____Date_____

Ashland Springs Hotel

212 East Main Street
Ashland, Oregon 97520
541-488-5558 / 888-795-4545
www.ashlandspringshotel.com

Northbound I-5, take exit 11 onto Hwy 99. Go 5 mile to down-town. Turn left on 1st. Southbound take exit 19 go right to 1st light, left at Hwy 99. Go 2 miles. The hotel is at 1st and E. Main Street.

The 1925 Ashland Springs Hotel, which is a historic landmark, offers a Sunday afternoon tea at the hotel's restaurant, LARKS Home Kitchen Cuisine. The tables are covered with floor-length linen cloths and are set with crisp napkins, silver accessories and fine china. Grand windows, the artwork and loom chairs painted in sage, olive and mustard give a casual, eclectic feel.

Afternoon tea, which began in 2000, offers a pot of Harney & Sons tea, assorted tea sandwiches, house baked scones with strawberry preserves, lemon curd and Devonshire Cream, smoked Oregon salmon, local cheeses, chocolate dipped fruit, apricot tart and your choice of raspberry cordial, dry sack sherry or sparkling cider. Tiered servers adorn the tables and the cost per person is $25. Special dietary needs can be accommodated with prior arrangements.

The Ashland Springs Hotel is conveniently located near the Shakespeare Festival venues and the Oregon Cabaret Theater. Also near the hotel are the many quaint shops and boutiques for which Ashland is known. Within walking distance is the beautiful Lithia Park which offers many walking trails and points of interest. I think it is apparent that a weekend at the Ashland Springs Hotel is the ideal place to relax and pamper yourself, and tea in the afternoon is the perfect way to spend a Sunday afternoon there.

Wheelchair accessible
MC/V/AE/DC/DIS/JCB/Checks
Room Charge Accepted
Lot Parking for Hotel Guests
Free Street Parking

The restaurant is open 7 days a week from 11:30 a.m. to midnight. Tea is served on Sundays from 2:30 to 4:30. Reservations are required. Large groups and private parties can be accommodated with prior reservation. There is a 24-hour cancellation policy.

Proprietor's
Autograph_____Date_____

Blue Angel Heavenly Delectables

10500 S.E. 26th # A33
Milwaukie, Oregon 97222
503-975-9744
blueangelbake@yahoo.com

Teas are on-location and the place is to be determined at time of booking.

Elise Hamilton offers private teas only, either at your location of choice or at the historic Broetje House in Milwaukie. Built in 1889, the home offers the perfect ambiance for your special tea. The banquet room can seat up to 150 people and is available for weddings, retirements, birthdays and other events.

Blue Angel Custom Bakery uses only the freshest, highest quality, natural ingredients to prepare your unique menu. Many of the recipes are one of a kind and each menu is made to order. The tea menu offers tea and scones or Afternoon Tea up to a High Tea package. All teas include scones and there is a list of 74 to choose from. Dessert is included in High Tea only but may be added to the other teas at nominal cost per person. Tea Zone is the house tea and coffee is available upon request.

Some of the tea choices include entrée soup or salad and the selection is extensive. Elise encourages you to make your event unique by offering you some basic packages to which you may add selected items. All packages include a choice of Premium Exotic Tea.

Specialty items are a tart, pastries and an old family recipe for potato cheese enchiritos. As for dessert ... just reading the list was a pleasure! There are bars, tortes, tarts, crisps, cakes, cookies, breads and muffins. Where to begin?

MC/V/Checks
Wheelchair Accessible at Broetje House
Large Parking Lot at Broetje House

Tea is by reservation only. A 50% non-refundable deposit is required at time of booking. Call for further information.

Proprietor's
*Autograph*_____*Date*_____

Boccherini's Coffee & Tea House

208 1st Avenue SW
Albany, Oregon 97321
541-926-6703
boccherine@peak.org

*From I-5, take the Albany exit and follow the signs for
Corvallis/downtown Albany. At First Street, take a left.
Boccherini's is one block down across from Wyatt's.*

This is one of the many charming shops that line the historic district of
downtown Albany. The building, which is deep and narrow, sports brick
walls on both sides and high ceilings that seem to go on forever. On the left
is a long, curved counter where coffee and tea as well as delicious pastries
and lunch items may be purchased. Once you get your order, comfortable
tables and chairs line the walls where locals visit, read the paper or just relax
for a while.

At the back of the building, tables may be put together for a more
comfortable group gathering. That is where Wendy Kirbey serves special tea
items to those lucky people who are her guests for a couple of hours.

Wendy's tea offerings are numerous and unlimited. All include tea and
you are invited to try as many as you like.. These are samplings of her tea
menu: the Light Temptations offers a cup of soup, finger sandwiches and
scone for $6.95; a scone with tea is $3.75; a cup of soup or small salad and
finger sandwiches is $5.75. The Temptation has pastries, cookies, cake and
cheesecake for $7.50. Finally, Traditional Afternoon Tea includes scone, tea
sandwiches, savories, small salad and dessert tray for $11.95. Those who
wish to do so can order off the lunch menu. Scones are served with cream
and jam.

Coffee may be ordered and dietary needs can be
accommodated with prior arrangements. A large
selection of teas is sold in bulk. Their house tea is
Montana Tea & Spice but they also sell Barnes &
Watson and Taylors of Harrogate.

Checks/ Cash   Wheelchair Accessible
Free Street Parking

*Tea is available 7 days a week 11-3:30 by reservations with 24-hour notice.
Groups from 2 to 12 can be accommodated and there is a one-day
cancellation policy. Holiday and theme teas are offered.*

Proprietor's
Autograph_____Date_____

Historic Broetje House

3101 S.E. Courtney Road
Milwaukie, Oregon 97222
503-659-8860
thebroetjehouse@aol.com
www.thebroetjehouse.com

From I-205, take exit 11. Turn left and go to the second stop light. Turn right onto Oatfield Road. Travel 3½ miles and you will see Broetje House on the left.

Lorraine and Lois offer teas in the Historic Broetje House, a Queen Anne Farm house, circa 1889. The original house has retained its historic elegance while a special-events facility has been added adjacent to the house. The two buildings are connected by a lovely glass and tiled breezeway, which offers a view of the beautifully manicured lawn and lovely gardens.

Teas may be arranged for groups of up to 80 person. A typical tea for 25 people would be $25 per person, which would meet the $475 minimum. This is a three-course tea and it includes tea, assorted tea sandwiches, fresh fruit, scones, and desserts. A tea and desserts event would have a $250 minimum. There is an assortment of tea labels to choose from to accompany your tea set. Coffee is also available.

If you are interested in booking a luncheon or dinner event, there is an extensive menu from which to choose. Groups of up to 150 can be accommodated. The location is also perfect for weddings, either inside by the fireplace or outside by the gazebo. Check their website for more details.

MC/V/AE/Checks
Wheelchair Accessible
Parking Lot

Teas are served by reservation with a two week notice. They are served Monday through Friday only.

Proprietor's
*Autograph*_____*Date*_____

Butteville General Store

10767 Butte Street. N.E.
Aurora, Oregon 97002
503-678-1605
forrestgalley@msn.com / www.buttevillegeneralstore.com

From I-5, take exit 282B (Charbonneau) and drive west on Butteville Road
for approximately 5 miles. The road follows the Willamette River.

Just a short distance from the freeway, in a lovely little oasis, sits a real gem called the Butteville Store. This 1863 building, with its French Prairie design, is a historical treasure. As you sit and sip, you are aware that not much has changed in this building in over 140 years. Others before you probably enjoyed our favorite beverage in the very same location by the window, overlooking the expansive front porch. You are grateful that Rob and Barbara chose to offer tea in this very special "spot in the road."

Afternoon Tea, which is $15 per person, offers a pot of tea, scones, Marionberry jam, Devon Cream, tea sandwiches and a variety of desserts. If you are looking for something smaller, you may choose a pot of tea and scones for $6. Tea is served in the rustic setting of the general store, surrounded by antiques and other memorabilia. Weather permitting, tea is served on the multi-level porch beside the building.

Besides tea, deli items are available and they include soup, sandwiches and salads, as well as numerous beverages and desserts. Friday night is Pizza night, and Candlelit Heritage Dinners are presented periodically.

After a leisurely tea, take a little extra time to look about the store at the many items that are available for purchase. They include items that you would find in a historic general store, candles, soaps, etc. The Forrest Gallery offers paintings, ceramics, hand-woven baskets, and blown glass, plus more local artists work.

The store is part of Champoeg State Heritage Area and is another Oregon treasure. Take time to admire and appreciate her!

MC/V/Cash   Wheelchair Accessible
Free Street and Lot Parking

Store hours are seasonal and teas are by reservation only. Call for specifics.

Proprietor's
Autograph_____Date_____

The Campbell House Inn

B & B and Tea Room
252 Pearl Street
Eugene, Oregon 97401 / 541-343-1119
www.campbellhouse.com / campbellhouse@campbellhouse.com

From I-5, take exit 194B onto I-105 then take the Coburg/Downtown exit. Stay left and follow City Center/Mall signs. Cross river, turn right at 2nd exit (Downtown/Hult Center-Hwy 126). Make an immediate right at the signal onto High Street. Turn left on 5th Avenue then turn right on to Pearl Street. You will see the Inn on the left side of the street. Pull into the drive at the sign and enter the large parking lot.

This lovely bed and breakfast is located at the foot of Skinners Butte, within walking distance to 5th Street Market and other spots of interest. An expansive Victorian House situated on a hillside, it immediately impressed you as you drive up to it. More delights await you upon entering. Beautiful antiques and room décor are featured in the 19 guestrooms as well as the charming public rooms. The lobby features a gift nook which offers sweatshirts, birdhouses, CDs, cards and more.

Afternoon tea begins with a delicious frozen mousse drizzled with berry syrup, followed by scones with jam and cream. The last two courses are served together on a tiered server and consist of three types of finger sandwiches and assorted desserts, which may be apricot truffles, cream puffs, fruitcake, fruit and nut bread or a chocolate truffle. Tea is poured by charming and friendly servers, who also offer additional sandwiches. Other beverages are available upon request. The cost of the tea is $25 per person, and the Christmas teas may includes carolers or a roving storyteller for entertainment.

Children's teas are offered at noon during the year at a cost of $18 per child, and they may have special character themes such as American Girl or Harry Potter.

Dinner is now served in the Inn Thursday through Saturday from 6:30-9, with entrees ranging in price from $12-$25 and featuring Northwest cuisine. Soups, salads, appetizers and desserts are also offered. Special diets may be accommodated.

MC/V/DIS/AV/DEB/Checks
Wheelchair Accessible   Lot Parking

Special teas are offered during the year including Mother's Day weekend and on specific weekends during December. Reservations required. Private teas may be arranged. Call for information regarding groups.

Proprietor's
*Autograph*_____*Date*_____

The Charms of Tea

333 First Avenue West
Albany, Oregon 97321
541-928-9475

From I-5, take the Albany exit. Follow the signs to Hwy 20 (Corvallis/ Albany City Center). Turn left on 1st Avenue and go 2½ blocks. The Charms of Tea is on the right-hand side, across from the Wells Fargo parking lot.

In 2004 Shannon Miller moved her tea room just down the street from its previous location. "Charm" certainly describes her new pink and white "eclectic, shabby chic and slightly retro" tea room. White furniture, rose-hued walls, and soft-pink roses placed liberally about the room invite you to leave your cares at the door. Should you be taking tea alone, I recommend that you head straight to the back of the shop. In that area, Shannon has recreated a very comfortable retreat, complete with wall shelves of memorabilia, a bird cage, books, a trunk of vintage hats, a fountain and a wonderful collection of ink drawings by her grandmother. You are invited to take in and enjoy the beautiful surroundings and cozy ambiance, where Shannon tries to take you back to when life was much slower-paced. She asks you to "relax, listen to music, smell the aromas and visit with your friends."

There are 5 tea sets to choose from: The Poet's Tea offers soup, salad and a scone for $7.25; the Pamper Yourself tea is sorbet, scone and 3 desserts for $7.95 and the Red Letter Tea includes soup, 3 finger sandwiches and a scone for $8.75. For more substantial teas, choose from the Empress Tea of sorbet or fruit, 3 finger sandwiches, a scone, 2 savories and 3 desserts for $9.95; or the Regal Tea which includes sorbet or fruit, soup, 3 tea sandwiches, 2 savories, a scone and 3 desserts for $11.95. All include a pot of tea. If you prefer, there is a lunch menu to select from as well. Coffee is available upon request and special dietary needs can be accommodated.

A small gift area sells tea-related items such as clotted cream and lemon curd as well as books, cards, tea accessories and large selection of loose teas. Outside catering is available and groups are welcome.

The tea room shares space with Aromatique - The Body Care Shoppe. Be sure to take time to check out the many "pamper yourself" items.

MC/V/DIS/Checks   Wheelchair Accessible   Lot & Free Street Parking

The tea room is open 11-4 Monday through Saturday. The last seating is 3. Sunday tea is available by reservation. There are also many evening events throughout the year.

Proprietor's
Autograph_____Date_____

34

The Coburg Inn

Restaurant and Events Center
91108 N. Willamette
Coburg, Oregon 97408
541-485-0711 / 541-905-2696
John@Coburginn.com
www.coburginn.com

From I-5, take the Beltline exit. From Beltline take the Coburg exit north and follow that road to Coburg. The inn is in the center of town on the left hand side of the street.

I was thrilled to hear that tea is again being served at the Coburg Inn. This lovely Italianate mansion, located in the center of town, is the perfect location to take a break from browsing the antique stores and gift shops.

Built in 1877 by the Van Duyn family, the Coburg Inn has a long standing tradition of hosting glamorous events. In the 1960s, this residential structure was turned into the 5-star Coburg Inn Restaurant, where locals celebrated their most cherished occasions. The current owners are now restoring the inn's tradition, and are offering guests a piece of Coburg's heritage.

Tea is served in the beautiful dining room, where tables are covered in burgundy linens and the chairs are draped in white covers that reach the floor. Lovely bows adorn the chair backs. White columns break up the main room, and a large entryway and expansive opening connects that room with the other dining area. Both rooms enjoy the natural light which comes from the many windows on three sides of the buildings main floor. When weather permits, tea may be taken on the wide porch that wraps around two sides of the inn.

The Afternoon Tea buffet, which is offered for $10, includes the following: a variety of scones with clotted cream and jam, an assortment of finger sandwiches, such as turkey/pecan, cucumber or smoked salmon, fresh fruit medley, a marinated vegetable salad, and a dessert selection. Unlimited tea, iced or hot, is also included.

The ambiance is comfortable, the service friendly and the food very tasty! This is a great way to take time for yourself on a Sunday afternoon.

V/MC/Checks
Not Wheelchair Accessible
Lot and Street Parking

Tea is served on Sunday afternoons between 11 and 4, by reservation only.

Proprietor's
Autograph_____Date_____

Columbia Gorge Hotel

4000 Westcliff Drive
Hood River, Oregon 97031-9970
541-386-5566 / 800-345-1921
cghotel@gorge.net
www.ColumbiaGorgeHotel.com

Take I-84 east from Portland to Exit 62 and follow the signs. Cross the freeway and the hotel is on the left. It is one hour east of Portland.

How nice it is to see another fine hotel offering afternoon tea. Time was when all the big resort and city hotels offered tea, but unfortunately many have ceased that tradition. This beautiful hotel, built in 1921, is referred to as a "Romantic Jazz-Age Hotel" and it is a national landmark. After your relaxing tea time, spend a little time walking around the hotel and taking in all the beauty she has to offer, both inside and out.

Tea is served in the beautiful dining room overlooking the grounds of the hotel. White linens, elegant china, sparkling crystal and fresh flowers grace the table, and tiered silver servers provide the finishing touch. The set consists of assorted Columbia Gorge Hotel specialty sandwiches, scrumptious scones with crème royale and jam, seasonal fresh fruit, gourmet chocolate-dipped strawberries, savory quiche, "guilty pleasures" from the pastry chef, seasonal fruit trifle and a pot of delightful tea. The cost is $24.95 per person. Special theme teas will be provided on request and changes in the menu may be made at the customer's request.

Brunch, lunch, dinner and appetizers are offered in other areas of the hotel and there is a gift shop for browsing and shopping.

Besides taking tea at the Columbia Gorge Hotel, you might want to add a weekend stay at this fabulous hotel! Their breakfast and dinner offerings are also wonderful and the rooms quite elegant!!

MC/V/DIS
Wheelchair Accessible
Lot Parking

High tea is served on Sundays 1-3, May through December, including holidays. Reservations are coveted Groups should reserve. There is a 24-hour cancellation policy.

Proprietor's
*Autograph*_____*Date*_____

The Country Cottage Café

and Bakery
205 Fern Valley Road
Medford, Oregon 97501
541-535-5113
countrycottage@charter.net
www.countrycottagecafe.com

From I-5 at Medford, take exit 24 toward
Phoenix. Watch for the neon sign directing you to shops at that exit. Your
next landmark is McDonalds...the tea room is right there!

After selling another successful business, Pamela Lawrence and Diane Linderman opened their bakery and tea room in 2003. With the help of their husbands, they continue their tradition of offering wonderful bakery items and afternoon tea. The decor, designed by David Linderman, is enchanting. With picket fences on the windows, a trellis in the dining area and floor-to-ceiling murals depicting outdoor scenes, the room has a true garden feel. What a charming place to take afternoon tea.

High Tea offers a selection of sandwiches (vegetarian is available), a scone, brown sugar shortbread, fresh fruit and 3 sweet surprises of the day. Since this is a bakery, you can count on fresh scones and breads, and many luscious dessert choices for $13.95.

After your afternoon tea, stop at the bakery and select something special to enjoy later in the evening or perhaps you will be interested in something really yummy for breakfast the next day!

Breakfast and Lunch are served every day, and the selections are numerous.

V/MC/AE/ DEB
Wheelchair Accessible
Lot Parking

The shop hours are 9-4, Monday through Saturday. Breakfast and lunch are
served 6 days a week. High Tea is served from 1:30 to 3:30 daily.

Proprietor's
*Autograph*_____*Date*_____

Country Cottage of Jacksonville

230 East C Street
Jacksonville, Oregon 97530
541-899-2900

From I-5, take the Medford exit and follow Hwy 238 (Jacksonville Hwy) into Jacksonville. The café is on C Street, across from the museum.

Country Cottage of Jacksonville was opened in 2000 and is now under the ownership of Pam Bock and Patty Keck. The ambiance in this vintage house in historic Jacksonville features garden murals and pink and lavender wisteria vines hanging from the ceiling. If the weather allows and the mood strikes you, tea on the lovely front porch is an option. To find Country Cottage, just watch for the white picket fence with the arched gateway.

There are two selections for afternoon tea and both require a reservation for a minimum of two people. The High Tea, which is $12.95, includes 2 selections from their Stash Tea list, fingers of flavored scones with cream, shortbread, and a tiered server of assorted tea-sized cakes from their bakery. The Queen's High Tea, which is served on a beautiful table setting of crystal and silver, is priced at $18.95. This special tea offers loose-leaf tea steeped to perfection, a bottle of Perrier Water, a bowl of fresh home-made soup, 3 varieties of savory tea sandwiches followed by fingers of scones and cream, shortbread and a tiered server of assorted tea-sized cakes from their bakery. The finishing touch for this extravaganza is a slice each of their 6-layer carrot cake and 6-layer Midnight Madness Cake.

Breakfast and lunch are served every day and the selection is extensive. Some breakfast choices such as stuffed croissant, omelet, quiche, crêpes, and Belgian waffles, are offered from $7.95 to $9.95. The lunch offerings include favorites such as the Reuben, Italian hoagie, Philly beef, French dip, Western BBQ, soups and salads which are priced between $6.95 and $8.95.

This is a bakery and the desserts cover everything from cookies and cakes to cheesecake and pies. Pam and Patty also offer business catering from 7 to 5 weekdays. Bulk teas and gift items are available for purchase.

MC/V/AE/DEB/Checks   Street Parking
Wheelchair Accessible

Open Mon. through Sun. 9-3. High tea is offered 11:30-2. Reservations are required 24-hours in advance.. Groups are welcome.

Proprietor's
Autograph_____Date_____

The Country Inn

4100 Country Farm Road
Eugene, Oregon 77408
541-343-7933 / fax 541-343-7783

From I-5, take exit 195B to Beltline West. From Beltline, take the Coburg Road exit and proceed about 1½ miles. The Country Inn is on the left near the exit of Coburg Road and Game Farm Road.

This was one of those wonderful, accidental finds! While driving home from afternoon tea in Eugene, my friend Sue and I decided to take the old "country route" through Coburg. Along the way we passed this charming inn, and curiosity got the best of us. I turned around and we went back to investigate. The staff was welcoming and gave us the "cooks tour" of this former private residence.

We started our tour outside where we wandered around the beautiful garden. It featured a large gazebo which was surrounded by roses and other colorful flowers. Set to the sides of the garden were smaller gazebos and ponds with trickling waterfalls. The lawns were manicured and the trees and bushes trimmed to perfection!

Everything about the interior was beautiful and elegant. The rooms were on different levels which broke them up into intimate spaces. Toward the back of the house, a reception room features a beautiful old carved bar which practically takes up one complete wall. This room, the garden and other areas of the Inn are perfect locations for any event or special occasion.

Before leaving, I of course mentioned afternoon tea. As luck would have it, that is one of their offerings. Private teas can be arranged for small or large groups by special arrangement. If you are interested in spending the afternoon in this lovely setting, give Lisa a call.

MC/V/AE/DEB/Checks
Wheelchair Accessible
Lot Parking

Tea is by reservation and there is a 72-hour cancellation policy. Holiday and theme teas are offered.

Proprietor's
*Autograph*_____*Date*_____

Cozy Café & Tea Room

3081 N. Highway 97
Bend, Oregon 97701
541-330-1881
www.cozycafeandtearoom.com

They are on Hwy 97 between the Shilo Inn
and The Riverside, across from the mall.

After operating a successful restaurant in Seattle, Glen and Jeannette Kelso decided to try to do the same when they moved to Bend in 2003. Their dream was to combine a café and espresso with an antique and gift store. They leased a building in front of the Riverhouse on North Third and completely renovated the interior and exterior before opening on April 22, 2005. The interior room is surrounded by "razzleberry" purple walls and the tables are covered in black and white checkered tablecloths. Some glass cases show off the luscious desserts and chocolates while others display antiques. What a fun environment to enjoy afternoon tea ... the latest addition to Glen and Jeannette's offerings.

High Tea, which is presented on a three-tiered server, consists of gourmet sandwiches, fruit, dessert and scones. A pot of tea is included and the cost is $19.95. A Spot of Tea, which is available each day without reservations, may be purchased for $7.95 and it includes a scone with clotted cream and wafer.

Breakfast and lunch items are available and range in price from $3.95 to $8.95. There is also a kid's menu.

Almost everything is home-made. The coffee beans are roasted on site. All of the chocolates are shipped from a family-owned factory in Washington state. One of their favorite ingredients is razzleberries - a combination of several Oregon berries. You will find them in scones, cobblers and other desserts as well as in their smoothies.

Major Credit Cards
Wheelchair Accessible
Lot Parking

The café is open 7 days a week from 6:30 to 3. Tea is by reservation only.

Proprietor's
*Autograph*_____*Date*_____

Creative Touch Tea House and Café

23855 S.W. 195th Place
Sherwood, Oregon 97140
503-502-9680 / www.teamap.com

Located off 99W between Sherwood and Newberg. Follow green Hwy signs to "Sleighbells." The cross street is Chapman Road. The tea room is located inside Sleighbells.

I have visited Sleighbells many times over the years and I am so pleased that there is now a tea room located inside. What fun it is to take a break from shopping for "tea time"!!

"A Creative Touch" was opened in 2004 by Heidi Marlin and is a much-needed addition to this wonderful destination. Since there are 10,000 feet of shopping space, one would welcome a chance to sit a bit and take tea. Heidi describes the ambiance as cozy and warm, and a "magical experience." The décor changes with the seasons with attention given to special holidays. A special effort is made to add little creative touches.

All of the teas are named for special people, from Joanne's Tea with tea and scones for $5, to the full Grandmother's Tea offering fruit, 4 tea sandwiches, 4 savories, 4 cheese appetizers, 3 scones with toppings, 5 desserts and tea for $20. Other selections are Brianne's Tea for children for $5, Billie Jean's Tea, which is a dessert tea, for $5, Ruby Marie's Tea of fruit, 2 finger sandwiches, 1 savory, scone and 2 desserts for $10 and Mabel Anne's Tea which adds a sandwich, 1 savory, 2 cheese appetizers and 1 scone to the last tea for $15.

Luncheon items such as soup, quiche, sandwiches and desserts are also available for $3 to $7. The house tea is Adagio, and coffee is available for non-tea drinkers. Dietary needs may be accommodated with prior arrangements. Outside catering is also offered.

After your inside shopping and refreshing tea are complete, take time to walk the beautiful Christmas Tree Farm. Better yet, come back in December and select that perfect tree.

MC/V/DEB/Checks
Handicapped Accessible
Free Lot Parking

Hours of operation are 11-4 Wednesday through Sunday, and any time is tea time. The last seating is 3:30. Reservations are suggested for individuals but necessary for groups. Large groups are asked to reserve 1 to 2 weeks in advance. All reservations require a 48-hour cancellation.

Proprietor's
Autograph_____Date_____

Cynthian Café and Catering

957 Main Street
Dallas, Oregon 97338
503-623-9445
cynthiancatering@aol.com

From Hwy 22, follow signs to Dallas. Once in Dallas, at the second signal keep to the left onto Main Street. From Hwy 99W, take the Dallas exit. Follow the road as it curves to the right when you get to town, then follow as it curves to the left at the hospital. Go straight to Main and turn left. They are across the street from the Dallas Public Library.

The Cynthian Café is a small establishment in the original downtown area of Dallas which fits nicely into the charm of that area. Surrounded by historic buildings, an antique mall, boutique shops and small dining establishments, the café is right at home. The owner, Carol Marshall, opened her café in 1991. She has decorated it with a homey feel ... antiques, pretty dishes and framed early pictures of Dallas, originally called Cynthian!

Each tea is a "catered affair" and Carol selects only the most popular tea foods for your event. A sampling of her dishes includes cucumber finger sandwiches, cubed chicken and pineapple sandwiches, fresh fruit, orange/cranraisin scones, lemon curd, clotted cream, raspberry jam, cinnamon apple scones, a variety of small homemade tea cookies and hot Tetley tea. Quiche and/or soup can be added to the above for a traditional High Tea. Carol also offers a variety of home-made soups served with warm scones and any of the above. Teas range in price from $12.50 to $17, depending on your selected menu. Coffee is available and dietary needs can be accommodated with prior arrangements.

If you are looking for a friendly, cozy place to take tea with friends, Cynthian Café offers that and more.

Checks/Cash
Wheelchair Accessible
Lot Parking (behind their building)

Teas are private events. Reservations are made in advance. Groups of 20-49 can be accommodated. There is a $50 deposited required to hold the date. It is refundable only if two-week notice is given.

Proprietor's
*Autograph*_____*Date*_____

Deepwood Estate

1116 Mission Street S.E.
Salem, Oregon 97302
503-363-1825
deepwood@open.org
www.historicdeepwoodestate.org

From I-5, take exit 253 (Mission Street) Go west on Mission. Turn left on 12th. The house is on the corner of Mission and 12th. The parking lot is on the corner of 12th and Lee.

Deepwood Estate, which is owned by the city of Salem, is a beautifully restored 1894 Queen Ann style home. Tea is served on antique china by costumed servers, in the oak paneled dining room ... the ambiance of Victorian times.

The tea hostess, Janice Palmquist, studied the Victorian and English traditions, and has developed menus which incorporate many period recipes. Attention to detail is evident at every tea Janice oversees, from the collection of teacups and saucers to the vintage linens which grace the tables. All of the afternoon teas are five courses and include seasonal fruit, cream scones, 2 savories, 3 sandwiches and dessert. The menu, which is of the highest quality, reflects the best of seasonal food available. The cost of the tea is $25 pre-paid, but it is so much more than a tea. The 3 1/2 hour experience includes a stroll of the ever-changing five and a half acres of English Gardens, and a tour of the house. Deepwood is considered one of the finest examples of a Queen Anne home west of the Mississippi and here you will experience tea as it was. Past attendees have said, "it was the best I have ever experienced - I feel thoroughly pampered!"

Several themed teas are presented throughout the year and benefit dinners are now being offered. Other offerings, made with prior arrangements and for specific numbers of guests are; Tea with cookies for $6, Tea, Dessert and Music for $12, Formal Buffet Tea or Afternoon Formal Tea for $25 and finally lunch or dinner in the dining room for $15 to $45. All events include a tour of the house. Special dietary needs can be accommodated with advance request. For those interested in learning the art of preparing tea foods, Janice offers private classes.

MC/V/DIS/Checks   No Wheelchair Access
Lot Parking   Gift Shop

Teas are by reservation; recommended 2 months in advance. Call Deepwood for dates and times of public teas. Private teas can also be arranged. If you are on the mailing list, you will receive information on teas and other events.

Proprietor's
*Autograph*_____*Date*_____

43

The Doll House Tea Room

3223 S.E. Risley Avenue
Milwaukie, Oregon 97267
503-653-6809
www.dollhousetearoom.com

Take I-205 to the Oregon City exit, turn right on 99E and go about 4 miles
toward Milwaukie. Watch for GI Joe's. Turn left at the next street (Risley
Avenue). The tea room is the first driveway on the right.

Opened in 2000 by Jeanine Nordling, The Doll House truly fits its name. Every room is decorated with whimsical painted chairs, tea pots with fresh flowers on the tables, and beautiful dolls. Pretty pastel tablecloths, attractive wall borders and soft curtains with floral touches complete the look.

Jeanine has been offering "Fabulous Dress-up Tea Parties" for little girls for 4½ years. The Fantasy Closet is complete with 150 gowns and accessories for girls of all ages, children or adults. The tea room can be reserved for private parties of 15 to 30 people at a cost of $15 per person.

Tea choices are the Lady Alexander's Tea for $13 which includes a scone with the trimmings, 6 tea sandwiches, fruit, and dessert; Story Book Tea of scone, 4 tea sandwiches and fruit OR Cupie Doll Tea of 3 tea sandwiches, fruit and desserts for $10: High Tea which offers an entrée or a main course salad, scones and dessert for $15. The High Tea is only offered for parties of 4 or more with 48-hour reservation. All teas include a bottomless pot of tea. The Shirley Temple Dress-up Tea for children under 10 when accompanied by an adult tea order, consists of a mini scone, sandwiches, fruit and cheese, dessert and lemonade or tea for $10. It includes a trip to the Fantasy Closet. Janine says her focus is on presentation (as well as quality and flavorful food) and a clean and calming atmosphere … and fun!

The house tea is Carnelian Rose and coffee is available upon request. Special dietary needs will be accommodated if possible.

MC/V/DEB/Checks
Not Wheelchair Accessible
Lot and Street Parking

Open Wednesday, Thursday and Friday for adult teas. Tea time is 11-3:30
with the last tea service at 2:30. Open Saturdays for dress-up parties.
Reservations are recommended 24-hours in advance. Groups of 12 or more
will be charged a non-refundable deposit if cancelled in less that 48-hours.

Proprietor's
*Autograph*_____*Date*_____

ERMATINGER HOUSE
(COURTESY OHS)

Ermatinger House

619 - 6th Street
Oregon City, Oregon 97045
503-650-1851
harding63@att.net

*From Hwy 99 in Oregon City, take 10th Street up Singer Hill (the street to
the upper level of town). At the top, 10th becomes 7th Street. Turn right and
go to 6th Street. Take a left and go to 619-6th. It is on the corner of 6th and
John Adams.*

Francis Ermatinger came to Oregon in 1835 as an employee of the
Hudson's Bay Company. He worked his way up through the ranks under Dr.
John McLoughlin, the father of Oregon, and was placed in charge of the
Company store in Oregon City in 1844. He was later elected treasurer of
Oregon's Provisional Government. His house, which he built in 1845, was
the first frame house built in Oregon and only the third in the entire Oregon
County. Due to the development around Willamette Falls, in 1910 the house
was moved to the upper level of town. In 1986, the Ermatinger House was
moved to its present location at 6th and John Adams.

The Ermatinger House welcomes groups for Living History Teas which
are conducted by Marge Harding. Marge takes guests back to the period of
the Oregon Trail and early Oregon history, and she speaks in first person
while sharing the "news of the day." Comments and questions by guests are
pertinent to "today." As Marge says, "you are eating in 1865."

The light tea, which is enjoyed during the presentation, includes scones
with lemon curd and Devon cream, fruit, shortbread and tea for $15. The
price of the tea includes a tour of the house and additional menu items can be
pre-arranged. This special tea is a fun learning experience with good
food - a perfect combination!

Checks/ Cash
Not Wheelchair Accessible
Street Parking

*Living History Teas are by special arrangement only. House tours, which
are offered year-round, are conducted Fridays, Saturdays and Sundays
11-4. Private tours may be arranged. Admission is $4 for adults and $3 for
seniors and students.*

Proprietor's
*Autograph*_____*Date*_____

Eve's Garden Café and Tea Room

15090 Highway 238
Applegate, Oregon 97530
541-846-9019
zackmancathy@yahoo.com/ www.edengatefarm.com

From I-5, take exit 58 at Grants Pass and proceed to intersection for
Williams Hwy/Hwy 238. Take that highway toward Murphy and continue to
the town of Applegate. From I-5 in Medford, take exit 30 and head west on
Hwy 238 through the town of Jacksonville. Continue another 15 miles to the
town of Applegate. They relocated to downtown Applegate.

Eve's Garden Café, which is owned by Cathy and Paula, opened in 2002 and is located at Eden's Gate Farms in historic Applegate. The quaint tea room is located in an 1890s cottage and boasts a whimsical décor complete with painted clouds on the ceiling and ivy on the floor. The windows are decorated with antique hankie valances, and the tables are covered with antique cloths. Outside seating is offered in the summer in their beautiful rose and flower gardens. What better setting for dress-up tea parties featuring Victorian hats, vintage attire, gloves and boas? Cathy and Paula call their parties, "a great escape for a few hours of fun."

"Tea Time" is offered all day for $12 and it includes a scone with Devon Cream and lemon curd, three tea sandwiches, two desserts and a pot of tea. Reservations are not required.

High Tea, which is by reservation only, would be the perfect event for an anniversary, shower, retirement, business luncheon, or any other special occasion. At a cost of $12 for children and $18 for adults, the tea offers scones with Devonshire cream and lemon curd, soup or salad, finger sandwiches and quiche, sorbet or fruit, an assortment of desserts and a selection of teas to choose from for your bottomless pot of tea.

Breakfast items such as French toast made with hazelnut bread or a croissant sandwich are also offered. Lunch specialties include quiche, salads, sandwiches and soups. You might be tempted to try Eatin' From the Garden, a double-decker vegetarian sandwich or Gobble Till You Wobble, the cook's favorite turkey sandwich.

Catering is available for groups up to 25 during the winter and for up to 125 in the summer. The tea room shares space with a gift shop so allow yourself time two browse in this "little bit of heaven."

MC/V/DEB/Cash   Wheelchair Accessible   Lot Parking

Summer hours: Wednesday through Thursday 8-3; Friday, Saturday and
Sunday   8-7. Winter hours are Wednesday through Sunday 8-3. High tea is
by reservation. Your credit card will be charged if you fail to show at the
appointed time. A gratuity is added for groups of 5 or more.

Proprietor's
Autograph_____Date_____

Gentle House

855 N. Monmouth Avenue
Monmouth, Oregon 97361
503-838-8673
gentlehouse@wou.edu
www.wou.edu/gentlehouse

From Hwy 99W, go west on Main Street (the four-way traffic light for
Monmouth and Independence). Travel six blocks to a four-way stop and turn
right onto North Monmouth Avenue. Travel through campus. Gentle House
is on the right, just past the Oregon Military Academy and Gentle Avenue.

This beautiful historic home, situated on nearly 4 acres of landscaped
gardens, was the home of Thomas Gentle and his family. Built in the early
1880s, the farmhouse was purchased by Thomas in 1914. He was the head of
Campus Elementary Training at Oregon Normal School, which is now
Western Oregon University. The home remained in the family until daughter
Catharine donated it to the WOU Foundation in 1981. She asked that it be
used by the college and community for "genteel entertaining." What better
way to use the home than for afternoon tea.

In 2004, an energetic committee started planning Tea Party Luncheons as
fundraisers for Gentle House. They planned menus, sewed tea cozies and
napkins, and started a collection of tea cups. Their efforts were well
rewarded, as each tea has been well attended. A typical tea is a buffet, and it
features a delicious choice of soups, quiche, scones, finger sandwiches, fruit
trays and a selection of petite desserts. Everything is presented on doily-
lined tiered servers and pretty serving plates. The cost of a typical tea is
between $14. and $20, an excellent value for a benefit tea.

The tables are set about the house, and are covered with soft-colored
tablecloths that coordinate with the napkins and cozies. Fresh flower
nosegays in teapots are set in the center of the table. Entertainment is
provided by the WOU music department.

How satisfying it is to take tea in an historic home while helping support
that home.

MC/V/Checks
Wheelchair Accessible
Lot Parking

Teas are offered occasionally during the year. Please call for more
information. They are by reservation only. There are a number of seatings
for each of the teas.

Proprietor's
*Autograph*_____*Date*_____

47

The Gordon House
at the Oregon Garden

P.O. Box 155
Silverton, Oregon 97381
503-874-6006 / 877-674-2733 ext. 6006
gordonhouse@oregongardens.org
www.oregongarden.org

The house is located at the Oregon Garden property, which is 15 miles east of Salem on Silverton Road.

We have had the pleasure of visiting both the gardens and the Gordon House in Silverton. Having grown up hearing about Frank Lloyd Wright, it was especially memorable to be able to visit the only house in Oregon that was designed by him. It is also his only building open to the public in the Northwest. How sad it would have been had the house been destroyed!

I met Molly, the coordinator, at a tea class we took together. Her interest in tea, and her desire to present teas which will benefit the Gordon House, are note-worthy.

Teas are presented during specific months of the year and reservations need to be made from two months to two days in advance, as available. The setting is a home that features Frank Lloyd Wright's "economic design for middle-class American families." It provides the tea attendees a unique and artistic setting for tea and lunch. How special it is for us to be able to sit down and relax as a guest of the Gordon House!

The tea venue changes from tea to tea and some of the menus follow a particular theme. An example would be the Russian Tea: Russian Caravan black tea, Georgia black tea, Honey Lemon Ginseng Herb tea, cream scones with fig jam and lime curd, salmon quiche with medium Cheddar cheese, and finger sandwiches of herbed cream cheese with cucumber, open-face Albacore tuna and smoked turkey and chutney roll-ups. A salad of mixed organic greens with Imperial Russian Vinaigrette dressing and Anastasia cake complete the meal, which costs $35 ($32 members). Sounds wonderful!

The best part about taking tea at the Garden is that the proceeds continue the restoration and preservation of this very special house.

MC/V/AE/DIS/Checks   Wheelchair Accessible   Free Parking

Tea is by reservation only and is offered in November, December and February on Saturdays at noon. Total seating capacity is 25-40 people and groups are welcome.

Proprietor's
*Autograph*_____*Date*_____

Green Door Antiques and Tea Room

113 W. Historic Columbia River Highway
Troutdale, Oregon 97060
503-666-7483

Head east on I-84 from Portland. Take exit 17 then go up the hill, past the outlet stores, to the Historic Columbia River Hwy. Turn left and the tearoom is in Green Door Antiques, the second business from the corner on the left.

We had the opportunity to do a book signing at Green Door Antiques and were so pleased that the owners, Charles and Janeane Reisner, were planning to open a tea room in the store. That became a reality in 2005. Now, one has the pleasure of taking tea in the Victorian atmosphere that includes a lovely chandeliers, faux fireplace, cloth linens with lace and velvet upholstered chairs. All are done in burgundy and cream and are set off by rich plum walls. The six tables, each with seating for four, are graced with fragrant fresh flowers.

The tea choices include a Cream Tea of scones with Devonshire cream and curd for $4.95, and a Demi Tea with three tea sandwiches, 2 scones with Devonshire cream and curd and seasonal fruit for $8.95. Afternoon Tea offers sorbet, assorted tea sandwiches, savories, fruit, 2 scones with Devonshire cream and curd and an assortment of sweets for $17.95. For the sweet tooth, the Dessert Tea has an assortment of sweets for $5.50. All teas include a pot of Taylor's of Harrogate house tea. For children, Janeane does a special Child's Tea consisting of a pot of "children's tea," peanut butter and honey sandwich, fruit, cheese and scone with jam and Devonshire cream and dessert for $6.95. Special dietary needs will be accommodated whenever possible.

Other lunch fare includes chicken salad croissant with seasonal fruit, ham and Havarti on marbled rye with fruit, quiche with fresh spinach salad and soup of the day with 2 garlic cheese biscuits. All are priced between $4.95 and $7.25. A pot of tea, iced tea or coffee may be purchased with a meal or separately.

Allow yourself plenty of time to wander through the antiques that fill this lovely store. It will be well worth your time!

MC/V/DEB/DIS/Checks
Wheelchair Accessible
Lot and Street Parking

The tearoom and retail store are open 10:30-5, Tuesday through Saturday. The retail store only is open Sundays 12 to 4.

Proprietor's
*Autograph*_____*Date*_____

49

The Heathman Restaurant

1001 S.W. Broadway
Portland, Oregon 97205
503-790-7752

Located in the Heathman Hotel at the corner of Broadway and Salmon in downtown Portland.

The Heathman is an elegant Old World hotel which offers tea in the elegant lobby amid crystal chandeliers, wood paneling and eucalyptus. A working fireplace adds to the charm of this historic tea room.

The afternoon tea, which is $21.75 per person, includes sandwiches, savories, congolais and cookies, cake, a scone, lemon tartlet and a pot of tea. The Peter Rabbit Tea for "little sippers" consists of a sandwich, cheese blocks, congolais and cookies, fruit, goldfish crackers, teddy grahams and hot chocolate for $8.95. Sparkling and Sweets by the glass are also available. The house tea is Fonte Coffee and Tea Co. out of Seattle, Washington, and there is a generous selection of regular and decaffeinated teas. Coffee is available upon request, as is a full lunch menu.

The Lobby is Wheelchair Accessible.
MC/V/DIS/CB/AE and Checks Accepted

Tea is served from September 24th through November 11th, weekends only at noon and 2. From November 24th through January 8th, tea is served daily at 11, 1 and 3.

Proprietor's
*Autograph*_____*Date*_____

Hoffman House

523 E. Main Street
Molalla, Oregon 97038
503-829-2640
hoffmanhouse@molalla.net
www.hoffmanhouserestaurant.com

From I-5, take the Woodburn exit and head east (Hwy 214). Continue for 20 minutes to Molalla, where the road changes to Hwy 211 Main Street. They are in the Historic downtown area on the corner of Main and Fenton, in the two -tory house with blue trim and the large front yard.

Originally built by the Robbins family in 1888, this Folk Victorian home housed the first library in Molalla from 1900 to 1906. Dennis and Debbie Hoffman took on the task of restoring this historic building and transformed it into the Hoffman House Restaurant, which they opened in 2003.

Debbie offers special teas, one for adults and another for children. The full Afternoon Tea, which is priced at $18, is prepared for a minimum of ten people and the reservation is required 2 weeks in advance. The four course tea is served on their best china and best linens, and it consists of fresh fruit, scones with clotted cream, jam and lemon curd, savories and tea sandwiches and sweets. Two different teas of your choice are served throughout the party. Please allow 2 to 1½ hours for your tea party.

The Children's Craf-tea is $16 per person and there is an 8 person minimum. Tea is served on fine china and there is a plate of fruit and sandwiches and other delights that children love. "Dirt cake" is served in a flower pot with gummy worms and a flower. After the cake is finished, the children enjoy a craft time of decorating their flower pot, which they take home with them. The birthday girl is treated to a tiara and a cape to make her feel special.

The dinner menu includes such items as Shrimp for $12.95, Country Fried Steak for $8.95 and Catfish for $10.95. They feature Prime Rib every Friday night starting at 5 while supplies last. Appetizers are available and the entreés include chefs' choice of vegetable and potato and your choice of soup or salad.

V/MC/Checks
Wheelchair Accessible
Street Parking

They are open Tuesday through Saturday 11-5. Tea parties are by special reservation only.

Proprietor's
*Autograph*_____*Date*_____

51

Julia's Tea Parlor

2280 Wallace Road N.W.
Salem, Oregon 97304
503-378-7060
juliastea@msn.ncom

Take I-5 to Hwy 22 exit. Proceed through town, and cross the Marion Street Bridge. Stay to the right. Take the West Salem / Dayton exit (Wallace Road). Go right, proceed approximately 1½ miles. The tea room is on the right.

If you are a history buff and incurable romantic, Julia's will give you a taste of both. This 150-year-old farmhouse on the outskirts of Salem has a wonderful story to tell. Ed will share the history of the house and how it got its name, while you sip tea and enjoy the attractive sandwiches and delicious scones prepared by his wife, Kathleen. Choosing your tea is a treat in itself, as you sniff the many small apothecary jars until you find just the right one. Savor your tea, listen to the tale of Julia's humble beginnings, and relax in the comfort of this charming tearoom. Perhaps you will be there on a cool day and can sit before the huge stone fireplace with its massive mantle. Or maybe it will be nice enough to take tea in the garden. Either way, atmosphere abounds at Julia's. And, if you have forgotten your hat, there are numerous ones resting on the backs of the chairs in the tearoom, as well as some proper wraps, should you get chilly.

The tea itself is a work of art, with seasonal flowers and rose petals scattered on the tiered servers. Five tea choices are available: a scone and tea for $5.95, Cream Tea which adds fruit to the above for $7.95, the Lighter Fare of tea, scone, tea sandwiches and fruit garnish for $10.95, the Light Afternoon Tea which consists of a scone, fresh fruit, 4 tea sandwiches and a selection of decadent afternoon desserts for $14.95 and finally, the Full Afternoon Tea, which adds a quiche of the day to the afternoon tea for $17.95. All include a pot of tea, Devonshire cream and lemon curd. For children 10 and under, Kathleen prepares a Wee People's Tea of hot cocoa or tea, peanut butter and jelly and cheese tea sandwiches, fruit and dessert for $6.95. Whatever your choice, all are delicious and attractive offerings!

While there, browse through the many gift items available for purchase in the tea room as well as the gift shop located in the entry area.

MC/V/AE/Checks   Wheelchair Accessible   Lot Parking

Tea room hours are Tuesday through Saturday 10-4. Reservations are requested 24-hours in advance and groups are welcome.

Proprietor's
Autograph_____Date_____

K.J.'s Tea House

337 Second Avenue S.W.
Albany, Oregon 97321
541-967-1829 / fax 541-967-0193

From I-5, take exit 234B and follow the signs to City Center onto Lyons
Street. Turn left on 1st Street, go 3 blocks to Ferry and turn left. Go one
block to 2nd and turn left again. The tea room is on the left side of the street,
across from Two Rivers market.

This bistro style restaurant which doubles as a tea room was a real find! Located in the historic district of Albany, Karen and Jessie bring fun to dining with their whimsical décor, flying chefs on the wall and hat collection in the "powder room".

Small tables dot the room, but for groups, Karen will set a single row of white linen topped tables down the center of the room. The tables are set with eclectic tea cups and saucers, and the tea is served promptly when you are seated. Thick clotted cream and lemon curd are pre-set, and the scones on which to spread them are served right after the tea. Edible art of grape clusters and strawberry fans surround the scones, making for a very attractive presentation. Though you are never rushed, sandwiches and savories follow the scones, and the dessert platters finish off the offerings. There are four types of sandwiches, all quite tasty, and four different desserts. The cost of the afternoon "Tea and Treats" is $10.50, and bottomless pots of tea are included. Off-site teas are offered and theme teas may be arranged. A special tea is offered during the Historical Home Tours for which Albany is noted.

When not presenting teas and running a very successful catering business, Karen arranges cooking classes for the public. Ethnic cooking, as well as kids cuisine and chocolate confections, are a sampling of the types of classes offered. To find out more about the classes, call or fax Karen.

MC/V/AE/Checks   Wheelchair Accessible   Street and Lot Parking

Tea served on Saturdays at 11, 12:30 and 2. Reservations are required
24-hours in advance. The cancellation policy is also 24-hours in advance.
Groups are welcome and if there are 6 or more, special times may be
arranged.

Proprietor's
Autograph_____Date_____

Kashin Tei Tea House

611 S.W. Kingston Avenue
Portland, Oregon 97201
503-223-9233
www.japanesegarden.com

Located west of the Rose Gardens and Tennis courts in Washington Park.
Call the Japanese Garden Society at 503-223-4070 for specific directions.

This authentic 4½ mat tea room from Japan, whose name translates to Flower Heart Hut, is owned and operated by the Japanese Garden Society of Oregon. The tea presentation may be viewed by the public May through September, on the 3rd Saturday of the month from 1 to 2. This is during the Japanese Garden operating hours.

Private party experiences for 5-10 guests are available for a fee of $100 and up. Guests will be served a Japanese tea sweet and bowl of Matcha, which is a powdered green tea.

To arrange a private experience of Chanoya (tea of water) or Chado (path of tea), call the Japanese Tea Society and they will provide the names and phone numbers of certified teachers.

The Japanese Garden has a gift shop for your enjoyment.

Not Wheelchair Accessible
Lot Parking and On Street Parking.

Call the Japanese Garden Society for specific information.

Proprietor's
*Autograph*_____*Date*_____

54

La Tea Da Tea Room

904 Main Avenue
Tillamook, Oregon 977140
503-842-5447
tea@lateada-tearoom.com
www.lateada-tearoom.com

The tea room is located at the corner of Main and 9th streets. This is Hwy 101, and is a one-way street going south..

La Tea Da is gaining a reputation as "the place to go" for tea. The beautiful tea room, opened in 2001 by Terry and Suzanne, says welcome, come in and relax. Its lavender and pale yellow walls, lovely floral arrangements, eclectic collection of antique furnishings, and lace window coverings are just the perfect touch. If seating is not available right away, you can take advantage of the wait by looking through the wonderful gift shop. It features hand-painted teapots and teacups, silver serving pieces, English bone china and imported jams, jellies and teas - the essential ingredients for taking tea at home. Unique picture frames, tassels, swags, Tiffany-style lamps, candles and bath products are also available for purchase. If you wish, complimentary gift wrapping is included.

Once seated in the tea room, sit back and take in the surroundings while you make your choice from the numerous tea sets, One may choose the Queen Mum's tea, which offers something sweet, or the Cuppa Tea, with its three scones, each of which is $7.95. The Villagers Tea consists of sorbet and soup with scones *or* tea sandwiches for $10.95 and the Governors Tea, preferred by gentlemen, consists of sorbet, a selection of sandwiches and savories, scones and a little sweet for $13.95. The tea that receives raves is the La Tea Da High Tea! This 4-course tea starts with sorbet, followed by sandwiches and savories. Then, one sweet and one Tillamook cheese scone are served, followed by a selection of dainty and ever-so-tasty desserts, all for $16.95. For the children, there is a Scamp's tea with bite-sized sandwiches and sweets, sorbet and a whimsical tot's pot of tea for $6.95. There is something for everyone and every morsel is delicious! Special event teas are offered.

MC/V/AE/DIS/Checks   Wheelchair Accessible   Free Street Parking

September to May, Tuesday through Saturday, 10-5:30. June to August - Monday through Saturday, 10-5:30. Tea is served from 11 to 4. Reservations are recommended, groups are welcome, and a party room is available for a small fee.

Proprietor's
Autograph_____Date_____

Lady Di's British Store
and Tea Room
20 Second Street
Lake Oswego, Oregon 97034
503-635-7298 / 800-357-7839
www.britishfare.com

From I-5/217, take Kruse Way to Boones Ferry. Follow signs to downtown Lake Oswego. From I-205, take Hwy 43 to West Linn then to Lake Oswego. Left at A Avenue then right on 2nd.

Lady Di, with its convenient location, has been a mainstay in Lake Oswego for a number of years. The store shelves are stocked with an extensive selection of British groceries and teas and there are frozen and refrigerated items available for purchase. An extensive catalog serves those who can't make it into the shop, but long for goods from their homeland.

Collectables, such as teapots, cards, miniatures, pictures and other English items are set about the store to tempt you.

Tucked away in a corner, enclosed by a friendly fence, is the vine-clad tea room, where one can enjoy a cup of tea and quiet conversation. Moya offers a varied menu from which one can select a tasty morsel to enjoy with tea. You may choose a sandwich with crisps and fruit for $4.95 or the Lady Di Tea which includes a tart, biscuit, shortbread, cake, fruit and tea sandwich for $9.95. If you prefer to have a scone, there is a Devon Cream Tea for $9.95, which also includes fruit and tea sandwich. A holiday menu is offered between Thanksgiving and Christmas. Groups of 6 or more are charged a 20% gratuity.

MC/V/Cash
Free Street Parking

Store hours Monday through Saturday 10-5. Teatime is 11-4. There is seating for 12 people in the Garden area. A separate parlor seats 4-5. Reservations may be necessary on Saturday and for groups of more than 6. Special teas for Mother's Day, Valentine's Day, etc. (see WEB page for more information)

Proprietor's Autograph_____Date_____

Lavender Tea House

and Gift Shop

16227 S.W. 1st Avenue
Sherwood, Oregon 97140
503-625-4479
LavenderTeaHouse@yahoo.com
www.lavenderteahouse.com

From 99W, turn south onto North Sherwood Boulevard (light). Follow for almost a mile (.8), turn right onto 1st Street. They are 2½ blocks down on the right. Located across from Veterans Park and Morehouse Museum.

The location of Lavender Tea House, an 1892 Queen Anne Victorian cottage, couldn't be more suitable ... across from a park with a huge aging tree, near the end of the street in a quaint neighborhood. The owner, Tamara Neill, says, "here you experience the soothing atmosphere of an era gone by." The tea room has an English country theme with lace-covered windows, and soft lavender walls in one room and pink in the other. Tea may be taken on the porch, at tables set for two, June through September.

High Tea is an English-style tea served in three courses. The first course is 6 tea sandwiches and soup, followed by a scone with jam and clotted cream and fruit. The final course is dessert and this tea is priced at $21.95. Afternoon Tea is a refreshing afternoon's repast of 6 tea sandwiches, scone with jam and clotted cream, lemon curd, and dessert for $14.95. Tea and gratuity are included. They promise to "keep your teapot filled until you are!"

For the smaller appetites, there are two other offerings on the luncheon menu. Queen Mum has 4 tea sandwiches, scone with jam and clotted cream and fresh fruit for $7.75. The Garden has 4 tea sandwiches, fresh fruit and a truffle for $6.95. Tea is not included but is available at $2 for one and $3 for two. There is a Children's Tea for $5.75 as well as other lighter fare items. Some items may be purchased à la carte or for take out. Selected desserts and Italian Soda's are offered June through September.

The gift shop offers that perfect gift or memento to commemorate your visit ... tea pots, books, linens and much more.

MC/V/DEB/Checks   Wheelchair Accessible   Free Street Parking

Tea is served Tuesday through Saturday 11-4. The last tea service is 3:30. Reservations are required 2 days in advance for small group or 2 weeks in advance for groups of 8 or more. 1-week cancellation policy. Groups are welcome. The maximum is 30 people.

Proprietor's
*Autograph*_____*Date*_____

Leach Botanical Garden

6704 S.E. 122nd Avenue
Portland, Oregon. 97236
503-823-9503

From I-5, take Foster Road exit East to 122nd Avenue. Turn right 1/4 mile to garden parking lot.

Though tea is only offered once a year, it is excellent and worth putting on your calendar well in advance. On one weekend in July, Leach Garden offers a fundraising tea for $20 per person. Tea is served in three courses with a first course of scones with jam, Devonshire jam and butter patties. The second course might consist of such delectables as a fruit cup, asparagus rolls, dilly cucumber rounds, Persian chicken packets, or tomato with basil and mozzarella cheese. For a finale, perhaps you will be offered poppy seed cake, lemon curd tart, raspberry shortbread or chocolate truffle. What ever the menu, and it changes each time, you will be pleased with the taste and presentation. The two seatings are at noon and 2:30 p.m. and the tea is in the Garden's East Terrace. Each table is uniquely decorated and the tea is graciously served by volunteers.

There is a gift shop, so allow yourself a little extra time to look around after you have toured the gardens and enjoyed this wonderful tea.

MC/V/Checks
Wheelchair Accessible
Free Lot Parking

The gardens are open Tuesday through Saturday, 9-4 and Sunday 1-4. Tea is offered in July, by reservation. A spring tea is a possibility, but please call to confirm.

Proprietor's
Autograph_____Date_____

Lord Wicklow's

inside "A Riverside Inn"

430 S. Holladay Drive
Seaside, Oregon 97138
503-738-8254
ariversideinn@people.pc / www.ariversideinn.com

Go north on Hwy 101 to Broadway, turn left at the light. Go 1 block to Holladay and turn left. Go 1½ blocks to "A Riverside Inn" on the right. Watch for the little picket fence. Ring the bell ... they are expecting you!

This charming Inn on the Necanicum River is one of the oldest and most recently restored inns on the North Oregon Coast. The owners, Richard and Margaret Mason, have put their hearts into this wonderful 1927 boutique hotel, and it shows in every nook and cranny. The main house, where tea is served, is home to the Lord Wicklow dining room. Generously decorated with floral wallpaper, numerous antique furnishings, beautiful dishes and crystal, gilt-framed pictures and elaborate serving pieces, the room is a gift to those of us who enjoy all things from days gone by.

Margaret serves elaborate teas in this olde world setting, and her love of what she does is evident in every morsel. She calls her food "wicked indulgences" and all of the recipes are Australian, as Margaret is. A typical tea consists of cut-out sandwiches, sweet and savory scones with flavored butters and at least 9 different desserts - from chocolate cappuccino towers to lemon cheesecake. At Christmas they have favorites such as mince tarts, plum pudding and marzipan. Of course, pots of tea are included and the house tea is Billy's Australian or Irish. Coffee is available upon request.

Special occasions, such as birthdays and showers, can be celebrated at the Inn. For a really special celebration, give yourself the gift of a stay at A Riverside Inn. The room choices are numerous and the amenities perfect. Oh, yes, and the owners are warm and welcoming!

Checks/Cash
Not Wheelchair Accessible
Lot and Street Parking

Tea time is 12-4 and the last tea service is 4. A 24-hour advance reservation is required for tea. Groups of 4 to 16 are welcome.

Proprietor's
*Autograph*_____*Date*_____

Lovejoy's Tea Room and Restaurant

195 Nopal Street
Florence, Oregon 97439
541-902-0502

Going north on Hwy 101, cross the Florence Bridge. Before coming to the
first stop light, turn right on Nopal Street. Continue on Nopal to the corner
of 1st Street. Going south, just before the Florence bridge, turn left on
Nopal.

Great things are happening for Lovejoy's. After moving to a new
location in "Old Town" Florence, the tea room is now owned by Judith and
Liam Kingsmill. Since 1994, tea time has been a tradition at Lovejoy's, and
it is great to see that continue.

This is a traditional English tea room, with an additional tiered dining
area for added seating. It is rich in color with its deep red curtains on the six
large corner windows and coordinating textured carpet. The walls are a
golden yellow, and large gold-hued roses serve as curtain tie-backs. Antique
furnishings, framed art and tables covered in floral cloths complete the
elegant look.

The tea choices begin with a Cream Tea for $6.95 and a Light Tea of one
sandwich, scones and a petite dessert for $8.95. An Imperial Low-carb tea
offers fresh salad greens, a selection of low-carb pinwheel sandwiches and
specially selected low-carb sweets for $9.95. High Tea, which is $11.95 for
1 and $19.95 for 2, includes two tea sandwiches, two salads, scones, and a
petite dessert. The final presentation is the Royal Tea - smoked salmon on
dark rye bread, stilton cream cheese, pear and walnut on whole wheat and
turkey with cranberries on white bread, savory creamed mushroom vol au
vent, scones and a selection of desserts at $26 for 2. All teas include your
choice of Taylors of Harrogate tea, and Double Devon and lemon curd or
preserves for your scones. The Wee Tea for children is offered at $7.95

There is also a lunch menu with daily hot items,
salads, soups and sandwiches. Coffee, beer, wine and
espresso are also available. Dietary needs can be
accommodated with advance arrangements. A gift area
carries tea-related items as well as bulk teas - Taylors of
Harrogate, P.G. Tips and Typhoo.

MC/V/Checks/Cash   Wheelchair Accessible
Street and Lot Parking

Open Tuesday through Sunday 11-5. Any time is teatime. The last service is
4:30. Reservations are suggested 48-hours in advance. There is also a
48-hour cancellation policy. Groups up to 30 welcome.

Proprietor's
Autograph_____Date_____

Mon Ami

490 Highway 101
Florence, Oregon 97439
541-997-9234
cindywobbe@msn.com

From Hwy 126 East, turn left onto Hwy 101. The tea room is located next to the Purple Pelican Antique Mall, at the corner of Hwy 101 and Rhododendron.

Mon Ami is among the many tea rooms making an appearance on the Oregon coast. A really adventurous soul could spend a couple of days just driving from one to the other while seeing the beautiful sights and listening to the wonderful sounds of the coast!

The tea room tables are located amid a wonderful collection of antiques and collectables, all of which will tempt you while you are waiting for tea to be served. Seems I never stay seated very long, as I find myself browsing between courses. Not to worry, Cindy never rushes you!

There are three tea sets from which to choose, starting with the Cream Tea of scones, shortbread, clotted cream and lemon curd for $3.95. The next offering is the Petite Luncheonette and it includes a delicious salad, two tea sandwiches (may include quiche if available), fresh scones and shortbread with lemon curd and clotted cream, and petite desserts. The High Tea, which is served in three courses, includes assorted tea sandwiches and canapés, Mon Ami's signature Waldorf salad, freshly baked scones with citrus curd, classic shortbread, delicate desserts and a pot of tea for $13.95. Dietary needs may be accommodated with advance notice and they are "Adkins friendly!" The house tea is Taylors of Harrogate and they offer that, as well as other labels, for sale. Holiday teas are presented and they would be "happy to do special theme teas" for your special occasion.

This is a great area of town to do some browsing, so allow yourself plenty of time to check out Mon Ami as well as the other stores around it.

If a stay in the area is in your plans, Cindy now operates a beautifully decorated guest cottage overlooking the ocean. It is 20 miles north of Florence near Yachats and is called Sea Mist Guest Cottage. Many of their out-of-town customers stay there and then go to Mon Ami for tea.

MC/V/DIS/Checks   Free Street and Lot Parking
Wheelchair accessible but please let them know you are coming.

Open 9:30-5 Monday through Friday and 10-5 on Saturday. Closed Sunday. All teas are by reservation only.

Proprietor's
*Autograph*_____*Date*_____

Moyer House Benefit Tea

East Blakely Avenue
Brownsville, Oregon 97327
541-401-0500
karenengel@comcast.net

The tea is held at the former Brownsville Elementary School, which is located on East Blakely Avenue in Brownsville.

The elegant Moyer House was built by John and Elizabeth Moyer in 1881. The house was inspired by Italianate Villa-style, popular at the time, but was an original design. The exterior is generously decorated with carved finials, corner boards, frieze boards and eave brackets.

The Moyers were early Linn County settlers who were influential in the development of Brownsville. Elizabeth was the daughter of Hugh L. Brown, for whom Brownsville was named. She met John while he helped her father build the house. They were married in 1857 and first lived in a house outside of town. They later moved to town and John ran a successful planning mill as well as the woolen mill. John and Elizabeth lived in the house together until his death in 1900. Elizabeth continued to live there until her death in 1920. In 1963 the Linn County Historical Society acquired the house with a grant and private donations. The house now belongs to Linn County and is designated a museum, under the care of the Parks Department and a group of volunteers.

Karen Engel, a devoted volunteer, heads-up the committee which puts on this annual benefit tea. She first found a location, as the tea can't be held at Moyer House, and now enlists hostesses to take care of centerpieces, dishes, linens and favors, all of which follow a theme ... most of them the holidays.

I had the pleasure of attending this tea where I enjoyed delicious scones, served with clotted cream and jam, 3 tea sandwiches, 2 cookies, 2 dessert bars, chocolates and unlimited tea. The menu changes with each tea and entertainment is provided. I can't think of a better way to honor a lovely old house than to attend a benefit tea in her honor and to visit Moyer House before or after tea in Brownsville.

Checks/Cash   Wheelchair Accessible   Lot Parking

The tea is held on the first Saturday in December. Seating is limited to 200 and is by advance ticket sales only. The cost is $25 and a portion of the cost is tax-deductible. Mail reservations to Karen Engel, 730 Washington Street S.E., Albany, Oregon, 97321. Include a self-addressed stamped envelope.

Proprietor's
*Autograph*_____*Date*_____

Mrs. B's Special Teas

55 West Grant
Lebanon, Oregon 97355
541-259-5100

From Northbound I-5, go east on Hwy 34 (Exit 228 / Corvallis). Stay right and get onto Main. Turn right at Grant. From Southbound I-5, take the Hwy 20 exit at Albany. Hwy 20 becomes Main Street in Lebanon. Stay on Main and turn right at the third light (Grant). They are the second building on the right.

The Tudor-style building on Grant Street beckons you to step inside and relax in a beautiful Victorian atmosphere. The owner, Barbara Brown, has dedicated the tea room to the memory of her very special mother, Gatha Viola, and her love of all things tea is evident in the food, ambiance and service.

Though delicious lunches are offered Tuesday through Friday, tea time is her specialty. The color scheme changes monthly to suit that month's holiday. Everything changes … tablecloths, glassware, teapots, candles, dishes and even the many collectables which adorn the shelves that encircle the room above you.

The tiered servers, with the appropriate colored flowers, feature a special sandwich to match the theme. There are a number of tea offerings: The Royal Tea of sandwiches and scone or desserts at $9.50, the Luncheon Tea with sandwiches, scone and assorted desserts for $14, the four-course Victorian Tea for $18 and the five-course Queen's Tea at $20. The latter two feature five desserts! All include Devon Cream, preserves and all the tea you can drink. Gourmet coffee is also available.

I recommend that you plan to arrive early or stay late, because the gift area is very large and ever so interesting. You will find everything from cards, books and teapots to boas, hats and a "sea of red and purple!" Take your time checking-out because all the fun jewelry is near the cash register and you are bound to get distracted!

MC/V/Check   Wheelchair Accessible
Street Parking and Lot

The gift shop is open 9-5 daily and lunch is served Tuesday through Friday 11-2. Reservations are required for all teas. Tea is offered Tuesday through Friday at 11 or after the lunch hour 1:30- 3, and on Saturday 11-3.

Proprietor's
*Autograph*_____*Date*_____

Newell House Museum

at Champoeg State Park
St. Paul, Oregon 97137
503-678-5537
NewellHouseMuseum@centurytel.net

From I-5, take exit 278 toward Champoeg State Park. The house is on the left before you turn into the park's main entrance.

For those of us who like all things historical, the Robert Newell House is the perfect place to enjoy two important jewels of the past … traditional teatime and an historic home. Owned by the Daughters of the Revolution, the home is a beautiful reminder of how things used to be, just as tea time is a reminder of what can be … a slower, gentler time. If you plan to visit the museum, invite a group of friends and enjoy an afternoon of tea and conversation in this wonderfully preserved 1850s farmhouse.

There are a number of different teas available ranging in price from the $12 Princess Tea which consists of tea, scones, and fruit to The Royal Tea which offers tea, 3 tea sandwiches,2 savories, scone w/jam and clotted cream, fresh fruit and dessert for $21. The prices are for a minimum of 10 and include admission to tour the house. During the summer, teas may be held in the garden, on the tea porch or in the Great Room. During inclement weather teas are presented in the Great Room only. We had the pleasure of taking tea inside and it was such a perfect setting … seated at antique tables covered with vintage linens and wonderful old mismatched china cups and saucers, surrounded by so many remnants of the past. Tea was served in courses and iced tea as well as hot tea was included.

During the course of the afternoon, our hostess, Judy, gave a detailed history of the house and its relationship to the town of Champoeg. After a leisurely tea, we were able to ramble about the house taking in all the history it had to offer. How I loved the temporary exhibit of inaugural dresses of former governor's wives that dated back to the 1850s. To top off your visit, take a tour of the grounds and see the jail and school house that have been moved to the property.

Checks/Cash
Wheelchair Accessible on the Porch
Lot Parking

Tea is by appointment only. A two-week deposit is required as is a 48-hour cancellation notice.

Proprietor's
*Autograph*_____*Date*_____

Once Upon a Time

Central Point, Oregon 97502
541-665-2808
dressup@cdsnet.net
www.princessparty.com

Tea parties are presented at clients' homes or other location.

What better way to introduce little boys and girls to the fine art of taking tea than a personalized tea party? Teri does just that with her dreamy, dress-up tea parties for children, which she calls "indulgent and elegant"! She offers parties in your home, as well as for organizations at their location of choice. Children get to dress up in high-quality costumes such as princesses (Royal Tea) or faux stoles and elegant vintage gowns, hats and jewelry (Sweet Tea). Teri also teaches etiquette classes, with a tea party at the end of the session.

An example of a themed tea is A Royal Princess Dress-Me-Up Party, which provides costumes and accessories for children aged 4-7. The guest of honor is given royal attire and a throne, a crowning ceremony, a Princess parade, a royal ball, an official Princess certificate and a special gift. Guests will receive personalized invitations that are addressed and mailed for you. The following amenities will be provided; a bubble machine to greet the guests, an instant camera with photo frames, a royal table setting, a fabulous castle cake, ice cream, 7-up and party favors. You simply choose a date, supply the guest list and relax … the rest is done for you! There is a non-refundable deposit on all events, and the cost of these all-inclusive parties is based on the number of children.

Besides private parties, Once Upon a Time does the annual children's tea for the Voorhies Mansion.

MC/V/DIS/Checks/Cash
Special dietary needs can be accommodated.

Most tea parties are held on Saturday and the most popular time is 1 p.m. Two-weeks advance reservation recommended.

Proprietor's
*Autograph*_____*Date*_____

The Oregon Tea Garden

305 Oak Street
Silverton, Oregon 97381
503-873-1230 / fax 503-874-0906
oregonteagarden@aol.com

Follow signs to downtown Silverton. The tea room is located at 1ˢᵗ and Oak Streets in the Silverton Realty Bldg. It is just 3/4 mile from The Oregon Gardens.

This is one of those tea rooms that you just can't forget once you have visited. The brick building on the corner is home to a wonderful "tea time" experience. The bright yellow walls and upside down floral umbrellas hanging from the ceiling make the ambiance fun. Beautiful white chair covers with large lovely bows on the back give the room elegance. It is a wonderful combination of beauty and whimsy. Oregon Tea Garden has changed hands and the new owner, Lennez Hitzemann, looks forward to continuing the tradition that Michelle started.

The generous use of fresh flower and vegetable decors make the tea plates works of art ... almost too pretty to eat. But, do! Besides being attractive, the food is delicious! High Tea, which is $20, offers a large selection of assorted tea sandwiches, fresh fruits, a medley of sweets (cake fit for a queen and the world's best bread pudding are among the selections), warm cream scones and a pot of tea.

Besides High Tea, there is a selection of lunch entreés such as quiche, salads, sandwiches, soup and of course, scones.

While dining, you will find yourself surrounded by an extensive gift shop. Stop to check out the Spode China, gift baskets, tea pots and handmade aprons and tea cozies, as well as assorted tea accoutrements.

MC/V/AE/DC/DIS
Wheelchair Accessible
Metered Street Parking

Tuesday through Saturday 10-4. The tea room may be reserved on Sunday or Monday for special occasions or private parties. They prefer reservations for groups of 5 or more.

Proprietor's
Autograph_____Date_____

The Primrose Tea Room

217 N.E. Third Street
McMinnville, Oregon 97128
503-474-1559

Take 99W to downtown McMinnville (Third Street). Turn right and proceed two blocks. The tea room is on the left-hand side of the street and shares space with Oregon Stationers. They are next to Boersma's.

This charming tea room was originally opened in 2000 by Richard Belgard, but he has been in his new location, a much larger facility, since 2003. Antique furniture, including a massive Duncan Phyfe table and sideboard, fills the British-style dining room. The seven tables, which are surrounded by large comfortable chairs, are covered with burgundy tablecloths, lace toppers and dressy silver accoutrements. The large windows, dressed in the appropriate lace, face the street and offer ample lighting without diminishing the cozy feel of the room. The biggest change with this location is that one can no longer visit with Richard as he prepares his delicious offerings! He is tucked away in his shiny new kitchen!

The tea, which is PG Tipps Cut Black, comes right away. It is piping hot and steeped to perfection. Afternoon Tea is the specialty of the house. The first generous course of sandwiches is served with Richard's signature coleslaw and fruit wedges. The sandwiches are followed by a delicious scone and a small plate of desserts. The cost of the tea is $14.50 and it includes bottomless tea, clotted cream and jam. There is also a Cream Tea for $5.25 and a Dessert Tea for $6.25. The menu includes a few other luncheon items such as soup, house salad, crust-less quiche, chef's special and Shepherd's Pie. The soup is a wonderful specialty called Queen Victoria Soup, and it is unique and delicious. Do try it!

Special dietary needs are accommodated with advance request. Gluten-free scones and quiche may be requested, as well as sandwiches prepared without bread.

Checks/Cash
2-Hour Parking in Back Lot
Wheelchair Accessible

The tea room is open Monday through Saturday, 10-4:30 and lunch is offered during those hours. Full afternoon tea is offered 2-4:30. Tea requires 24-hour advance reservation. Groups are welcome. Please call to cancel.

Proprietor's
*Autograph*_____*Date*_____

Rose's Tea Room

155 S.E. Vista Avenue
Gresham, Oregon 97080
503-665-7215
rosestroom@comcast.net

Take I-84 to exit 16 -Wood Village/238th Drive. Go right off the freeway onto 238th Drive. Go south on 238th for 5 miles then go right on Powell. Take the first left onto Vista Avenue. Sunbelt Rentals is on the corner.

Tucked away in a quaint neighborhood in Gresham sits this delightful and charming tea house which opened in 2001. Though it looks small from the outside, once you are inside you find that it grows with every step. Cindy and Tonia say that their tea room reflects "gracious living inspired by the 20s and 30s" and that is apparent in the floral tablecloths, china cups and seasonal flowers that grace the tables, as well as the very friendly hospitality.

The menu choices are varied and interesting. The Royal High Tea is served in four courses and includes soup and scones with jam and cream, assorted tea sandwiches and savories with fresh fruit, a dessert course, and a chocolate course for $21.95. The Tea Luncheon Plate offers assorted tea sandwiches, including a cranberry chicken salad puff, fresh fruit, freshly made desserts and a scone for $10.95. Also for $10.95, one may choose the Chicken Salad Luncheon or the Caribbean Chicken Salad. Both salads are served with fresh fruit and a scone. The Ploughman's Lunch consists of soup of the day, assorted cheeses, fresh fruit, freshly made desserts and a scone for $10.25 and the Earl's Sandwich is honey ham with cheddar cheese on soft rye, fresh fruit, freshly made desserts and scone for $10.90. All of the above include a pot of Carnelian Rose Tea., which they also sell in bulk. A cup of soup may be added to any item for $1.50. Many items may be ordered à la carte or take-out. Sugar-free and vegetarian are available with prior arrangements.

There is a small gift shop to tempt you while you wait to be seated or to delay you on your way out! Take time to check it out!

Checks/Cash
Wheelchair Accessible
Street and Lot Parking

Hours are Tuesday through Saturday, 11-4. The last tea service is at 4. Reservations are not required but are highly recommended.

Proprietor's
*Autograph*_____*Date*_____

68

Royal House of Orange Tea Co.

316 E. First Street
Newberg, Oregon 97132
503-554-5620
kimzout@verizon.net

They are located on Hwy 99, on the one-way heading east toward Portland.
The tea room is on the corner of First and Blaine, at a controlled railroad
crossing.

A tea room in Newburg is a perfect blend with the antique and collectable shops that are scattered about town. You can browse a while, stop for a tea break, then head back out for more browsing. Just my kind of day!

This Dutch-themed tea room was opened by Kimberly Zoutendijk in 2005 and it is a celebration of her husband's heritage. Light and airy blue sheers dress the six enormous windows, giving a full view of the passing traffic and people. The tables are set with navy blue table cloths and white linen napkins. In keeping with the theme, Van Gogh prints decorate the walls and other Dutch accents are set about the room.

After being seated and making your menu selection, you choose your tea cup from a china hutch. The menu choices are numerous. The smaller teas are the Van Gogh - 2 tea sandwiches and sorbet for $5.95; Lisse's Tea - 2 scones for $5.95; M.J.'s Tea - a children's tea for $6.95; and Anna's Tea - 4 tea sandwiches, sorbet, chocolate and scone for $10.95. For a larger tea set, one may choose Beatrix's tea which includes 4 tea sandwiches, cheese selection, sorbet, assorted chocolates and 2 scones, or the Dutch Tea which has a Dutch tea sandwich, cup of chicken curry soup, Dutch cheese selection, assorted Belgian chocolates, warm stroopewaffels and almond fingers for $21.95. The teas include a pot of tea, and scones are served with sweet cream, jam and lemon curd. The Dutch Tea requires a 48-hour reservation.

Kimberly has a number of party plans for adults and children to choose from, and she offers classes on tea and etiquette and tea history, as well as a tea-tasting seminar. A special teas is presented in December for Christmas and on the Saturday before Mother's Day. More theme teas are planned.

MC/V/AE/ DEB   ADA Accessible   Street Parking

February through September: Monday through Friday the hours are 11-4
and Saturday 11-3. October through January: Wednesday through Friday
the hours are 11-4 and Saturday 11-3 and Sunday 10-3. Tea is served from
opening until 1/2 hour before closing. Reservations are not required but are
recommended.

Proprietor's
Autograph_____Date_____

Ruthie B's Tea Room

346 Main Street
Springfield, Oregon 97477
541-988-4791

From I-5, take exit 194A. Take the first Springfield exit. Go right on Pioneer Parkway. Take a left on 1st Street, a left on 4th street and a left on Main.

This is so much more than a tea house … *still*! After moving just two blocks from her former location, Ruthie B has managed to keep the same fun and interesting ambiance she was famous for at her original site. Ruth describes her tea room as "Fun with Tea and Art" and that is an understatement.

The new location is HUGE! The massive room is divided up into large cubicles and each has shelves laden with everything imaginable for the collector. Each also has a table and chairs set and ready for tea. The area is roomy and comfortable, and one can view, and perhaps shop for the items around them from a comfortable distance.

Once you are seated, your server brings glasses of water, then scatters lavender on the table and blows bubbles to lighten the moment. The service is fun *and* efficient, and your order is taken in a timely manner.

There are two tea sets to choose from:The Garden Tea, which includes your tea of choice, soup, 4 tea sandwiches, 2 savory salads and a shortbread treat for $12, and the High Tea which includes your tea of choice, a warm scone topped with Devonshire cream and jam, a cup of soup, then the main course of 4 assorted tea sandwiches, two savory salads, a compote of winter cranberry fruits, and an assortment of special desserts for $18 per person. Special teas are presented throughout the year, and there is a children's menu which is available to "big and little kids." The Mad Hatter's Children's Tea is by reservation only and it includes children's theme tea sandwiches, carrots with ranch, creamy chicken noodle soup, fruit compote, mud with worms and a pot of tea or cocoa. Desserts are available à la carte, and one may choose a soda, coffee, Italian Soda, or Cremosa in place of tea. Just remember, when you arrive, plan for a very long visit!

MC/V/DEB/DIS/Checks
Wheelchair Accessible
Street Parking

Hours of operation are Monday through Saturday 10-5:30 and Sunday 12-4. Tea is served all the hours they are open. Reservations for tea are recommended. For parties of more than 6 people, they are required.

Proprietor's
*Autograph*_____*Date*_____

Savouré

201 W. Broadway
Eugene, Oregon 97401
541-242-1010
cpotter@savouretea.com
www.savoure.com

Savouré is located near the downtown district at the corner of Charnelton and Broadway. Check the website for more information.

If you have not visited a French tea room in the past, you will immediately sense the difference upon entering Savouré, a lovely tea room which was opened by Cindy Potter in 2000. The rich red walls, floor-to-ceiling white drapery, huge picture windows, and many gold accents suggest that this tearoom visit is going to be different. Cindy has visited France many times and her attention to detail reflects those journeys. As you enter, on your left you will see a wall showcasing their signature tea selections, including teas from Mariage Freres. The adjacent showroom displays teapots, books, dishes and other necessities for the "tea lover."

In the dining area, tea is served on small tables draped with crisp white linens. The beautifully upholstered chairs and couches are comfortable and inviting spots for taking tea. Tables are set with white English china and the tea sets are presented on silver tiered plates with dainty silver servers.

The tea sets are numerous and include the Proust's Tea which consists of 2 scones for $7.50, the Dessert Tea for $9.75, Tea Savories for $8.75, the Very Nearly Tea for children at $8.50, and the Salon Tea for $18. A typical Salon Tea includes a petít four and 2 other sweets, 2 scones and 4 savories. The menu changes monthly and you can check their interesting website (www.savoure.com) each month to find out what that month's offerings will be. One thing you can count on … it will be delicious and interesting!

MC/V/DIS
Wheelchair Accessible
Metered and Lot Parking

Open Monday through Saturday 10-6 and Sunday 12-5. Tea is served until 1/2 hour before closing. Tea is first-come-first-served!

Proprietor's
*Autograph*_____*Date*_____

Shelton-McMurphey-Johnson House

303 Willamette Street
Eugene, Oregon 97401
541-484-0808 / fax 541-984-1413
director@smjhouse.org
www.smjhouse.org

From I-5, take Eugene/U of O exit over the Ferry Street Bridge. Go right on 3rd. exit to Pearl Street. The house is located off 3rd and Pearl.

This is the perfect ambiance for afternoon tea ... a stately Victorian mansion located in the heart of Eugene. The Shelton-McMurphey-Johnson House offers specialty teas in honor of Valentine's Day, Mother's Day and Christmas. The traditional high tea menu may offer cucumber tea sandwiches, egg salad tea sandwiches, banana nut bread and cream cheese tea sandwiches, lemon tartlets, chocolate baby cakes, Madeleines and mini scones with toppings. The tea offerings are catered in by some of the areas finest caterers and cost $20 per person. Since these teas are very popular, they fill up quickly, so plan ahead and make reservations well in advance.

Their Sampler Tea for groups of 10 to 30 is offered for $10 per person, and it is available only with prior arrangements. This tea includes one sandwich, one sweet-treat, a mini scone, tea and a tour of the historic house. You bring the group and they provide the ambiance and food!

Plan to allow yourself time to take the tour of this beautiful reminder of our elegant past. It is quite large but well worth your time.

Checks and Cash Only
Wheelchair Accessible
Lot Parking

Holiday teas are offered in February, May and December. Reservations required up to one month in advance. Cancellation policy. Private teas for groups of 5-30 people are also available.

Proprietor's
Autograph_____Date_____

Sister Act Party Specialists

Catering and Teas
Corvallis, Oregon 97333
541-752-7624 / 541-757-6525
jacobt@peak.org

Alicia and Deanna cater off-site, at your home or other location of your choice.

As the name implies, Alicia and Deanna are sisters with a broad background in the catering business. They started at an early age, helping their mother with her catering business, then ventured out on their own when they became mothers themselves.

Though they do all types of catering, presenting teas is their main focus. This duo has done a tea for as few as two people and as many as seventy-five. A typical afternoon tea includes sandwiches, savories, fruit, scones with Devonshire cream, lemon curd and jam, assorted desserts and, of course, tea. Some of their special tea items are tomato and fresh basil on crostini, egg salad pocket, rotisserie chicken wrap, ham and asparagus roll, Florentine square and their signature bacon ranch pinwheel.

Other types of teas are available depending on your needs, and price is dependent on what type of tea you choose. The average range is $10 to $15. They also enjoy doing theme teas such as Mother's Day, Valentine's Day, Christmas, Birthday Parties, Bridal and Baby Showers as well as your personal theme choice. Teas for children are of special interest to these moms, and the tea features peanut butter and jelly sandwiches, meat/cheese stacks, shaped cheese sandwiches, fruit, mini cupcakes, cookies and a party favor for $6.50 to $8. Additional items which they would be happy to provide for a minimal fee are linens, tableware, teapots and other tea accoutrements, dishes, and decorations.

Besides teas, Sister Act does catering for groups and individuals at the client's home or at another location. Call for prices and specific information.

One-week notice on teas is appreciated.

Proprietor's
Autograph_____Date_____

Society Woman

29970-B S.W. Town Center Loop W.
Wilsonville, Oregon 97070
503-582-0646 / 800-361-0944
barbrasharp@msn.com
www.societywoman.com

From I-5, take exit 283 east to Town Center Loop West. Turn left then an immediate right turn. You will see the shop in front of you. It is behind Boston's Pub.

This is the ultimate Red Hat store, where you sit for awhile and enjoy one of Barbara Sharp's custom-made teas ... then shop 'til you drop! Or if you prefer ... shop first! Then you can share your treasures during tea.

For $14 per person, you may enjoy one of Barbara's three tea selections. The first is Red Hat Tea and it includes finger sandwiches, fruit and three different desserts. The next choice is Raspberry Chicken Salad with three desserts, and the last is Garlic/Herb Chicken Salad with 3 desserts. All of the meals include tea.

Groups of up to 18 people can be accommodated. Society Lady does door prizes and really caters to her guests. You may stay as little or as long as you would like and enjoy the ambiance in a 100% Red Hat store. Although they are closed on Mondays, Barb will open for a tea for a group.

Holiday and theme teas are also offered.

V/Checks/Cash
Wheelchair Accessible
Lot Parking

The store is open Tuesday through Friday 10-6, and Saturdays 12-5. Closed Sunday and Monday. Teas are by reservation and are served between 11 and 3.

Proprietor's
Autograph_____Date_____

Stratford House

207 East Main Street
Hillsboro, Oregon
503-648-7139

From I-5, take exit 292 toward Beaverton (Hwy 217). Take the ramp onto US-26 (Sunset Highway). At exit 65, keep right onto the ramp. Turn left onto Cornell. Bear right onto E. Main Street.

This is one of the many tea rooms appropriately located in the historic district of town where renovations have drawn people back to the community's roots. Stratford House, owned by Steve and Alice Stratford, was opened in 2000. It dwells in one of the old buildings where brick and wood, high ceilings and deep rooms set the tone for a trip back to the past. A recessed entryway, set off by double sided display windows, greets you. The tea room shares space with an antique business, so one is surrounded with history in the form of furnishings, decorations, clothing, linens and household items from yester-year. The area where tea is served reminds one of an old-fashioned soda fountain. The counter is on one wall, and an array of tables, covered with linens and lace, fill the room.

The tea set is presented on tiered-servers and tea comes in mismatched pots. None of the teacups and saucers came from the same set.

The afternoon tea , called Tea For Two, offers tea sandwiches, fruit, scones with Devon cream and lemon curd, petite desserts and a pot of tea. The price is $25 for two people but it may be purchased for one at $12.50. There is also a Cream Tea for $6.95 and a Tea Place offering soup, sandwich and petite dessert for $8.95. Their signature soup, Hungarian mushroom, brings customers back again and again!

Besides tea, Stratford House offers light breakfast items including a breakfast sandwich special. Quiche, sandwiches and soup may be purchased for lunch. A variety of hot and cold beverages is also available.

V/MC/Checks
Wheelchair Accessible
Free Street Parking

Afternoon Tea is by reservation. The shop is open from 8 to 4.

Proprietor's
Autograph_____Date_____

The Tea and Herb Shop

Water Street Market
151 N.W. Monroe Street
Corvallis, Oregon 97330

From I-5, take Exit 228 to Corvallis (Hwy 34). Go 10 miles and cross the bridge into town and take a left at 2nd Street. Take a left at Monroe, and The Water Street Market is on the corner of Monroe and 1st. Streets.

This successful business has made a few location changes throughout the years, but it is now settled into a new and exciting location on the waterfront in Corvallis. Water Street Market was completed in 2005 and houses a number of boutique-style businesses - a wine cellar, fish market, Danish bakery, gourmet foods store and more. Tucked into a corner of the market is this wonder gem, which is owned by Peggy Leedberg. Peggy sells an extensive and interesting selection of teas and herbs.

The shop is small but comfortable, and well laid out. An abundance of windows keeps the room light and cheerful. One long wall holds shelves of large glass jars filled with fragrant whole-leaf teas. A large portion of them is organic. Near the counter, shelves hold a nice selection of herbs.

Peggy offers teas from China, Japan, Kenya, India, Ceylon, South Africa, and Latin America. She also has many blended teas. The selection includes black, green, white, herbal, red and other teas, and they range in price from $1 to $10 per ounce. On Friday and Saturday, a station is set up where one can sample one of the many tea choices.

Besides teas, Peggy has a nice selection of tea accoutrements from strainer to pots. She also has a Tea of the Month newsletter which customers may sign up for.

Cash and Checks
Wheelchair Accessible
Lot and Metered Street Parking

Hours of operation are Tuesday through Friday 11-6, and Saturday 9-6.

Proprietor's
*Autograph*_____*Date*_____

Tea and Treasures

1145 N. Oak Street
Sisters, Oregon 97759
541-549-TEAS (8327)

From the west, the tea room is on Oak Street, just off the main street (Hwy 20), soon after you enter town. From the east, you travel almost all the way through town then make a right on Oak Street .

Sisters is one of those towns where you spend the whole day walking from shop to shop, just for the fun of seeing all that they have to offer. Of course, you always find just the right gift for a friend or the perfect gadget or decoration you need for yourself. This is the perfect place to take a break from shopping for a cup of tea.

The owners, Steve and Barbara Wilson, built their Tea Room just off Main Street, around the corner from Steve's Business, Mountain Man Mercantile. The yellow, two-story building has a western-looking façade which blends into the theme of this western-themed town. The entry-way to the tea shop features a beautiful door which welcomes you to a large room with shelves and tables laden with beautiful and useful tea accouterments, gift, books, children's treasures, jewelry, hats and just about everything imaginable item. Specialty foods and bulk teas are also available for purchase.

The upstairs tea room, decorated in deep green and burgundy, has a very "Titanic" feel to it. Beautiful damask or green cloths on round tables set for four, forest green walls with wainscoting, green carpet with burgundy and gold accents and lace covered windows with sheer burgundy toppers that drape to the floor. Tall plants, many of them palms, dot the room, and wall sconces and chandelier, reminiscent of the Victorian Era, complete the look.

The two tea offerings which are offered in this lovely setting are a cream tea for $5.95 and a light tea, which consists of soup, scone and tea, for $9.50.

The shop is open Monday through Friday 10-5, Saturday 10-5:30 and Sunday12-5. Tea is offered Wednesday through Saturday11-4. The last seating is at 3.

Proprietor's
Autograph_____Date_____

Tea Events

P.O. Box 7102
Bend, Oregon 97708
541-279-1023
www.StartATeaBusiness.com
www.TeaEvents.com

Dawnya Sasse is the creative force behind Tea Events, a tea business training company. Tea Events offers a variety of programs aimed at training new tea entrepreneurs in the tea business of their dreams. Tea Events flagship program, "Start a Tea Business" ™ , offers complete on-line tea business training from the comfort of your own home.

The "Start a Tea Business"™ class offers students a firm foundation in tea concepts, tea cupping, tea history, business planning and in-depth education on 17 different types of tea-related businesses. Everything you need to begin in the tea industry is available in this class, including inside information on over 200 wholesalers longing for your business.

Dawnya Sasse is a highly trained tea professional, beginning in the tea industry in 1997 during its "pioneer days." She has successfully owned and operated a British tea room and a by-reservations tea room (for 7 years), led British Tea Tours and trained hundreds of students on-line and in person. Dawnya has been educated by a Who's Who in the tea industry including Pearl Dexter, James Norwood Pratt, Jennifer Peterson, Ron and Donna Lasko, Tomislov Podreka, Bill Waddington, Richard Gusauska, Elizabeth Knight and Edward Brahma of the Brahma Tea Museum in London, England. She has received numerous certificates from programs all over the world.

Dawnya has also been featured in numerous publications including; *The Country Register, The Gilded Lily, The Teahouse Times, Tea Experiences, The Bend Bulletin, The Vancouver Columbian* and *The St. Louis Post-Dispatch.*

For more information on her tea classes both on-line and in person, be sure to visit:

www.TeaEvents.com and
www.StartATeabusiness.com

Proprietor's
*Autograph*_____*Date*_____

The Tea Party

716 N.W. Beach Drive
Newport, Oregon 97365
541-574-0545 / 877-7T-Party
www.theteapartycompany.com

From the Hwy 20/Hwy101 intersection, go west to Coast Street. Turn right on Coast then left on Beach. You will be at the turn-around in Historic Nye Beach. The tall Tudor building on the right is your destination.

I was thrilled to see Claire McNeely and her daughter Lucinda Chapman open their tea room in June 2005. The absence of a tea in Newport was felt by many tea enthusiasts like myself, and our need has been met! They have done a wonderful job of transforming this historic Tudor building into their own special 'Alice in Wonderland' place, starting with the bright yellow door that welcomes us to tea. The windows are adorned with soft miniature floral yellow curtains with yellow plaid tie-backs. The plaid pattern is carried out on the half-wall room divider just inside the door. A charming bench in the gift area is provided for those waiting to be seated. Speaking of gifts, the selection is interesting and extensive.

For tea, the selections start with Sweet Delights for $6.95, which offers a sorbet followed by five dainty sweets. The Classic Tea includes sorbet, four finger sandwiches, two hot savories, scone with all the fixings and three small desserts for $12.50. A Non Sweets Delights is much like the Classic Tea only the sweets are replaced by 3 additional finger sandwiches or savories and a scone, and is priced at $14. All teas include a pot of tea, and all the fixings for the scones. All hot teas may be served with a glass of ice as well. Special dietary needs may be accommodated with prior arrangements. For guests 12 and under, there is a seasonally themed Mad Hatter Tea for $6.95. It includes sorbet, a peanut butter and jelly sandwich, cookie, fruit and a beverage.

For large groups, a party room is planned for the back of the tearoom. Small children already have one!

V/MC/AE/DEB/DIS
Wheelchair Accessible
Lot Parking

The tea room is open Tuesday through Saturday 11:30-5.

Proprietor's
*Autograph*_____*Date*_____

The Tea Zone

510 N.W. 11ᵗʰ Avenue
Portland, Oregon 97209
503-221-2130
teazone@teazone.com
www.teazone.com

I-5 to 405 N(299B) Take exit 2B to Everett Street. The exit will merge onto 14ᵗʰ Avenue. Follow 14ᵗʰ about 4 blocks to Hoyt Street and turn right. Go to 11ᵗʰ Street and turn left. The shop is on the left side.

Located in the historic Pearl District, The Tea Zone offers over 65 loose-leaf teas, bearing their own label, and ranging in price from $2.25 to $7 per ounce. There are also some specialty teas and artisan teas which are individually priced. If you are looking for prepared tea, it can be purchased at $2.65-$3.70 for a one-person pot and $4.30 to $6.40 for a two-person pot. They now feature Fruit Tea Blasts, Tea Lattés and tea tonics, and were voted Portland's best Bubble Teas. To accompany your beverage, you can purchase scones (they say the best in town!), tart, cookies, desserts and other treats.

This European-style establishment also offers hardier fare, and the choices are numerous. They include empanadas, galettes, pasties, quiche, grilled panini sandwiches and a Southwest tuna sandwich. These entreés range in price from $2.75 to $6.95 and a mixed greens side salad may be added for $2.25. Daily specials are also available. When possible, dietary needs can be accommodated.

For those of us who enjoy the event called "Tea Time," monthly High Teas, excluding summer months, and Holiday high teas are offered.

MC/V/AE/DIS/Checks
Wheelchair Accessible
Gift Shop   Metered Street Parking
Self-serve Pay Lot is Available.

Weekdays open at 8 a.m. / weekends open at 10 a.m. Sunday to Wednesday - close at 6 p.m. / Thursday to Saturday - close at 8 p.m. Call for dates and times of High Tea. They are offered the three weeks prior to Christmas.

Proprietor's
Autograph_____Date_____

Tranquility Tea Room

134 S.W. 4th Street
Corvallis, Oregon 97330
541-738-1100

From I-5, take exit 228 (Hwy 34). Go west toward Corvallis. When you get
into town, turn left on 4th Street. Get into the right lane and go 2½ blocks.
The tea room is on the right hand side of the street.

This tea room changed hands in 2005 and is now under the ownership of
Tracy Thompson. She has brought her own personal touches to this
charming tea room, including intimate tables for two, set by the front
window. The wall colors, yellow in one area and soft green in the other, give
the tea room a warm and welcome feeling. The rooms, featuring very high
ceilings, are divided by a half wall which separates the dining area from the
extensive gift shop. French doors at the back lead you into a special room
which has soft yellow wallpaper covered with dark pink roses. The paper is
set off with a wide, coordinating tea cup border. Plants and soft floral
arrangements are set about the entire tearoom and give it a cozy garden feel.

The tea sets include a Relaxation Tea of sweets and a scone for $6.95;
Simplicity Tea which has 3 finger sandwiches and a scone for $8.95; and the
Meditation Tea offering 2 finger sandwiches, soup or salad and a scone for
$9.95. Other larger teas are the Serenity Tea with 2 finger sandwiches, fruit,
2 savories , a scone and 2 desserts for $9.50; the Reflection Tea which
includes 3 finger sandwiches, fruit, 2 savories, a scone and 2 sweets for $12;
and Tranquility's Afternoon Tea which offers 3 finger sandwiches, soup or
salad, fruit, 3 savories, a scone and 3 desserts or their Weekly Specialty
Cake for $15.25. Clotted cream, jam and marmalade is served with the
scones and a pot of tea is included. If you are just dropping by for a cuppa,
for $6.95 you may want to include a Scottish Tea - 2 scones, an English Tea
- 2 crumpets, or a French Tea - a hot croissant, all served with your pot of
tea. They proudly serve Harney & Sons Tea.

Tracy's goal is to create an atmosphere for all her
customers that is relaxing and tranquil while enjoying
excellent tea and scrumptious delicacies. She knows that
a tea room is a place where friends and family share
thoughts and memories.

VISA/MC/Checks   Wheelchair Accessible
Free and Metered Street Parking

The tea room is open Tuesday through Saturday from 11 to 6. The last tea
service is at 5. Reservations are needed for 8 or more. Holiday and theme
will be offered. Other menu's can be arranged with prior arrangements.

Proprietor's
Autograph_____Date_____

Tudor Rose Tea Room

480 Liberty Street S.E.
Salem, Oregon 97301
503-588-2345

*From I-5, take the Mission Street (Hwy 22) exit and go to Liberty Street.
Turn right, go a few blocks, and watch for the tea room on the right. From
Hwy 99, go across the bridge and turn right on High Street. Go past the
hospital and take the next right. Proceed to Liberty and take another right.
The tea room is just down the street on the right-hand side of the street..*

    Located in the back of an attractive English Tudor style building, Tudor
Rose Tea Room is a charming and comfortable place to take tea or any of the
other afternoon lunch items that are offered. The real challenge is getting to
the back! You must first pass through one of the most tempting gift shops in
the area. There are so many tea-related items that it is difficult to choose just
which ones you "can't live without." There are many other "necessities," too
numerous to describe, as well. For those who like a bit of England, Bob
carries a large selection of British foods to tempt the palate. Of course, those
are to take home, because after you have enjoyed the generous tea, you
won't be able to taste another morsel.

    The full afternoon tea consists of a first-course salad or savory served
with traditional English sandwiches. This is followed by a generous scone,
then trifle or other special pudding. To end the meal, a tiered server brings a
sampling of delicious desserts and a chocolate-dipped strawberry. The price
of the full tea is $13.95. There is also a smaller luncheon tea for $7.25.

V/MC/DIS/Checks
Wheelchair Accessible
Lot Parking

*The shop is open Monday through Friday 11-5:30, Saturday 11-5 and on
Sunday 12-4. Afternoon Tea is served on the 3rd Saturday of the month
between 12 and 4 by reservation only. Groups are welcome..*

*Proprietor's
Autograph*_____*Date*_____

The Vintage Vine Tea Room

101 S.W. Court Street
Dallas, Oregon 97338
503-623-3415
tvv@djsbodyshop.com / www.thevvine.com

Traveling west on Hwy 22, take the Dallas exit after the stoplight at Hwy 99.
Follow the left fork to Main Street at the main stoplight. Follow to the heart
of downtown. They are located diagonally across from the Courthouse.

The Vintage Vine was opened in July 2003 by Jackie and David Lawson. Featuring delicious homemade Italian cuisine, The Vintage Vine also carries a large assortment of fine wines, microbrews, teas and desserts.

Afternoon Tea is offered for $5.95 and includes assorted tea sandwiches, scone with toppings, tea cookies and tea. A modified tea for children 11 and under, with a 2-person minimum, is $4.95. It is the same as the above tea with smaller portions and "children's tea." Hats, boas, gloves and beads are included for fun "dress up."

The house tea is Davidson's and a Teapot for One may be purchased for $1.50, and a scone with jam and whipped cream is $2.95 while available. Assorted desserts, including daily specialties, are $3.95.

Numerous appetizers and salads, as well as quiche and sandwiches, may be purchased for lunch for $2.95 to $65.95. Dinner entreés range in price from $8.95 to $12.95 and are served after 5.

They are set up for large gatherings and catering, and special requests are gladly accommodated!

While waiting to dine, you may browse through the restaurant's unique gift items. These items include home accents to the perfect gift for the "hard to buy for."

MC/V/DIS/ Checks
Wheelchair Accessible
On-Street Parking

Open Monday and Tuesday 11-2, Wednesday through Friday 11-8:30 and
Saturday 12-8:30. Tea is available anytime by appointment with 24-hour
notice. A reservation made is a reservation paid. Groups are welcome.

Proprietor's
Autograph_____Date_____

Wakai Tea Room

1633 S.W. Skyline Boulevard
Portland, Oregon 97221
503-242-1557

Directions will be given at time of reservation.

Tea and Inspiration is offered once a month, usually on a Sunday, in this 8-mat Japanese Tea Room, located in a private home. The suggested donation is $15, and reservations are required one week in advance.

June serves a Japanese sweet and a bowl of Matcha, which is a high-quality powdered green tea, and the experience is reflective of the season. In the quiet setting of a garden and teahouse, guests contemplate words on a scroll, view the flowers in the alcove and enjoy a bowl of tea

Chado, the way of tea, is the practice of preparing, serving and drinking tea. This elegant yet simple practice reflects the philosophy of the four principles of tea: Harmony (Wa), Respect (Kei), Purity (Sei) and Tranquility (Jaku).

Also, the teachers of the Wakai Tea Assn. host a Guest Evening on the last Tuesday of each month at the Wakai Tea Room. Donation is $10 per person. Private group experiences, as well as lessons, are available through the Urasenke Certified Teachers of Wakai.

Checks Accepted
Off Street Parking

All teas are on the last Tuesday of the month at 7 by special reservation only. When you call, ask for June. Reservations are required 1 week ahead and there are no refunds.

Proprietor's
*Autograph*_____*Date*_____

The Windsor House of Tea

1004-C Marine Drive
Astoria, Oregon 97103
503-338-6900
sgeorge975@msn.com / slwindsor@aol.com
www.thewindsorhouseoftea.com

From west on Hwy 30, which becomes Marine Drive in Astoria, go to 10th
Street. The tea room is on the right side at the corner. From Hwy 101, which
becomes Commercial, proceed through town to the downtown area. Turn left
on 11th then left on Marine. The tearoom is at the corner of 10th and Marine

In 2004, Shirley George and Susan Windsor Widawski opened their tea room in the completely renovated Sanborn Building. The interior of the building appears like a town, with each business sporting a store façade. Two of the 'buildings' house the tea room and its separate gift shop. The interior of the tea room, with its eclectic tables and chairs, tea sets and dishes, antiques and colorful linens, looks out onto the 'street' and their 'courtyard,' complete with picket fence, lamp posts and additional seating.

The tea choices start with Lady Taylor's Tea for $6.95 which features scones with Devonshire cream, lemon curd and jam, and The Windsor Tea for $7.95, which is a dessert tea. The next selection is a Ploughman's Plate, and it includes a cup of tea, scone or finger sandwiches and a sweet dessert for $8.95. The Queen's Tea is $10.95 and it offers sorbet, miniature quiches, a scone with Devonshire cream, lemon curd and jam, and a selection of desserts. Finally, there is the Royal High Tea which starts with a trio of sorbets, followed by a tiered server of sweets and savories consisting of a variety of finger sandwiches, two scones with Devonshire cream, lemon curd and jam, and ending with a selection of desserts for $14.95. All teas include a pot of tea, perhaps their house brand ... Metropolitan-Windsor Castle. Some dietary needs may be accommodated with prior arrangements. For children, Sir Aidan's Tea includes finger sandwiches of peanut butter and jelly and cheese, fruit, cookies and choice of hot chocolate or apple juice for $5.95.

The gift shop, which is 'around the corner,' offers a wide variety of teas, selected gifts and tea accessories and accouterments.

MC/V/AE/DEB/DIS   On-Street Parking
Wheelchair Accessible (elevator)

The tea room is open Tuesday through Saturday 11-4, and Sunday (during
summer) 1-4. Any time is tea time. The last tea is served at 3. Reservations
are required for groups 72-hours to 2 weeks in advance, depending on size
of party.

Proprietor's
Autograph_____Date_____

Welcome

to

Washington

A Touch of Elegance

508 W. Bell Lane
St. John, Washington 99171
509-648-3466
jfk@stjohncable.com

St. John is approx. 55 miles south of Spokane. From Hwy 195, turn west on Steptoe and go 14 miles. Turn south on Saint. John Endicott Road, go 2 short blocks and turn right on Liberty. It becomes Bell Lane at the Catholic Church. They are the last house on the right.

Chintz-covered table cloths and chair backs, and servers in white starched aprons, greet you as you enter this charming Victorian-style tea room. These are some of the special touches that Barb Kite offers to those looking for gracious hospitality for their special event. Not just a tea room, but also a place to have a memorable luncheon with friends and family.

A catered lunch consists of two menu items of your choice: soup, salad or dessert, with sorbet and bread, for $20 per person including tax. If you choose to have soup, salad, bread and dessert, the cost is $25. With so many soup, salad and bread choices, selecting one will be a challenge! Everything, including the breads, is made from scratch by Barb.

Tea time, which is served in a gracious and elegant setting, offers a wonderful Victorian Tea that includes fresh from the oven scones, heart-shaped sandwiches, quiche, heart-shaped cheeses, sorbet, truffle, carrot cake, pecan tart, fancy sugar cookies and seasonal tarts. Assorted jams and jellies, spun honey butter and Devon cream are served with the scones. The desserts are garnished with Barb's signature chocolate lace butterfly and all this is available for only $25, including tax. Special themed teas are offered for holidays and birthdays and special dietary needs can be accommodated upon advance notice. Coffee is available.

Barb has been a florist for over 30 years and she makes all of her beautiful floral decorations and door wreaths. They add a special touch to tea.

After dining, guests are invited to browse through the Creative Workshop Boutique which features gifts, bulk teas and fine furnishings.

Checks/Cash   Not Wheelchair Accessible   Lot Parking

Tea time is 11-3 Monday through Saturday. Reservations are required 2 weeks in advance, with a minimum of 6 and maximum of 18. For the months of May and June, reservations need to be made 2 months in advance. Large groups require a one-week cancellation. You are responsible for the number reserved unless cancellation is made 48-hours in advance.

Proprietor's
Autograph_____Date_____

Abby Garden Tea Room

1312 - 11th Street
Bellingham, Washington 98225
360-752-1752
abbygardentea@fidalgo.net

I-5 North - take the Fairhaven Exit and turn left. Turn right at 2nd light (12th Street). Go 2 blocks. to light (Ham's Street). Turn left, go 1 block. then turn left onto 11th Street. You will be in the Fairhaven Historic District.

In 2005, Anne Winfrey moved her tea room next door to a beautiful new building where it blends perfectly into the Historic Fairhaven District. Here the tearoom shares space with "Creativitea", a business offering paint-your-own pottery, glass fusing and a tea bar. A big change from the former location, this "British inspired" tea room is now on the street level. The décor offers rich mahogany wainscoting, brown velvet chairs, gold curtains and burgundy tablecloths with white runners. Anne uses a wonderful assortment of mismatched china, and the tables are adorned with seasonal fresh flowers. Besides the main tea room, there is a mezzanine where private parties may be held.

There are numerous tea sets to choose from: the Cream Tea for $7.95; Abbey Tea of scone, 3 tea sandwiches and fresh fruit for $10.95; Savory Tea with tea sandwiches, sausage roll or Cornish pastry and dessert for $12.95; Afternoon Tea which includes 3 tea sandwiches, assorted tea cookies, dessert choice and fresh fruit for $14.95; Gentleman's Tea of 3 double tea sandwiches, sausage roll or Cornish pastry and dessert choice for $14.95; and High Tea which includes raspberry or lemon sorbet, 3 tea sandwiches, sausage roll, quiche or pastry, desert choice and fresh fruit for $16.95. All teas include tea, and scones are served with cream and jam. For children, Anne offers the Lil' Tea which includes 3 tea sandwiches, assorted tea cookies or mini lemon tart and a pot of tea or cocoa for $7.95.

Anne offers over 60 types of tea, both British brands and their own label, which may be purchased in bulk, and coffee is available. Lunch items such as soup, sandwiches, salads and savories are priced from $4.95 to $8.95. Delicious desserts are available for $3.95.

MC/V/Local Checks Only   Wheelchair Accessible
Free Street Parking and a Shared Lot

Tea is served Tuesday through Sunday 11-6. The last seating is at 4:30. Closed Monday and holidays. Reservations are not required. They offer party contracts for catered affairs and an upstairs party room is available.

Proprietor's
*Autograph*_____*Date*_____

89

All About Tea
Cyrilla Gleason
360-690-1811
cyrilla4tea@yahoo.com

The location for the etiquette class will be determined at the time of booking.

Cyrilla Gleason is a trained and certified Tea Etiquette Consultant and is the founder and director of *All About Tea*, a company specializing in tea education and etiquette. Classes, tea tutorials, and programs for groups are customized to the needs of the client. Mrs. Gleason has a BA in education and is a certified teacher. She is a member of the Colonial Williamsburg Foundation and is a graduate of the Protocol School of Washington in McLean, Virginia, which is the leader in etiquette and protocol services.

All About Tea classes provide an entertaining opportunity for men, women and young people to learn proper etiquette for taking tea in business and social situations. As Mrs. Gleason states, "taking tea provides a special opportunity to spend quality time with friends, family, and associates."

Programs include the history of tea, the proper preparation of tea, and the etiquette used while taking tea. Antique tea items and new tea accessories are demonstrated in their use of preparing tea. You will learn how to make a perfect cup of Green, Oolong, and Black Tea and why incorrectly prepared tea is bitter. Programs and classes may be held in tea shops, churches, businesses, clubs or homes.

Samples of programs are Afternoon Tea, High Tea, Friendship Tea and Etiquette, Traveling Tea Basket, Victorian or Colonial Days, Young Men's Manners, and Teddy Bear Tea and Etiquette. There is also a program for church and civic organizations which is perfect for brunch, lunch, tea or dinner meetings and can be given with or without a devotional.

For more information or to arrange a program, call or email Cyrilla. Classes are pre-arranged by reservation.

*Proprietor's Autograph*_____*Date*_____

Anna's Tea Room

606 N. Main Street
Coupeville, Washington 98239
360-678-5797
annastearoom@verizon.net

From Route 20, turn onto North Main Street. The tea room is on North Main between 6th and 7th on the left side as you drive toward the water. They are next to the United Methodist Church on 7th and Main.

How appropriate to find a tea room which honors the 7th Duchess of Bedford who started it all for us! This charming 1903 Victorian home, with its shuttered windows, manicured yard and white picket fence, does just that. The tea room, opened in 2002, features soft green carpet, lace-curtained windows and antique furnishings ... the perfect setting for tea

The owner, Kristin Schriker, invites customers to first select their tea cup from a glass case filled with both antique and modern pieces. They are then seated at a linen-covered table, or if they prefer, a lush settee or an elegant Victorian chair, in the bright and cheery parlor. The tea sets, which are served on antique china, range in price from the Light Tea of scone with cream and jam and a slice of tea bread with lemon curd for $5.75, to Anna's Royal Tea, which includes six tea sandwiches, scone with cream and jam, slice of tea bread with lemon curd and choice of sweet for $14.95. For an additional dollar, Anna's Luncheon Tea includes a teacup of soup or choice of salad. If you prefer just sandwiches, The Earl for $7.95 is perfect, or if you are taking children to tea, Auntie Anna's Schoolroom Tea is available for $4.95. Special theme teas are presented throughout the year.

If a tea set is not what you are looking for, soups, salads, lunch plate du jour and sandwich du jour are available. The tea items may be purchased à la carte. Catering is available, including picnics with advance notice.

MC/V/Checks
Free Street Parking
Not Wheelchair Accessible

Open 7 days a week. Summer hours are 11-5 and winter hours are 11-4. Any time is tea time! Reservations are not required. However, they are happy to take them. Reservations are recommended for parties of 6 or more.

Proprietor's
Autograph_____Date_____

Attic Secrets Café & Tea

4229 - 76th Street N.E., Suite 101
Marysville, Washington 98270
360-659-7305
atticsecrets-tearoom@yahoo.com

I-5 to exit 200. From north turn left, go to State Avenue, turn right, go to 76th (light). Turn left, it's 1/2 block on left side next to Van Dam Floors. From south, same except turn right at exit.

This is Snohomish Countys oldest tea room and was selected by the *Everett Herald* as one of the "top 10 places to dine" out of 200 restaurants, as well as, Best Tea Room by the *Marysville Globe*. Owners Happi and Rick, who purchased the tea room in 1998, refer to the ambiance as "Hollywood Romantic," and each of the four rooms is decorated in a different style. One has Waverly Print table cloths, fresh flowers, tulle-wrapped chairs and flowing floral draperies, while another takes you outdoors with its 'shuttered inside windows,' brick wall and wonderful murals. All are perfect rooms with all the finishing touches!

The tea offerings are numerous, from The Grand Lady Tea which consists of scone, four tea sandwiches and a specialty dessert for $14.95 and the Serenity Tea featuring a scone, three tea sandwiches and assorted Tea Room sweets for $12.95, to an Afternoon Tea of scone, sweets and fruit for $7.95. A unique feature is the selection of Peaceful Teas which offer various numbers of sandwiches with a sweet. All of the above teas include a choice of Tea Time Garden tea. Children can enjoy the Little Darling Tea for $5.95, and children's birthday parties are welcome. Dietary needs can be accommodated with advance notice. A full lunch menu is available all day, and catering is offered.

Sweet Peas Gifts, which shares space with the tea room, features a very large selection of gifts and tea items, including bulk tea.

MC/V/DIS
Wheelchair Accessible
Lot and Street Parking.

The shop is open Monday through Friday 10:30-4:30 and Saturday 10:30-4. Reservations are recommended. Walk-ins are welcome, though there may be a short wait. The last tea is served one hour before closing.

Proprietor's
Autograph_____Date_____

92

The Brambleberry Cottage
and Tea Shoppe
206 Pacific Avenue
Spokane, Washington 99202
509-926-3293

Take I-90 to Division Street exit. Go north on Division to Pacific. Go east on Pacific and they are on the third block.

Melanie and Dawn have combined their experiences to offer those of us who think tea time is a "necessity," just what we are looking for. The Victorian Cottage décor welcomes you while flowers, greenery and the eclectic décor make you feel right at home. They offer tea as it is intended to be, a step back from your busy life to a time when things were simpler and people enjoyed afternoon indulgences.

The tea offerings are Tea and Light Refreshments for $14, A Special Tea for $17 and High Tea for $20. Traditional cucumber, as well as chicken almond, artichoke bruchetta, and ham and Swiss are among the sandwich choices. Desserts vary as well.

The ladies traditionally have a theme tea once a month that consists of an entirely different menu to fit the theme of the tea. Their house tea is Cottage Blend but they offer other teas. Coffee and special dietary needs may be requested in advance.

While there, take time to check out the gift and antique area and ask about the classes that are offered.

MC/V/Checks
Wheelchair Accessible
Street and Lot Parking

Shop hours are Tuesday through Saturday 10-5. Afternoon tea is served Wednesday through Saturday 11-3, by reservation only.

*Proprietor's
Autograph*_____*Date*_____

93

The British Pantry, Ltd.
Bakery, Deli, Restaurant and Gift Shop
8125 - 161st. Avenue N.E.
Redmond, Washington 98052
425-883-7511
alvia@thebritishpantryltd.com
www.thebritishpantryltd.com

Go north on 405 to 520. Take the Redmond Way exit and turn left at the light. Proceed to 161st and turn right. Go 1/2 block and the tearoom is on the left in a row of shops. Look for the British flag!

Opened in 1978 by Mavis Redman, the British Pantry has earned a reputation for good food, friendly service and a wonderful selection of groceries and gift items straight from the United Kingdom. If a traditional English afternoon tea room is what you are seeking, you will find it here. Afternoon Tea is offered from 2:30 to 4:30 daily and the set menu consists of cucumber sandwiches, scone with jam and Devon cream, small cake, fresh fruit and house tea for $9.99. The Devon Cream Tea has a pot of house tea, scone with Devon cream and jam, fresh fruit and a tart for $7.95. We recommend that you allow room for dessert, because the trifle is absolutely wonderful. We started a chain reaction when we ordered it!

The British Pantry shares space with Nevell's Restaurants. The restaurant lunch menu features British favorites such as pasties, sausage rolls, fish and chips and Ploughman's, as well as sandwiches, soups and salads. For the sweet tooth, the list is extensive ... trifle, tarts, cheese cake, pies, cakes and much more. For dinner, you may choose from the above as well as other more substantial items.

MC/V/Cash
Wheelchair Accessible
Lot Parking

They are open 7 days a week from 10 a.m. to 9 p.m. The shop closes early some days, and they are closed all day for major holidays. Call ahead for those dates.

Proprietor's
Autograph_____Date_____

The Brits

A British Tea Garden and Gift Shoppe
1427 Commerce Avenue
Longview, Washington 98632
360-575-8090

From I-5, take exit 432 and proceed into town. Take a right at 15th then a right on Maple. Go one block and turn right on Commerce. From the Oregon side, cross the bridge and stay on Oregon Way. Turn right on Hudson and left on Commerce.

We were traveling north on one of our tea tours when we stopped in Longview to try this tea room. We were so glad we did! The room, with its distinctive British feel, was warm and inviting. Eclectic tables and chairs, crisp linens, an elevated fireside area and hats galore add to its charm. Joy Harris, who has owned the tea room for eight years, was very friendly and the service was efficient and timely.

The high tea tables are covered with linens and fine china, and the tea set is presented on tiered servers. The tea menu includes sandwiches, scones, tart, fruit and desserts for $12.95 plus gratuity. The scones are delicious, and are accompanied by double Devon cream and very tasty jam. A piping pot of tea is included.

There is also a nice selection of lunch items, including many traditional British dishes. One of Joy's specialty items is a savory scone which she tops with one of a variety of items, such as chicken.

After tea, take time to do a little shopping in the gift area. On one wall is a nice array of British foods and a selection of English teas. Beautiful tea pots, as well as cup and saucer sets, are available for purchase along with other tea accoutrements.

For a photo op, be sure to check out the red phone booth in the front of the store!

MC/V/Local Checks
Wheelchair Accessible
Street and Lot Parking

The shop is open 11-4 Monday through Friday. High tea is offered all day by reservation. Saturdays are available for groups of 15 or more.

Proprietor's
Autograph_____Date_____

Carnelian Rose Tea Co.

1803 Main Street
Vancouver, Washington 98660
360-573-0917
tea@carnelianrosetea.com
www.carnelianrosetea.com

Take I-5 to Vancouver City Center and go west. At Main Street, go right to
1803 Main. It is near the Clark County Historical Museum.

Supplying wholesale signature tea blends to tea rooms, the Carnelian Rose Tea Co. has a tea, antique and gift store, which is located in Uptown Village. It is also the location of the West Coast's premier Tea Business School. Tea samples are always available, and only the finest grades of specialty teas are served. An array of gift items, tea hats, candles and tea accoutrements is inviting to both men and women. Jennifer says, "my shop is a non-gender specific place, where fancy laces and down-home denims are both welcome."

Summertime seating is on the front porch amongst the botanicals, while winter weather asks you to step inside the cheery interior of the tea shop. Only the finest grades of specialty teas are served, and an eclectic assortment of teacups and teapots is available for purchase. There are also numerous other items such as glassware, garden items and decorative objects to please the eye. Featured artists are Kenneth Ray Wilson and Aquila Art Glass.

For a truly special treat, a full afternoon tea is available by reservation. A light luncheon menu is available from 11 to 2 and tea with scones or sweets is available from 11 to 5. Having experienced it, I can only say, "Get together a group of friends." The cost is from $9.95 to $18.95 and everything is made just for your event. A catering service is also available. Call Jennifer for details.

MC/V/AE/Checks
Wheelchair Accessible
Free Parking

Open Monday through Saturday 10-4. Tuesday and Friday open until 6.
48-hour advance reservations required for afternoon tea. Groups are
welcome.

Proprietor's
Autograph_____Date_____

The Cheshire Cat
British Tea Room & Restaurant
2801 Fort Vancouver Way
Vancouver, Washington 98661
360-735-1141
cheshirecattearoom@yahoo.com

From I-5 either direction, take the Fourth Plain Boulevard exit and head east. Turn left on Fort Vancouver Way and proceed to red stop sign. The shoppe will be immediately on the right corner.

This charming British-style tea room was purchased in 2005 by Sharon Harbeck and her daughter Chantelle Button. They were both born and raised in Reading, England, and have decorated their tea room to reflect their homeland - light and airy rooms where the tables are covered with white linens and the windows are adorned with lace.

The tea menu choices are numerous and there is something for everyone. For the lighter appetite, there are three choices priced at $6.95: Gwyneth's Devonshire Cream Tea; Poly the Parlor Maid, an array of desserts; and Fred the Footman, a selection of tea sandwiches. The other teas are; The Butler Tea which offers finger sandwiches and scones for $9.95 and the Sir Albert & Lady Myrtle's Tea which includes a selection of sorbet, an assortment of tea sandwiches, quiche, sausage roll, sweet and savory scones and a variety of desserts for $12.95. All of the above include a pot of tea, and the scones are served with jam, cream and lemon curd.

Lunch offerings include shepherd's pie, Ploughman's Plate, quiche, Cornish pastry, soup and sandwich, and more, all priced at $4.95 or $7.95. There is also a selection of desserts for $3.95 each. Carry-out is available.

Bulk teas as well as gift items, most of which are imported, abound in the tea room, so be sure to allow yourself time to look around.

MC/V DIS/Local Checks
Wheelchair Accessible
Free Parking Lot

The hours of operation are 11-4:30, Wednesday through Saturday. Tea time is 11-4. Reservations are not required but they are recommended. Holiday and theme teas are offered.

Proprietor's
*Autograph*_____*Date*_____

Christine's Tea Cottage

735 Burlington Boulevard
Burlington, Washington 98233
360-757-4889
chris@christinesteacottage.com
www.christinesteacottage.com

From I-5, take exit 230 and go east to Burlington Boulevard. The tea room is a few blocks down on the right.

Not far from the freeway, situated on the main street of town, sits this warm and welcoming cottage tea room. Christine Yerigan, who opened the establishment in 2002, calls it a "magical and relaxing atmosphere," and we have to concur. The three rooms offer a different feel, from the more formal front room to the fun and colorful party room. Everywhere you look there is beautiful stenciling ... over the doors, up the walls and around the room! Each room is brightened by windows dressed in lace, and different hued tablecloths with lace toppers. Even the lovely ribbon-bedecked menus, which hold a wealth of information about tea, tea time and tea classes, show the attention to detail.

The tea sets start with a Cream Tea, which includes a scone and soup or a garden salad, for $7.95. The next three are named for Christine's three daughters - Stephanie's Tea which consists of a scone with two tea sandwiches, sweets and fruit at $5.95 for children and $9.95 for adults; Madison's Sweets and Tea for $9.95; Alexandra's Best Friends' Tea which offers a scone, four assorted tea sandwiches, sweets and fruit for $12.95; and the Victorian Delight, which includes choice of soup or garden salad, scone, assortment of four tea sandwiches, sweets and fruit. All of the teas include Devon Cream, lemon curd, jam and a pot of tea. The presentation is very attractive and the scones are large and delicious! Fresh-made soups as well as sandwiches and a large selection of teas are available all day.

The tea room offers over 170 loose leaf teas to enjoy there or to take with you, and they represent numerous labels. Etiquette classes, readings and seminars can be arranged and Christine is now certified by the Specialty Tea Institute, Foundations of Tea Level I and II.

MC/V/Checks   Wheelchair Accessible
Lot Parking

Open Tuesday through Saturday 11-4 and tea is served all day. Reservations are recommended for groups of 4 or more. Theme teas that are offered are Ann of Green Gables, Fairy Tea, American Girl and Tea with Mrs. Claus.

Proprietor's
Autograph_____Date_____

Delicate Pleasures -A Tea Room

702-B Metcalf Street
Sedro Woolley, Washington 98284
360-855-0727
information@delicatepleasures.com
www.delicatepleasures.com

From I-5, take the Cook Road/Sedro-Woolley exit. Follow to second light (Hwy 20). Road changes from Cook to Ferry at intersection. Go straight on Ferry. At stop sign, turn right at Metcalf. The tea room is on the right-hand side.

Shelly and Michael Sterba have created a beautiful tea room in the heart of the historic district in Sedro Woolley. The unusual color scheme is very striking, with peach-colored walls that reach to the white picture rail, where the walls become dark green, a color that also covers the ceiling. Large gilt-framed pictures and period mirrors hang from green cords that are attached to the picture rail. Square antique English tables with eclectic chairs sit upon green carpeting, and are dressed in crisp white cloths and napkins. A fireplace is set on one wall where a pair of comfy green chairs may beckon you. There is also a cozy sitting area with couches and chairs near one of the front windows. Wall sconces and lovely chandeliers are the perfect finish.

There are four tea offerings, from the Cream Tea for $4.95 to the High Tea, which includes Entrée du Jour, scones and two fresh baked sweets for $16.95. Other teas are Afternoon Tea of soup, finger sandwiches, scones and fruit for $14.95 and the House Tea which has a scone and baked sweet for $6.95. All include a pot of tea. For children, the Teddy Bear Tea has an English muffin pizza, cinnamon toast or finger sandwich, two sweets and tea, milk or lemonade. Other offerings include Soup du Jour and sandwiches. Milk and cookies can be purchased for $2.95. The house tea is Harney & Sons and coffee is available. Special dietary needs can be accommodated.

A gift area offers bulk tea, as well as lovely gifts and tea accoutrements.

MC/V/AE/DEB/DIS/ Checks
Wheelchair Accessible
Free Street Parking

The tea room is open Monday and Tuesday from 11-2 and Wednesday through Sundays 10-4. Reservations are not required. Groups are welcome, up to 20 guests.

Proprietor's
Autograph_____Date_____

E.J. Roberts Mansion

W. 1923 First Street
Spokane, Washington 99204
509-456-8839 / 866-456-8839
bob@ejrobertsmansion.com
www.ejrobertsmansion.com

From the north, take the Maple Street bridge route, take the 1st right at the light after you cross the bridge. Continue straight ahead on 2nd Avenue to Cannon Street, turn right on Cannon, go to 1st Avenue, turn right on 1st. The Mansion is on your right.

The E.J. Roberts Mansion, long considered Spokane's best example of Queen architecture, is now open to the public for corporate events, private dinner parties, weddings and Afternoon Tea. The Mansion continues the fine tradition of elaborate entertaining begun by Mrs. Roberts at the turn-of-the-century. Whether you desire an intimate dinner or a large out-door wedding, the mansion's staff will attend to every detail with care.

You may experience the elegance of the Mansion personally by staying in one of the luxurious bed and breakfast suites. Relax in the parlor, antique-filled library, billiard room and sun-porch. A delightful five course breakfast awaits you after a restful night's sleep.

A Victorian High Tea is served four times per month for the public and private teas are easily arranged. The tea is served by staff dressed in period clothes. Chadwick, the theatrical English butler, entertains you with piano playing prior to the tea. A tour of the Mansion and a short history talk follow the tea. The cost of this special event is $25 plus applicable taxes.

Secluded from the street, the beautifully landscaped grounds include lush lawns and gardens; a rose garden; a private gazebo and ornate pergola. A  carriage house and an enclosed Secret Garden round out the estate. Twenty-four years of meticulous private restoration have resulted in national recognition for this historic home. Your event, such as a private tea, could not be held in a more luxurious setting.

V/MC/Cash
Not Wheelchair Accessible
On-site Parking and Limited Street Parking

Tea is by reservation.

Proprietor's
*Autograph*_____*Date*_____

Elegant Catering N.W.

425-238-0016
fax 360-653-9096
elegantcatering@yahoo.com

From I-5, take exit 202.Travel east on 116th, cross Smokey Point Boulevard (State Street, RR tracks). Continue 1/2 mile and 116th will turn north and becomes 47th Drive N.E. Take a left on 118th, which is the 2nd cul-de-sac on the left. Your destination is the 2nd house on the right.

It's taken two years, but Betty Martin is back! The former owner of Hattie's in Stanwood is now the proud owner of Elegant Catering where she specializes in Victorian afternoon teas. Her grand opening will be in October 2005. All events are at the location of your choice.

Betty has trans-formed her new establishment into a first-class catering business. In her updated kitchen, she can prepare anything and everything you may need for your special occasion. Future plans include Culinary Classes.

Her tea menu consists of: the Countess Cream Tea from $7 to $9; the Duchess of Sweets Dessert Tea which offers an assortment of pastries for $10; the Lady Eleanor's Tea which includes scone, fruit, 3 finger sandwiches and an assortment of pastries for $15; The Timeless Afternoon Tea, which is served in the British Tradition - soup, scone, 4 finger sandwiches, fruit, individual quiches, Cornish pasty, a glass of imported French fruit spritzer, and a selection of English and French pastries for $25 to $50 per person. A special treat is the Baroness Breakfast Tea - punch, assorted scones, fresh fruit, individual quiche, tartlets, éclair, lemon bread, oatmeal, croissant and bacon or sausage for $15 to $20 per person. All teas include a pot of tea, and the scones are served with clotted cream, lemon curd and berry preserves.

Other menu selections are available, so if a luncheon with friends or a dinner for a special group is what you need, Betty will be happy to accommodate you. A 50% deposit is required upon signing of the event contract. The balance is due 7 business days prior to the event.

MC/V//Checks

Catering is available 7 days a week. The catering kitchen is open to the public by appointment only. Holiday and theme teas are offered.

Proprietor's
Autograph_____Date_____

Elizabeth & Alexander's

English Tea Room
23808 Bothell - Everett Highway
Bothell, Washington 98021
425-489-9210
deanandsuehale@aol.com
www.e-a-englishtearoom.com

From I-405, take exit # 26. Turn toward Bothell and go one mile. The tea room is on the right. Look for the double-deck red London bus next to the tearoom. The nearest attraction is Country Village.

Dean and Sue Hale ask you to, "imagine yourself and an intimate friend slipping away to a quiet tranquil place where gentle music drifts in upon your ear while you sip a cup of fine English-style tea as the sweet discourse of your friendship lifts your heart. Here is a place where you unburden your cares and let time slip sideways." Such is the atmosphere of their tea room and gift shop. Each of the three rooms offers a unique ambiance. The Parlor boasts a fireplace, the Churchill Room, with its hunting theme, is decorated with bookcases and wingback chairs, and the Alexander Room offers an intimate atmosphere with its seating for only 10.

Once settled in, you select your tea from the variety offered under the Barnes and Watson label. Teatime offerings range in price from $6.95 for the Cream Tea to $21.95 for a tea that includes a scone, crumpet, jam, lemon curd and whipped cream, lemon tea cake, lemon tartlet, shortbreads, chocolate raspberry rum torte, fresh fruit and tea sandwiches. Other teas are Elizabeth's Tea for $10.95 offering a small scone with trimmings, fresh fruit, tea cookies, lemon/lime curd tartlet and lemon tea cake, and Alexander's Tea with assorted tea sandwiches, fresh fruit, crumpet w/lemon curd and short-breads for $11.95. The Children's Tea, for those under 12 years of age, is offered for $8.95. Dietary needs will be accommodated with advance notice and groups are welcome.

Lunch offerings include Quiche, Windsor Torte, Specialty Salads, Chicken Salad Croissant and Ploughman's Lunch. All are priced from $9.50 to $12.95. Desserts are also available à la carte for $3.50 to $5.95.

MC/V/DEB/Checks
Wheelchair Accessible
Lot Parking

Mon. through Fri. 9-3 and Sat. 8-4. They serve breakfast, lunch and afternoon tea. Tea time is from 11 to closing. Group reservations suggested 2 weeks in advance. Cancellations will result in the loss of a $25 deposit.

Proprietor's
Autograph_____Date_____

Everything Tea

1015-B First Street
Snohomish, Washington 98290
360-568-2267
everythingtea@prodigy.net

Take Hwy 9 east to Snohomish Exit. Turn right on 2nd Street and right on Avenue D. Go one block to the 4 way stop and turn left on First Street. Go 2 blocks (count blocks on the north side of the street). They are on the south side of the street (river side) in the middle of the third block, across the street from the parking lot.

Chris and Patricia call their business, Everything Tea, "1200 square feet of Tea Lover's Paradise." How right they are! There are over 200 loose teas available in this shop as well as a very large selection of tea accessories.

The shop is chock full of the "fun stuff" ... tea pots, kettles, cups and saucers, cozies and lots of unusual and handy accessories (those Drip Catchers really do prevent the spout from leaking!).

There are far too many tea labels to list but some examples are Bewley's, McGrath's, Ahmad, Barry's, Rishi Teas, Market Spice, Metropolitan Tea Co., and India Tea Co. Their house blend is Duncan's Ultimate Herbal Blend. As you can see, every kind of tea is represented and free tea sampling is available on Saturday and Sunday.

On one side of the room there is a cozy alcove with couches and tables, where you may take time for a little conversation, or you may choose to pick up one of the magazines on the "tea" table and get in a little reading while you sip.

Whatever your reason for visiting Snohomish, be sure to take time to check out this very friendly business, and catch up on the newest trends in teas.

MC/V/Cash
Wheelchair Accessible
Free Street Parking

The shop is open 7 days a week, Monday through Thursday 10-6, Friday and Saturday 10-7 and Sunday 11-5.

Proprietor's
*Autograph*_____*Date*_____

The Exhibitors Mall & Trellis Café

10312 - 120th Street E, # 4
Puyallup, Washington 98374
253-841-0769
mscampbell5@lycos.com
kimariejohnson@yahoo.com
exhibitors.mall.com

Take Hwy 512 to Eatonville exit. Follow Meridian to 120th Street E., turn left, go one block. The building is on the right-hand side of the street.

The Exhibitors Mall was initially established as an art gallery with antiques. When Joe and Kimarie purchased the business in 1994, they intended to add a restaurant, but first started expanding by inviting local artisans to show their wares. There are now 80+ cottage industries sharing space in the mall, along with major retail lines. Customers can shop from all the booths and check out one time!

The on-site café is now managed by Shelley Campbell, and has been named The Trellis Café. The menu offers soup, salad, sandwiches, dessert and afternoon tea. The Afternoon Tea offers fancy finger sandwiches, fresh baked scones, decadent chocolates and seasonal fruit, all served on a tiered serving tray, complete with endless tea for $12.95.

Children's tea parties, which are $9.95 per person, are similar to After-noon Tea but are scaled to fit the "little prince or princess".

I have always believed that antique stores are the perfect locale for a little tea room, and here you will find just that. Shop a little, take a tea time break, and shop some more.

MC/V/Checks
Wheelchair Accessible
Lot Parking

Store hours are Monday through Saturday 10-5, Tuesday until 7. Café hours Monday through Saturday 11-3. Tea is by reservation only.

Proprietor's
*Autograph*_____*Date*_____

Fairmont Olympic Hotel

411 University Street
Seattle, Washington 98101
206-621-1700 extension 3169
olympic@fairmont.com
www.fairmont.com

From the south, as you near downtown, get into the left lane. Take exit 165
(Seneca Street). From the light, go straight 2 blocks and move into the right
lane. Turn right on 4th Street and go one block to University Street. Turn
right and the hotel is on your right.

The luxurious Fairmont Olympic opened its doors in 1924, and has been considered Seattle's premier luxury hotel ever since. Boasting impeccable service, splendid Italian Renaissance architecture and two award-winning restaurants, the Olympic, listed on the National Register of Historic Places and a member of Historic Hotels of America, well deserves its reputation as Seattle's Grand Dame hotel. This and additional information is available on their website.

An elegant Afternoon Tea is offered for $35 for adults and $18 for children, plus tax and gratuity. Included in the tea set are the following sandwiches: citrus prawn salad on rosemary bread, tarragon and almond chicken salad on eight grain bread, smoked salmon and Dungeness crab salad on white pin wheels, and cucumber and heirloom tomato Roquefort mousse on French country bread. The luscious desserts are a strawberry Bavarian Tart, almond Tosca, apricot spritz cookie and coconut lamington.

The featured scone is a chucker cherry with Devonshire cream and raspberry jam. Your tea is selected from a list of loose-leaf teas which includes such traditional flavors as English Breakfast and Earl Grey to Japan Sencha and Kea Lani Orange Pineapple.

MC/V/AE/DIS   Wheelchair Accessible
Valet Parking - $16 for 2-3 hours
Hotel Lot - $13 for 2 to 3 hours
Limited Metered Street Parking

Tea is offered daily 11:30-2:30. Reservations are recommended.

Proprietor's
*Autograph*_____*Date*_____

Fireside Room at The Sorrento Hotel

900 Madison
Seattle, Washington 98104
206-622-6400
charlie.evans@hotelsorrento.com
www.hotelsorrento.com

North on I-5, take Madison Street exit. They are on the corner of Madison and Terry. South on I-5, take James Street exit, go left on James and right on Terry.

Tea at The Sorrento is served in the Beautiful Fireside Room, where you are surrounded by opulence reminiscent of the early 20th century. The Fireside Room is very traditional for afternoon tea. Honduran Mahogany walls add to rich fabrics and plush surroundings. Charlie Evans, the Hunt Club manager, calls the ambiance "modern posh."

Reservations are required for Afternoon Tea and you may even reserve the day you plan to attend. However, certain times of the year they take credit card reservations. At those times, 24-hour notice is required for cancellation or there will be a $15 charge.

Afternoon Tea includes your choice of Numi Tea, and a selection of sweets and savories including salmon roulades, chicken curry barquettes, celery root salad in cucumber cups, fresh fruit tartlets, madelines, mini cream puffs, petít fours, chocolate pralines, miniature cookies and fresh baked apricot and cherry scones with Devonshire cream and preserves, for $32 per person. With any luck, you will be fortunate enough to take this exceptional tea by the 19th century Rookwood fireplace in one of the overstuffed leather chairs.

The Hunt Club, which adjoins the Fireside Room, is a full-service restaurant. Perhaps you will return for a stay at the Sorrento and a chance to try their other culinary creations.

MC/V/AE/DEB   Wheelchair Accessible
On-Street Parking   Some are Metered
Parking Lot - $7 Validated Parking

Tea is served at 3 p.m. every day of the year except Thanksgiving and Christmas. The last tea service is 4:45. They extend their hours during December and Mother's Day.

Proprietor's
Autograph_____Date_____

Foxwood House

125 Foxwood Drive
Newport, Washington 99156
509-447-2346
rjshawgo@povn.com

Foxwood House is on Hwy 2 between mile markers 328 and 329. They are a 35 minute drive north of Spokane. Watch for the billboard at Foxwood Drive.

When you see Foxwood House B and B, it is hard to believe that the owners, Roger and Jeanine Shawgo, did ninety percent of building it themselves. This modern day "victorian" is absolutely beautiful, and the attention to detail amazing. Though only 5 years old, it looks like a home from the turn of the century. The furnishings are original items from the 1880s. They started offering afternoon tea to the public in 2004, and how lucky we are!

The dining room where tea is served is stunning. It boasts elegant antiques, and reproduction wall paper from the 1880s. Vintage Lenox Rose china, finger bowls at each place setting, 3-tiered servers, vintage linens, and ribbon bedecked dining chairs complete the elegant décor. For a really special touch, Roger and Jeanine dress in original clothing from the late 1880s and early 1900s while they serve you with great attention to detail.

A sample tea menu would include a first course of tea and scones with Devonshire cream, lemon curd and preserves. This is followed by 3 varieties of tea sandwiches which are served with fruit. Then comes a portion of raspberry sorbet. A second flavor of tea arrives with a 3 tier tray of desserts-usually cake, lemon tart, mini cheesecake, fruit cookie, chocolate-covered strawberry and a truffle. This generous menu changes weekly and guests receive a small gift to take home to remember tea at Foxwood House.

Special theme teas are offered throughout the year and the cost is $25. Janine sets the menu based on the occasion. Special dietary needs can be accommodated whenever making a reservation.

Checks/Cash
Not Wheelchair Accessible
On Site Parking

Tea is offered by reservation any day of the week. There is required 3-4 day advance notice with a 24-hour cancellation policy. There is an 8-person minimum and 30-person maximum.

Proprietor's
Autograph_____Date_____

Hattie's Restaurant

51 Cowlitz Street West
Castle Rock, Washington 98611
360-274-7019
www.hatties-castlerock.com

From I-5, take exit 48 west into town on Huntington Avenue (approx. 1½ miles). At Cowlitz Street turn left, travel 2 blocks and you will see the Restaurant on the left-hand side of the street, across from True Value.

Hattie's is gaining a reputation as a fun and interesting place to visit, whether for tea time, breakfast, lunch or dinner. The owner, Linda, offers what she calls, "Uptown class ... down-home cooking", and that is precisely what you will find!

The atmosphere of the restaurant, ice cream parlor, Garden Room (complete with back porch and clothes line!), and Victorian "house" afford you the opportunity to choose your setting. The Victorian House, which is off the main dining room, boasts deep purple wall paper, period furniture, touches of lace, and décor that represents the Victorian era. This is a very special room set aside especially for tea. The main dining room is delightful and is the setting for a small re-creation of a country kitchen and parlor, complete with a fireplace. Hard to describe but delightful to see! As the name seems to imply, hats are everywhere, so if you feel a little under-dressed you may be tempted to don one of them, just as the servers did.

The breakfast menu is extensive and now features Linda's 'national award winning' Almond Stuffed Orange Glazed French Toast! For lunch you may choose from soup, salad, deli sandwiches, wraps, stuffed pitas, fish and chips, burgers or a custom-made baked potato. The signature chicken salad is one of the favorite offerings, whether served on a bed of lettuce or in a sandwich. Reservations are recommended for dinner and, again, the menu is extensive. If you plan to reserve for a group, Hattie's boasts the largest table in the Northwest at 16 feet 3 inches. It is a sight to behold!

Should tea time be your meal of choice, a special menu is prepared just for you. It consists of a scone, salad, a selection of small sandwiches, fruit, vegetables, cheese and sweets, plus a fragrant pot of tea, for $11.95 per person. This is just what I am looking for when seeking out the event called tea time!

MC/V/AE/DC/DIS/Checks   Wheelchair Accessible
Free Lot and Street Parking

Tea is by reservation only with a 48-hour notice required. There is a 24-hour cancellation policy. The restaurant hours are Monday through Saturday 8-8. Closed Sundays and most holidays.

Proprietor's
Autograph_____Date_____

Healing Garden Tea Room
and Flowers
111 N. Tacoma Avenue
Tacoma, Washington 98403
253-274-0861

From I-5, take the City Center exit, move right and follow direction for Schuster Parkway (705 N.). Get to the right and take Stadium Way exit. Turn right on Stadium Way, follow the road as it curves to N. 1st and N. Tacoma Avenue. Drive past the high school and turn right. They are 4 doors down.

This tea room opened in 2003 under the ownership of Fannie Kelley and it offers just the ambiance "tea people" are looking for. Fannie calls her tea room an elegant, peaceful and quiet setting, and she invite you "to enjoy a beautiful tea experience with her."

The tea room features lavender and sage-green walls, floor-length sage-green tablecloths, floral top cloths and plants and greenery throughout. A second floor room is available for large groups or special functions. Special functions require a 30-day notice.

The afternoon tea menu has three tea sets to choose from. The Crème Tea of scones, fruit and nuts is $6.50; The Traditional Light Afternoon Tea includes scone, fruit cup, nuts and dessert for $9.50; and the Healing Garden Light Afternoon Tea offers a scone, assorted savories, fruit cup and nuts for $12.95. The Full Afternoon Tea consists of a scone, assorted savories, fruit cup, nuts and assorted desserts for $18.50. Assorted savories are tea sandwiches, crackers with spreads and mini quiche. All teas include a pot of tea and lemon curd, preserves, creamed honey and Devonshire cream for the scones. The tea selection is extensive and it includes Republic of Tea, Ahmad Tea of London, Taylors of Harrogate and Market Spice.

Lunch items are on the à la carte menu and include sandwiches such as chicken salad, smoked salmon and cream cheese, and honey baked ham, priced from $5.50 to $7.50. Soups and salads are available for $2 to $4.50, and desserts are priced at $2.25 and $4.50. Beverages other than hot tea are also available.

Fannie's gift shop carries tea related items and silk flowers. Her tea shop adjoins the Custom Framing Company and Gallery.

MC/V/AE/DEB/DIS/Checks   Wheelchair Accessible
Street Parking

Hours are 11-6 Tuesday through Saturday. The last tea service is 4:45. Anytime is tea time! Reservations are recommended for groups of 6 or more.

Proprietor's
Autograph_____Date_____

The James House

1238 Washington Street
Port Townsend, Washington 98368
360-385-1238 / 800-385-1238
info@jameshouse.com
www.jameshouse.com

The James House sits on the bluff overlooking the Port Townsend-Keystone ferry. Centrally located in the historic district, it is just a short stroll to the downtown shops.

Sitting high on a bluff, with unsurpassed views of the beautiful water and majestic mountains of Puget Sound, the James House is the perfect setting for high tea. Sitting in the parlor of this 1889 Victorian mansion, it is not hard to imagine the past, with tall sailing ships in the harbor, and streets bustling with activity of a busy Victorian seaport. Tea is served in the dining room, surrounded by warm rich woods, an ornately carved fireplace, and the rich history that lives in this 115-year-old mansion.

The inn was opened as a bed and breakfast in 1976 and just began offering tea in 2005. Patricia Minish, the tea hostess, is taking "Just Pretend" tea parties and starting "Tea at the James House." Her tea offering will consist of tea sandwiches, savories, scones with Devonshire cream, fresh fruit, tea breads and tea for $25.

After this delightful tea, one can spend hours walking the historic streets of this delightful and charming town, venturing in and out of the many shops and markets that line the main street. Be sure to check the side street

for more boutique shops. If quiet time is your desire, you may enjoy sitting by the dock and watching the ferries as they enter and leave Port Townsend. Whatever the reason for your visit, be sure to include tea at The James House in your plans.

MC/V/ AE/Checks
Not Wheelchair Accessible
Off-street Parking

Tea is served in a private inn, so please call for information.

Proprietor's
Autograph_____Date_____

110

La Connor Flats - A Garden

15920 Best Road
Mt. Vernon, Washington 98273
360-466-3190
bobhart@fildago.net

From I-5, take exit 230. Follow Weston Hwy 20 for 5 miles to Best Road.
Turn left on Best Road and go 2 miles. La Connor flats will be on the right
hand side of the road.

A short drive in the country brings you to this very special place. This oasis in the country is really beautiful and the hostess, Marjorie, most gracious. It must have surprised her to find two strangers knocking on her door in the late afternoon inquiring about her tea room. Actually, her tea room is a "retired" granary that has been converted into a charming and cheerful room … perfect for tea. Refinished hardwood floors and rustic barn board walls greet you, along with matching oak chairs and tables, set with double white linens and fresh flowers. The room, rich with light and a feeling of the outdoors, overlooks the beautiful garden.

The set tea is served on depression glass, and Marjorie has over 200 cups and saucers, which she uses for teas, in her collection. The tea, which is served in three courses, consists of a fruit cup, hot scones and jam, a trio of sandwiches and assorted desserts for $11 plus gratuity. Other items may be substituted upon request.

In the summer months, tea is served outside on the porch or in the beautiful English Country Garden. At one end of the garden there is a large gazebo which is used extensively for weddings and other celebrations. The gardens are open and in bloom, March through October, and the carpet of color is always changing. We found it enchanting when we visited during the month of September.

Checks/Cash
Lot Parking

The granary is open during April and serves soup/sandwiches during the
Tulip Festival. Tea is by reservation, preferably at 2, throughout the year.
Small groups should give at least 24-hour notice, 8-10 people minimum.

Proprietor's
Autograph_____Date_____

111

La La Land Chocolates

32279 Rainier Avenue
Port Gamble, Washington
360-297-4291
lalalandchocolates@yahoo.com

From downtown Seattle, take the Washington State Ferry Service to Bainbridge Island. Follow Hwy 305 through Poulsbo to Hwy 3. Turn right (north) and continue to Port Gamble. Turn left at Gamble Bay. The nearest cross street is Hwy 104.

Janie started making her chocolates around 1996 for holiday craft shows. When the sales volume grew, she moved her business into a house in the historic town of Port Gamble. Customers commented that, the sitting room would make a wonderful tea room, and the rest, as they say, is history. The tea room opened in 2002 and has developed a loyal following of very happy customers.

Since they were already serving scones, tea, coffee, cookies and fresh fruit with chocolate fondue, they incorporated a Chocolate High Tea into their offerings. For $16.95 per person, the tea includes a variety of tea sandwiches (smoked salmon, English cucumber with mint butter and Cotswold cheese with Roma tomatoes), cranberry pecan scones with home-made jam and clotted cream, orange blossom cookies, truffle of your choice, fresh fruit with chocolate fondue and a pot of loose leaf tea. French-press coffee or Mayan hot chocolate may be substituted at no extra cost. A new feature is Breakfast Tea which is offered for $14.95. It includes a variety of individual quiches - quiche Lorraine, quiche Florentine and lobster quiche, cranberry pecan scones and fruit tart served with home-style clotted cream. Special dietary needs can be accommodated with prior arrangements.

Besides high tea and chocolate, you may enjoy a tea-tasting once a month on Saturday from 10 to noon. The cost is $6.95 and reservations are required. Seating is limited, so call early!

V/MC/Checks
Not Wheelchair Accessible
Free Street Parking

Open daily, except major holidays, 9-5. Tea time is by appointment. Please call or email for reservations, at least the day before. Notice of cancellation is appreciated.

Proprietor's
Autograph_____Date_____

La Tea Da Teas

at the Bradley House B and B
61 Main Street
Cathlamet, Washington 98612
360-795-3030
bradleyhouse@centurytel.net
www.bradleyhousebb.com

Take I-5 to Long View and Long Beach to SR 4, which will bring you right into Cathlamet. From Astoria, cross the Astoria Bridge then turn right to SR 4 to Cathlamet. They are near the last ferry to Oregon!

It just seems natural to me that a bed and breakfast would offer afternoon tea in the same tradition as the grand old hotels. Many B and Bs are in turn-of-the-century or early 1900's homes, with vintage furnishings and collections of memorabilia from the past ... a fine setting for tea. Bradley House is just such a place. Built in 1907 as a gracious home of a lumber baron, this elegant home sits on a knoll overlooking the historic town of Cathlamet, Puget Island and the mighty Columbia River. Tea is served in the dining room with its expansive fireplace and large lace-covered windows with floral valances. Shades of rose and pink give the room a soft, welcoming feel.

Audrian offers a large selection of themed teas from holiday to special occasion and each is custom-made to suit your wishes. A sample menu for High Tea might include jicama, green onions, slivered onions and parmesan cheese on Hawaiian bread, English cucumber marinated in rice vinegar and sea salt on white bread with cream cheese, mini quiche, grain cracker with fresh brie and dried apricots, orange cranberry scones with lemon curd, raspberry jam and Devonshire cream. The selection of desserts could be any of the following: petít four, mini cheesecake cube, cream puff or white chocolate macaroon. A selection of teas is included. All of this for $14.95 plus tax and gratuity. The tea menu varies and special needs may be accommodated. A gift shop is available for browsing.

Checks Accepted
No Wheelchair Accessible
Street and Lot Parking

Open Monday through Saturday, 11-3. High Tea is by reservation only, with a 24-hour advance request. There is a 72-hour cancellation policy. House Teas are offered at Christmas, Valentine's Day, Easter and Mother's Day.

Proprietor's
*Autograph*_____*Date*_____

113

Lynden's Cup of Tea

517 Front Street
Lynden, Washington 98264
360-354-2446
lyndenscupoftea@verizon.net
www.lyndenscupoftea.com

From I-5, take exit 256A toward Lynden. Go Right on Hwy 539 North for 10½ miles. Turn right on Front Street and go 1½ miles. They are across from the Lynden Chamber of Commerce.

With the many individual "rooms" and the lovely main dining area, this is a tea room where you can almost choose your ambiance. Jeri Martinsen, who opened her tea room in 2003, chose beautiful shades of burgundy, rose, lilac and soft green, which complement the rich, dark wood of the furnishings and wall features. Many lush green plants compliment the Victorian theme Jeri has chosen. There is even a children's room complete with miniature furniture and a period cradle.

The tea offerings are numerous and start with the Petite Choice of fruit and scones for $6.95 or the Lynden Special which adds 3 tea sandwiches to the above for $8.95. Fruit, quiche and scone or an English pastie, salad and tart are $9.95. For $10.95 there is The Hydrangea Tea which includes fruit and assorted cheeses and 3 sandwiches. Lynden's Choice has fruit, 3 tea sandwiches, scone, and dessert for $12.95. For a heartier meal, there is Afternoon Tea consisting of fruit, soup, scone, 3 tea sandwiches and assorted desserts for $15.95 or High Tea which offers fruit, soup, sorbet, savories and cheese, scone, 3 tea sandwiches and assorted desserts for $19.95. All teas include a pot of tea for one. For children there is the Butterfly Tea, which

includes sandwiches, fruit, dessert and beverage for $6.95 or the Little Tots Tea, for those 5 and under, which offers peanut butter and jelly or egg salad sandwich, fruit, dessert and beverage for $4.95.

There is an interesting lunch menu, and items may be ordered à la carte. An extensive gift shop will give you reason to linger a bit longer at this lovely tea room.

MC/V/Checks/Cash
Wheelchair Accessible
On-street Parking

Tea time is Monday through Saturday 10-5. The last tea is served at 4:30. Reservations are preferred. Afternoon Tea is served from 11 to 4 and High Tea is served from 12 to 4. Reservations are requested for High Tea.

Proprietor's
Autograph_____Date_____

Makenzie's Tea Room

at Between Friends

9111 State Street
Marysville, Washington 98270
360-658-9407
shayla@makenzistearoom.com / www.makenziestearoom.com

From I-5, take exit 200 (Quilceda and 88th Street). Go east to State Avenue. Turn left. Go north to 911 State Street - just before the next light. The tea room is set back on the left in the green and white house, next to Precision Tune.

Makenzie's, which was purchased by Shayla Ratté in 2004, is named for her charming and capable daughter. Upon entering you may choose the setting that suits you, because each of the rooms offers a unique ambiance. The English Garden Room has a small fountain and a mural-covered wall, and the other room is called the Tuscan Room, for those who would like to take tea in a "piazza."

When you find your niche, you get to make another choice from the large number of tea sets. The Cuppa Tea, with fruit and sweets is offered for $4.95, and if you add a scone, you have the Coral Tea for $7.95. The Afternoon Tea includes soup, a scone and sweets for $8.95, while the Duchess Tea adds salad and fruit to the Cream Tea for $9.95. The Garden Party offers green salad, two vegi-delight tea sandwiches, fruit and sweets for $10.95 and the Contessa Tea consists of scone, four assorted tea sandwiches, savories, fruit and sweets for $12.95. The full Victorian Tea has choice of soup or salad, scone, four assorted tea sandwiches, savories, fruit and sweets for $14.95. Choice of tea is included in all of the above, and scones are served with Devonshire cream, lemon curd and jam. This tea room is very kid friendly and offers the Lady Bug Tea for $5.95 for children under 12. It includes a scone, two tea sandwiches, fruit, tea room sweets and a beverage.

The à la carte items are available by request. Specialty salads and sandwiches may also be ordered and range in price from $5.95 to $7.95. You may add a scone for $1.50. Bulk teas and specialty gifts are also available.

If you are looking for Friday night entertainment, Jazz Night is offered on selected Friday nights.

MC/V/AE/DIS/DEB/Checks   Wheelchair Accessible   Lot Parking

Tea time is Monday through Saturday 11-5 and Sunday 12-4. The last tea service is 4:55 Monday through Saturday and 3:55 on Sunday. Reservations are not required except for groups. If you must cancel, a call would be appreciated. Themed teas are offered throughout the year.

Proprietor's
*Autograph*_____*Date*_____

Mount Rainier Railroad

P.O. Box 921
Elbe, Washington 98330
360-569-2351 or 888-STEAM11
www.mrsr.com

From Tacoma, take I-5 south and at exit 217, merge onto WA-512 going toward S. Tacoma Way. Take WA-7 / Pacific Avenue exit toward Spanaway. Turn right onto Pacific Avenue S. / WA-7 and stay on that highway 35 miles to Elbe. From Portland, take I-5 north to exit 68 and go east on US-12. Continue for 31 miles. Turn left onto 2nd street / W-7 and follow 17 miles into Elbe.

Those of us who like to go to tea, like to go to tea anywhere! Can you think of a more fun and appropriate place to enjoy our favorite past-time than on a train? The Mt. Rainier Scenic Railway had its first Mother's Day Tea in 2005 and plans to make this an annual event.

Tea is served while enjoying a 2½ hour excursion on trains being pulled by vintage steam locomotives. Should you choose to step outside while on the trip, an 80-foot long converted passenger car will fill the bill. It is a fully open-air car where photo opportunities abound and the smell of fresh mountain air delights the senses.

The menu for the Victorian Tea includes dainty sandwiches and dessert, along with a pot of tea. Additions to the menu may be made in the future. The cost of the excursion *and* tea is $35 for adults; $20 for children 4-12; and free for children 3 and under.

When you return from the trip, take time to walkabout the tiny town of Elbe and, of course, stop and visit the Mount Rainier Railroad gift shop.

MC/V/DIS/Checks
Wheelchair Accessible
Lot Parking

The train operates Memorial Day to July 3rd on Saturdays and Sundays only; July 4th to Labor Day 7 days a week; and on weekends in September on Saturday and Sunday only. Special events are scheduled during the summer. Seasonal and Theme Trains run during October through December. Please arrive 1/2 hour before departure.

*Proprietor's Autograph*_____*Date*_____

Mr. Spots Chai House
Home of Morning Glory Chai
5463 Leary Avenue N.W.
Seattle, Washington 98107
206-297-2424
info@chaihouse.com / www.chaihouse.com

From I-5, take the 50th Street exit, head west and take a left on Phinney Avenue. Then take a right on 46th, which becomes Market Street, and continue down the hill. Take a left at Leary Avenue and the shop is on the right next to the park.

This may not be what most of us think of as a tea room but they do offer a very large selection of bulk teas. The owner, Jessica, refers to the décor as "Gypsy Funk," which to me implies fun and a change of pace. As for teas, they offer 45 single herbs, 35 blacks, green, 13 high-grade oolong and scented. The house tea is Morning Glory Chai. There is something for everyone's taste!

Besides tea, a selection of food items are available, including pasties, samosas, falafel, calzones, soups, grilled cheese sandwiches and bagels. If dessert is what you are craving, cheese cake with chai and fancy cakes are also on the menu. Beer and wine as well as an espresso bar round out the beverage selections.

It seems like this could be the place to stop before heading to the Bay Theatre, or perhaps a picnic at Bergen Place Park is in order. Whatever your desire, this tea house offers a good selection of food and beverages to suit everyone's taste.

There is a gift area on the premises offering bath items, imports, incense, candles, and herbs. Bulk tea is also available for purchase.

MC/V/AE/Checks
Wheelchair Accessible
Metered and Free Street Parking

Monday through Thursday 7 a.m. to 10 p.m., Friday 7 a.m. to 11 p.m., Saturday 8 a.m. to 11 p.m. and Sunday 8 a.m. to 8 p.m. Anytime is tea time!

Proprietor's
Autograph_____Date_____

Mrs. Pennycooke's Tea Room

922 First Street
Snohomish, Washington 98290
360-568-5045 / Website being developed.

Snohomish is located 30 minutes north of Seattle or 10 minutes east of Everett, off State Route 9, which is easily accessible from I-5 or Hwy 405. Snohomish is also 5 minutes west of Monroe, off Hwy 2.

Mrs. Pennycooke's, which opened in 2002, is a wonderful addition to the charming shops and dining establishments in historic Snohomish. This lovely tea room, with its soft 'Feathery Green and Divine Blue' walls, sparkling white furniture and pale yellow plaid table cloths, is set off by very large windows facing the often busy street. The exclusive use of silver teapots, flatware, and cream and sugar sets gives the room a rather regal touch. That is quite appropriate considering the sizeable collection of Royal Family memorabilia.

Located in the heart of "The Antique Capital of the Northwest," this is the perfect place to stop for a break from shopping, to enjoy a cuppa or partake of a delicious tea set. For a romantic tea, or if the company is special, request the charming Alice Room, which seats 2 to 4 people.

Light breakfast items are served from 10-11:30 Monday through Saturday. The luncheon menu features attractively presented soups, salads and sandwiches priced from $4.75 to $7.75. Tea offerings range from the Cuppa Tea (tea and sweet) for $6.75 to Mrs. Pennycooke's Traditional Afternoon Tea for $16.50. The latter includes an assortment of tea sandwiches, cheese and fruit, scones with clotted cream, jam, lemon curd, special sweets, cake of the day and pot of tea of your choice. There is a Prince or Princess Tea for $10.25. Desserts and scones are available à la

carte. Mrs. Pennycooke's serves and wholesales their own tea label. Tea-related items, including antique and vintage English bone china cups, saucers, plates and Royal Winton Chintz, are available for purchase.

MC/V/Checks
Wheelchair Accessible
Free Street Parking

Open Monday, Wednesday, Thursday and Friday 11-4, Saturday 11-5 and Sunday 12-4. Tea trays are served after 2 except for Sunday when it is noon. Reservations are recommended for parties of 5 or more though groups are welcome if space is available.

Proprietor's
*Autograph*_____*Date*_____

Once Upon a Tea

14612 N.E. 4th Plain Road
Vancouver, Washington 98682
360-892-4832
michelle@onceuponatea.net
www.onceuponatea.net

From I-5, take the WA-500 E/39th Street exit (number 2), towards Orchards.
Merge onto WA-500E. And take it for about 5 miles until you get to N.E.
Fourth Plain Road Bear right and take Fourth Plain Road for 1½ miles.

Tea parties for little girls and adult ladies are the specialty of Michelle Albright, the owner of this unusual tea service which opened in 2005. You set the date and provide the guests and Michelle will do the rest! Customized invitations, guest book, fresh flower decorations, karaoke, digital pictures, party favors customized thank-you notes and games are all included at teas presented in her specially decorated shop. Linens, crystal, china and silver are taken care of, and a special gift is given the guest of honor.

The catered luncheon includes tea sandwiches, fresh fruit, pretzels, petít fours, cheese and crackers, pastries, tea cookies and beverages of punch, coffee or tea. A teapot cake is available for $25, and the plates, forks and napkins are included. Parties are scheduled for a minimum of 6 guests. A Premium Party Package costs $250. and includes all of the above. Each additional guest costs $20, up to a maximum of 12 guests. However, all parties can be customized to include as much or as little of the extras as needed. They will attempt to accommodate food allergies.

A $50 deposit is required to secure your reservation. The balance is due at the time of the party.

If you want to hostess a party without all the work, give Michelle a call. She will be happy to take care of you and your special guests.

MC/V/AE/Checks
Wheelchair Accessible
Limited Street Parking on Weekdays

Parties are by reservation only and there is a cancellation fee. If you must cancel, an alternative date can be arranged if it is within 4 weeks of the original party date.

Proprietor's
*Autograph*_____*Date*_____

Peach Tree Bakery & Tea Garden

in Country Village
740 - 238th Street S.E.. Suite B
Bothell, Washington 98021
425-483-2005
ivahawthorne@hotmail.com.
www.peachtreebakery.tripod.com

From I-405, take exit 26 and drive south for 1 mile. They are the only tea room in Country Village, and are located in the back left near the fountain. Look for the black and white chicken!

Kristine, the owner of the bakery and tearoom and a graduate of the prestigious Culinary Institute of America in New York, runs the bakery with the help of her mom, Iva. Kristine is kept very busy baking, especially their delicious signature peach scones, while Iva enjoys visiting with the patrons. The tea room is decorated with soft green walls and window toppers in shades of coral stripes and floral print. The large tablecloths match the window valances, and are topped with pretty white cloths. An abundance of light from the windows, flower arrangements, and the use of pastels and white make the room warm and inviting. For a whimsical setting, ask for the Sir Mumford Room, which is set off with lace, wicker, greenery and a charming wall mural.

For tea, one may choose the Veggie Tea which includes a garden salad, herb cheese/cucumber and hummus/tomato sandwiches, sundried tomato spread with provolone cheese and roasted peppers for $12.50. The Afternoon Harvest Tea offers a cup of soup and 2 tea sandwiches for $11.98 and the Afternoon Garden Tea has a choice of salad or soup, and 4 tea sandwiches for $12.98. All of the teas also include tea (hot or iced), a warm scone topped with English cream, and an assortment of desserts.

Sir Mumford's Grand Afternoon Tea, which is $15.95, includes a basket of scones with English cream, a cup of soup, fresh seasonal fruit, five tea sandwiches and a grand assortment of tarts, cookies and pastries. For children there is Penelope's Tea priced at $7.95. If you are seeking something other than tea, there is also a generous selection of soups and sandwiches to choose from and coffee is available.

A baker's case is laden with a selection of scones and other desserts to purchase, and gifts and tea related items are set about the room to tempt you.

MC/V/Checks   Wheelchair Accessible   Large Parking Lot

Regular hours are Tuesday through Sunday 11-4. Tea time is 11:30-2:30. The last tea service is 2:30. Holiday or theme teas are offered. Reservations are required 24-hours in advance on weekends and for large groups.

Proprietor's
Autograph_____Date_____

The Perennial Tea Room

1910 Post Alley
206-448-4054 / 888-448-4054
Seattle, Washington 98101
tealadies@perennialtearoom.com
www.perennialtearoom.com

*Take I-5 from the north or south. Follow downtown exits to Pike Place
Market.*

Finding the Perennial Tea Room, which opened in 1990, was easy! We
just followed the sidewalk at Pike Place Market north to the end. We then
saw the bright floral windsock and very colorful window boxes strategically
placed on the historic brick building. Both were an indication of the friendly
and welcoming atmosphere we were about to enter.

The owner, Sue, engaged us in conversation and shared with us the
extensive selection of 70 bulk teas which they retail. They carry their own
Perennial Tea Room label as well as Barnes and Watts. Each day four teas
from their unique selections are brewed up, and one can have it served hot or
iced.

Four small tables are set out for your relaxation, two inside and two
outside. Should you wish to have a treat to go along with your tea, packaged
shortbreads, Eccles cakes and McVitties biscuits are available for purchase.

While there we took time to look at the eclectic collection of gift items
which were neatly placed on the many shelves that occupied the tea room. I
was particularly interested in the selection of tea-related books while my
daughter Alicia was fascinated by the art deco tea pots and tea cups. The gift
choices were interesting and unlimited.

I would recommend that you take a bit more time to explore Pikes
Market, which is a veritable hub of activity, but be sure to take a break and
have a cuppa at Perennial Tea Room. You will enjoy both the tea and the
visit with the owners, Sue and Julee.

There is limited on-street parking as well as a pay-parking garage.
Customers receive validation with a $20 purchase.

MC/V/DIS/AE/DEB/Checks
Wheelchair Accessible

Open daily from 9:30 to 6.

*Proprietor's
Autograph_____Date_____*

Piccadilly Circus

1104 First Street
Snohomish, Washington 98290
360-568-8212
piccadillycircuswa@yahoo.com

Snohomish is located 30 minutes north of Seattle or 10 minutes east of Everett, off State Route 9, which is easily accessible from I-5 or Hwy 405. Snohomish is also 5 minutes west of Monroe, off Hwy 2.

In the back of the store, through the magical doorway, one enters the charming room where afternoon tea is served. The domed ceiling with its cloud covering, and the walls with their Yorkshire Dales Murals, are complimented by the relaxing sound of a fountain. The Afternoon Tea set is priced at $15.95 and includes scones, finger sandwiches, cake, pastries, confections, fruit, sorbet and tea. Scones and desserts are offered à la carte.

Breakfast, which is served from 9 to 11, offers a traditional English breakfast for $7.95. There are other selections as well. For lunch, one may choose from such English favorites as Welsh Rarebit, Ploughman's Lunch and Meat Pies to chicken dishes and sandwiches. Dinners are offered Thurs., Fri., and Sat. nights and their steaks have been voted "Best in the Northwest." There are too many menu choices to list here, so I recommend that you check out Piccadilly Circus yourself ... more than once!

Exciting news for Jeff and Marion is the addition of a pub. The gift area has been cleared, and coming in December 2005, the pub will be located in the front of the store. We wish them luck with their new venture as well as continued success in their tea room.

MC/V/AD/DIS/DC/Checks
Wheelchair Accessible
Street Parking

Open Sunday through Wednesday 9-5 and Thursday through Saturday 9-8. Tea time is 11-5. Reservations are recommended but not required.

Proprietor's
*Autograph*_____*Date*_____

Poulsbo Tea Room
and Art Gallery
19132 Jensen Way N.E.
Poulsbo, Washington
360-598-6100

From Bainbridge Island Ferry, take Hwy 305 north 11.2 miles. Turn left on Hostmark Street. It becomes Front Street as you approach historic downtown. Turn right on Jenson and the tea house is about 1½ blocks down on the right.

This charming cottage, situated just a few steps from the sidewalk and the charming lamp post, was opened by Kimberlee Crowder in 2004. Once inside, you feel the warmth of the ambiance; antique tables, linen tablecloths and napkins, tapered candles and a variety of treasured tea cups. All of these features are the makings for a traditional afternoon tea. You will also enjoy the works of the resident artist, Beverly Hooks, whose Romantic Impressionist art adorns the walls.

There are three teas to choose from starting with the Cream Tea for $6.95, and the Sweet Tea, an array of delicious desserts for $8.95. Traditional High Tea, which is $18.95, includes fruit sorbet, an assortment of delicate tea sandwiches, scones and an array of miniature desserts. All teas include tea, and the scones are served with Devonshire Cream and preserves.

If lighter fare is what you are seeking, Kimberlee offers quiche, scones, handcrafted, sandwiches, and an assortment of tea sandwiches priced from $3.95 to $9.95. Dessert selections include an assortment of petít fours for $8.95, a dessert special for $4.95, miniature key lime tart for $2.50 and handmade chocolates for $1.50. Hot chocolate and iced or hot tea are available for $3. The teas are all loose leaf and there are many to choose from.

Dietary needs can be accommodated with prior arrangements. Coffee is available as is outside catering. There is a gift area with teacups, cozies, bulk tea and dolls to tempt you.

Special teas are offered throughout the year - Mother's Day, Red Hat, Graduation, Christmas and Children's Dress-up Parties. Come for tea for any occasion knowing that, as you pass through the door, you will feel comfortable and pampered.

MC/V/Checks   Wheelchair Accessible
Lot Parking With Handicapped Permit
Free Street Parking

Hours are Monday through Saturday 10-5 and Sunday 12-4. They serve traditional High Tea and luncheons all day. Reservations are not required but if you reserve, they ask that you cancel if you are not

Proprietor's
Autograph_____Date_____

Pomeroy House Carriage House Tea

20902 N.E. Lucia Falls Road
Yacolt, Washington 98675
360-686-3537
pomeroy@pacifier.com / www.pomeroyfarm.org

Directions on the next page.

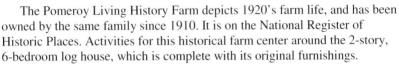

The Pomeroy Living History Farm depicts 1920's farm life, and has been owned by the same family since 1910. It is on the National Register of Historic Places. Activities for this historical farm center around the 2-story, 6-bedroom log house, which is complete with its original furnishings.

This is a fully operational farm, but special events are open to the public during the year. Seasonal activities include a Spring Herb Festival and a Pumpkin Festival. The farm is open to the public on the first full weekend of each month, June through September. All gratuities are gratefully accepted as a donation to the Pomeroy Living History Farm's school programs.

The carriage house, where tea is served, is also the location of a charming British Gift Shop. Though tea is primarily served upstairs, handicapped seating may be arranged in the gift shop. There are four offerings in the tea room: Tea and Scones for $6.95, a Dessert Plate with fruit and tea for $7.95, a Tea Plate which includes tea, scones, assorted tea sandwiches, sweets of the day and soup or fruit for $10.95 and a Ploughman's Lunch of tea, scones, cheese, roll, pickle, sweets of the day and soup or fruit for $10.95. In England, a ploughman's lunch referred to the bread and cheese that was taken into the fields for lunch. Later this became "pub lunch," and it was served on a plate with pickled onions or pickled eggs. Today you may choose a sweet or dill pickle, pickled onions or English pickles. Dietary needs will be accommodated if possible, with prior arrangements.

There is an extensive tea list, but, if you prefer, a latte cappuccino or mocha may be purchased for $2.50.

MC/V/DIS/Checks
Lot Parking
RV Parking
Handicapped Accommodated

Tea room hours are Wednesday through Saturday 11:30 -3. They do not take reservations and there is a minimum $6.95 charge. The gift shop is open Monday through Saturday 10-5, and Sunday 1-5.

Proprietor's
Autograph _____Jane Brink_____ Date 2/15/06

Directions to Pomeroy House Tea Room

From the south, take I-5 north to the Battle Ground exit (exit 9). Go straight ahead at the traffic light (you're on 10th Avenue). Turn right at the traffic light at 219th. Follow that to Battle Ground, turn left at the traffic light between Safeway and Fred Meyer (also SR-503). Go north on SR-503 for 5½ miles. Note Pomeroy Farm sign, and turn right onto N.E. Rock Creek Road. Follow that for 4½ miles (it eventually becomes Lucia Falls Road). The farm is on the left.

Alternate from the south, take I-205 north to exit 32 and take Padden Parkway East to the second traffic light which is 117th Avenue (also SR-503). Turn left and follow SR-503 north to Battle Ground. From Safeway in Battle Ground, continue north for 5½ more miles. Note Pomeroy Farm sign, turn right on N.E. Rock Creek Road. and follow that for 4½ miles (it eventually becomes Lucia Falls Road). The farm is on the left.

From the north, take exit 14 off I-5 south and turn left. Go to 10th Avenue. Turn right then turn left at the traffic light onto 219th. Follow that to Battle Ground. Turn left at the traffic light between Fred Meyer and Safeway (SR-503). Go north on SR-503 for 5½ miles. Note Pomeroy Farm sign, and turn right onto N.E. Rock Creek Road. Follow that for 4½ miles (it eventually becomes Lucia Falls Road.). The farm is on the left.

Queen Mary Tea Room

2912 N.E. 55th Street
Seattle, Washington 98105
206-527-2770
QueenMary@queenmarytearoom.com
www.queenmarytearoom.com

From I-5, take exit 169 (45th Street) toward University of Washington. Pass U.W., cross the overpass and immediately follow the loop to the right at the bottom. Go 1/2 block, turn right on 25th. Proceed to 55th and turn right, then go about 4 blocks.

Established in 1988, Queen Mary's is an authentic English Tea Room serving breakfast, lunch and traditional formal afternoon tea. The owner, Mary, calls her tea room, "theatrical Victorian fantasy," with its dark wood "ivy topped" wainscoting, and floor-to-ceiling draperies in floral shades of deep green and burnt orange. Lace curtains and cream-colored table linens, as well as silver teapots with flowers, give the room its finishing touches.

Formal Afternoon Tea, Priced at $22.99, starts with a trio of sorbets served in a champagne glass, with a finger of shortbread on the side. This is followed by a tiered server laden with a generous trio of sandwiches: chicken almond, fresh cucumber and mint, and smoked salmon with cream cheese. Also on the server are a miniature scone, crumpet, English muffin, thumbprint jam cookie, London sugar cookie, lemon curd tart, chocolate raspberry teacake and assorted fresh seasonal fruit. The tea includes homemade whipped cream, jam, marmalade and a pot of tea. For an additional $5, the Royal Afternoon Tea includes a Mimosa, Dir Royale, Magnolia or Royal de Framboise. Queen Mary herself would have been impressed! Dietary needs may be accommodated with prior notice. Seasonal and themed teas are offered during the year and groups are welcome.

Breakfasts, which range from $5.99 to $9.99, include Bangers 'n' mash or Smoked Salmon Quiche The lunch menu, which is extensive, also offers a variety of English favorites priced from $6.99 to $10.99.

The house tea is Queen Mary label, and it is available for purchase in the gift area, along with many other special items. Be sure to allow yourself time to look around.

MC/V/Checks   Wheelchair Accessible   Street Parking

Open Wednesday through Sunday 9-4. Anytime is teatime! Reservations are strongly recommended. There is a 24-hour cancellation policy. Seasonal and themed teas are offered during the year. Groups are welcome.

Proprietor's
*Autograph*_____*Date*_____

The Rose Room

at the Rosalie Whyel Museum of Doll Art

1116 - 108th Avenue N.E.
Bellevue, Washington 98004
425-455-1116 / 800-440-3655 / fax 425-455-4793
dollart@dollart.com / www.dollart.com

I-405 to Bellevue. Take N.E. 8th Street West exit. Turn right on 108th Avenue. The museum is two blocks further. Bellevue Square Mall is just 4 blocks from the museum.

The Museum of Doll Art provides enjoyment to all ages and genders. They are internationally known, and have received many awards including the prestigious Jumeau Award for the Best Private Doll Museum in the World. This recognition was presented in Paris in 1994 and it is a 10-year award.

Besides being a premiere doll museum, the facility is available for dinners, weddings, luncheons and other private events. It is the perfect location for a catered tea, with its elegant Victorian ambiance and collection of antique furnishings and dolls. Somehow dolls and tea parties just go together!

Three packages for children's teas parties have already been established the Birthday Party, the English Tea Party and the Do-It-Yourself Party. The Museum works with a select list of caterers to provide the best teas and luncheons both for children and adults. For more information on reserving this beautiful building or any portion of it for your next tea, call or email the Museum directly.

MC/V/AE/Checks
Wheelchair Accessible
Free Parking

Tea is by reservation. The museum hours are Monday through Saturday 10-5, and Sunday 1-5. Closed New Year's, Easter, July 4th, Thanksgiving and Christmas.

Proprietor's
*Autograph*_____*Date*_____

Rose Tree Cottage Tea Room
and Gift Shop
645 W. Washington Street, Suite 3
Sequim, Washington 98382
360-683-2522

From Hwy 101, take Sequim Avenue Exit. At 1st light turn left onto Washington Street. Continue on Washington to 7th Street. They are on the corner of 7th Avenue and Washington Street directly across from Burger King.

Marci Columbia-Hibbard, who opened this tea room in 2003, offers "indulging tea parties that have been prepared for you to enjoy." She asks that you sit back and relax while they treat you to a no-rush experience and an abundance of freshly prepared delightful treats. Sounds like just the kind of tea room we are looking for!

The tea room, with its Victorian décor, is done in shades of burgundy and emerald green and is dressed in Victorian wallpaper, lace curtains, white china and antique furnishings. The atmosphere is cozy, with only six tables and a pair of burgundy wingback chairs that are tucked away by the window. Reserve early if you wish to take tea in the chairs!

There are five tea sets to choose from. The English Rose is soup, green or Caesar salad and a scone for $7.95. A Light Tea offers soup and scone for $7.95 while the Afternoon Tea includes scones and indulgent sweets for $6.95. For vegetarians there is a Garden Rose Tea with 2 vegetarian sandwiches, scone, seasonal fruit and sweets for $11.95. Then, there is the Victorian Rose Tea which includes 3 sandwiches, scone and indulgent sweets for $11.95. Finally, the Royal Rose Tea includes 4 tea sandwiches, scone, specialty dessert and indulgent sweets for $15.95. All teas include choice of tea. The tea labels are Republic of Tea and Olympic Lavender Farm.

Besides tea, a luncheon menu offers sandwiches served with salad or soup and a baked sweet for $6.95 (half for $5.95), or specialty salads for $7.95 (with a scone for $8.95). Oh, yes! On Friday nights you can reserve for the Chocolate Fondue, which is offered at $12.95 for two.

Since they are in the Lavender Capitol of North America, you might want to take time to visit the lavender farm in Sequim.

MC/V/ DEB//Checks/Cash   Wheelchair Accessible   Lots of Parking

Open Tuesday through Friday 10-5 and Saturday through Sunday 11-4. Closed Monday. All day is tea time with the last service 1/2 hour before closing. Reservations are recommended. For large groups, reservations are required 5 days in advance.

Proprietor's
*Autograph*_____*Date*_____

Sadie's Tea for All Seasons

2711 Meridian
Bellingham, Washington 98225
360-223-6646

Coming from the south, take I-5 to the Meridian Exit, turn left and go south on Meridian approximately 1 mile. Sadie's is on the right-hand side of the street. It is a two-story, light pink, Victorian building. The nearest cross street is Illinois.

This charming Victorian, with its soft pink color and large second-story porch, says welcome as soon as you see it. The owner, Arlene Doeden, has kept the Victorian theme in the tea room where she has used eclectic antique furnishings, linens and assorted china tea cups and saucers to decorate the numerous rooms. Soft green walls, lace curtains and a painted rose border under the expansive front windows, add to the charm.

There is a large party room in the back of the shop with a whimsical garden décor, where a children's party or a fun adult party can be held. In the middle of the house, in the formal party room, standing in a place of honor, is a corner cupboard that belonged to Arlene's Aunt Sadie, for whom the tea room is named. It seems that whichever room you choose, your surroundings will be interesting and comfortable.

Arlene has three tea sets to choose from and they are: a Cream Tea offering one or two scones for $2.25 and $3.90; Afternoon Tea with sorbet, a scone, sandwiches and a dessert for $12.95; and the Sadie's High Tea which includes Sorbet, a scone, sandwiches, soup and a dessert for $16.95. A pot of tea is $1.95.

There are numerous shelves and tables covered with gift items, specialty foods, tea accoutrements and quality bulk teas for your shopping pleasure. Take time to check them out!

MC/V/AE/DC/Checks/Cash
Wheelchair Accessible
Street and Lot Parking

Open Tuesday through Saturday 11-5. Anytime is tea time! Reservations required 24-hours ahead for Sadie's High Tea and for parties of more than 6. No refund if cancellation is less than 24-hours.

Proprietor's
Autograph_____Date_____

Sassy Teahouse and Boutique

16244 Cleveland Street
Redmond, Washington 98052
425-885-3581
kathleen@sassyhouse.com
www.sassyhouse.com

SR 520 east to Redmond Way exit. Turn left. After the light, get in the left lane and turn left, after Leary Way, into Windermere parking lot. The teahouse shares that lot. Town center clock is nearby.

Kathleen has opened what she calls "a gathering place for friends big and small." Located in Redmond's historic 1814 Stone House, this charming cottage-style tea house offers a shop where you can purchase a gift for a friend or a decorative accessory for your own home. Afterward, relax in a comfy chair and enjoy a beverage from the espresso bar or a hot cup of tea. You can stay for lunch or tea, but if time is an issue, opt for take-out!

There is a nice assortment of hearty sandwiches at $7.95 and $8.95, as well as tea sandwiches at $6.95. Both include a side of salad or fruit. Entrée salads for $8.95, baked goods, quiche and desserts are also offered.

Sassy Tea Decadence includes tea and a 3 tiered tower of sandwiches, scones, sweet cream and jam, and a variety of decadent petite tarts and sweets for $14.95. The Little Sassy Tea, for children 3 and up, consists of warm Sweet Vanilla Cream Tea or Teas 'R Us organic fruit tea, tea sandwich fingers, fruit and mini pastry for $6.95. There is even a children's corner designed for Sassy's littlest friends!

Remember the gift shop! You are sure to find something you can't live without.

MC/V/DIS/Checks
Not Wheelchair Accessible
Due to Historic Designation.
Lot and Street Parking

Open Monday through Wednesday 9-5. Thursday and Friday 9-10, Saturday 9-5, and Sunday 10-4. There are no formal tea times. Reservations required for parties of 6 or more. Catering is available.

Proprietor's
Autograph_____Date_____

The Secret Garden Tea Room

4041 Factoria Mall
Bellevue, Washington 98006
425-746-4557
secretgardentearoom@msn.com / www.sgtea.com

From I-405, take exit 10 (Coal Creek Pkwy). At the end of the ramp, go east and follow the signs to Factoria Mall. The tea room is located in the mall.

Opened in 2003 by Wendy and Elizabeth, this "oasis" is conveniently located inside a busy mall. The shop is quite charming, with its floral and lace draperies, white linen table covers and floral accents. The décor is English cottage, which makes one feel comfortable and welcome.

The smallest tea set is the Duchess Tea, which is scones with Devonshire cream, jam and lemon curd for $6.95. It is only available before 1 and after 2:30. The Princess Tea is $17.95 per person, and offers assorted tea sandwiches, savory bites, fresh fruit, plated sweets and scones with Devonshire cream, jam and lemon curd. The Queen Tea is $19.95, and it adds a cup of soup and orzo pea salad to the previous tea. The final tea set is the Ladies' Afternoon Tea, and it is only available after 2:30. With that tea you receive assorted tea sandwiches, fresh fruit, petite dessert plate and scones with Devonshire cream, jam and lemon curd for $12.95. All of the above teas include a pot of tea. For children under 6, Secret Garden offers a Teddy Bear Tea for $6.95, which has peanut butter and honey and a cheese tea sandwiches, orange slice, grapes, scone with Devonshire cream, jam and lemon curd, teddy bear cookies and lemonade or tea. A slightly larger children's tea is the Tinkerbell Tea, which adds a sliver of quiche, fruit, cheese wand, and assorted sweets for $9.95. Inquire about their party packages.

Besides tea, luncheon items of soups, salads, sandwiches, quiche and petite desserts are offered. Their special is the Secret Garden Sampler which includes half a sandwich, cup of soup, orzo pea salad and frosty cranberry salad for $9.95. There is a minimum charge of $5.95 per person.

Allow plenty of time to stop next door at their extensive gift shop. The selection is wonderful!

MC/V/AE/DIS/Checks
Wheelchair Accessible
Lot Parking

Open Tuesday through Saturday, 10-4 and Sunday, 11-4. Anytime is tea time! Reservations are recommended but walk-ins are welcome if space allows. Cancellations would be appreciated.

Proprietor's
*Autograph*_____*Date*_____

Steeped In Comfort

11016 Gravelly Lake Drive S.W.
Lakewood, Washington 98499
253-582-1336
steepedincomfort@msn.com
www.steepedincomfort,com

Southbound I-5, take exit 125 (Mc Chord AFB), turn right on Bridgeport
Way, left on 112th S.W., right on Gravelly Lake Drive S.W. to 11016.
Northbound I-5, take exit 124 toward Gravelly Lake Drive. Go right on
Nyanza and right on Gravelly Lake Drive S.W. to 11016.

We were thrilled to find this tea room, because we make occasional trips to Mc Chord AFB, and it is a short trip to a great afternoon tea. This charming tea room, which has a Colonial appearance from the outside, was opened in 2004 by Elsie Camp and Judy Heidal. They have know each other since Junior High and did research for years to prepare for opening their very own tea haven.

The interior, which they call a "nostalgic country look," offers a light and inviting place to take tea. White shelves and racks are laden with a large selection of gifts and your "necessiteas." Large windows frame the rooms, and the white tables and chairs, some wood and others wicker, give the room a warm and friendly feel. Seasonal table toppers add to the ambiance.

Tea offerings are numerous, starting with the Tranquilitea, which offers fruit and scones for $5.95. The Towne Center Faire, which is $12.95, includes fruit, assorted sandwiches, savories and scones. Making Memories has fruit, assorted sandwiches, savories, assorted desserts and scones for $17.95. All of the teas include a pot of tea. If you would prefer a lunch item, there is an à la carte menu offering soup, sandwiches, quiche, a fruit cup and scones. For children, there is a separate menu. The house teas are Harney & Sons and Blue Willow. Coffee is also available.

Judy and Elsie invite you visit so you can relax, refresh, and renew! Be sure to take time to shop, too!

MC/V/DEB/Checks/Cash
Wheelchair Accessible
Lot Parking

Hours of operation are 11-4 Monday through Saturday. The last tea is
served at 3. Reservations are recommended. Groups are welcome with a
minimum of 20 and a maximum of 50. The tea room is closed to the public
for larger groups.

Proprietor's
Autograph_____Date_____

Tamara's Tea Room

at the Painters Cottage

321 Wellington Street
Walla Walla, Washington 99362
509-200-1166
intimatedinners@hotmail.com

Take the Wilber Street exit off Hwy 12 in Walla Walla. Drive 2 blocks to Isaacs Street (1st stoplight) and turn right. Stay in the right hand lane. Turn right at Wellington Street. Turn right between Arby's and the Rent-a-Center. They are the cottage on the left side of the road.

In 2004, Tamara Krieger opened her tea room inside the Painters Cottage gift shop, where she presents monthly teas as well as themed teas and birthday parties for little girls. One of her special theme teas is presented in October. It is her "all about chocolate" month and everything for the tea is chocolate … bread, chocolate themed sandwiches and chocolate dessert buffet with a chocolate fountain.

The monthly High Tea menu, which is planned by Tamara, includes 4 finger sandwiches/savories, 3 types of breads or scones, sweet biscuit, coffee cake or muffin and 4 or 5 bite-sized dessert items for $15. With a private tea, the customer chooses all of these items. Special dietary needs will happily be accommodated with advance notice.

They are a full-range catering company, run by Intimate Dinners and the tea room is available for all types of events. Besides her busy tea and catering business, Tamara teaches etiquette classes to adults and children. She will be attending the Protocol School of Washington in the fall of 2005. Then, during the first part of 2006, Tamara plans to have a full-time tea room with gifts, live music at special themed teas, and a specialty cheese shop to enhance your tea time experience.

Major Credit Cards/Checks
Wheelchair Accessible with Assistants
Large Parking Lot

The Painters Cottage is open 7 days a week from 10:30 to 5:30. Tamara presents teas once a month by reservation only. There is a 48-hour advance reservation policy. You may also request a private tea for 6 or more people any time. Tea time is noon to 3:30.

*Proprietor's
Autograph*_____*Date*_____

Taste & See Tea Room

903 W. South Dragoon Drive
Colbert, Washington 99005
509-939-1856
tziegler@spocom.com
A non-profit endeavor.

From Spokane Wandermere Shopping Center, go 10 miles north on Hwy 395
to Deer Park, Washington. Left on South Dragoon Drive, first driveway on
the left.

Thada Ziegler opened her tea room in 2003 as a non-profit venture. The only expense is the cost of the food, as Thada volunteers her time to this endeavor. All funds raised are solely for the benefit of Anna Ogden Hall, which is a shelter for women and children in Spokane.

Thada says that the tea room offers an elegant Victorian warmth and charm, in a beautiful country setting. She asks that you "take some time to enjoy the taste of yesterday."

The four-course Afternoon Tea includes a choice of many specialized teas, fruits, signature scones, a variety of finger sandwiches and elegant desserts for $15 per person. Teas may be arranged for just two people or up to a group of 20. On Saturday, there is a minimum of 8 people or more for a group reservation.

The house tea is Harney & Sons and coffee is available. Special dietary needs can be accommodated with advance arrangements.

There is a gift shop for your browsing pleasure.

Checks/Cash
Limited Wheelchair Accessibility
Lot Parking

Tea is offered from 11-2, Wednesday through Saturday. Reservations are
required three days in advance. There is a 24-hour cancellation policy.
Less than 24-hours is non-refundable.

Proprietor's
Autograph_____Date_____

Taste The Moment

Restaurant and Tea Room
8110 - 164th Avenue N.E.
Redmond, Washington 98052
425-556-9838 / fax 425-881-3334
tastethemoment@nwlink.com
www.tastethemoment.com

From Seattle, take Hwy 520 east, WA. 202 W. exit towards Woodinville.
Turn left onto Redmond Way / WA. 202N. Turn right onto 164th Avenue
N.E.. They are located on the right-hand side of the street a couple of blocks
down.

A spring break tea room tour in Washington brought this tea room right to us. We were driving around Redmond, trying not to get lost, when we just happened upon this little gem. The new owner, Toni Monroe, opened for business in December 2004 as a restaurant. You may now reserve for tea!

The building is quaint and the two rooms quite pretty. White dominates the color scheme with white walls, linens, dishes and window covers. Even the gas fireplace at the end of the room is white. The ambiance is French formal with lovely gilt touches around the room. Windows line one wall and give the room a light and airy feeling.

Afternoon tea is served in the small side room with the decorated arched entry. Toni decorates the tables with seasonal touches and uses pretty tiered servers and china to make tea special. The Royal Tea has a hot entrée, savory salad, fresh fruit, and an assortment of pastries for $29.95. The Victorian Tea offers a tiered tower with assorted tea sandwiches, scones with crème fraichê and jam, and petite pastries for $19.95. Finally, the Taste the

Moment Tea includes a raspberry or chocolate crepe, selection of breads, scone with crème fraichê and seasonal fruit. All teas include a pot of Metropolitan Tea. For children, a pot of tea or apple juice, peanut butter and honey sandwich, fresh fruit and scone with jam is offered for $7.95

MC/AE/V/DIS
Wheelchair Accessible
Lot Parking

Open Wednesday through Friday 10-2 and 5-7, Saturday 9-2:30 and 5-9
and Sunday all day, 9-8. Reservations are not required but are preferred.

Proprietor's
Autograph_____Date_____

Tea by the Sea

102 - 5th Avenue South
Edmonds, Washington 98020
425-771-2601

From I-5, follow the signs to downtown Edmonds. They are located by the fountain at 5th Avenue S. and Main.

This establishment is a retail gift shop which offers a huge selection of teapots, kettles, trays, teacups, mugs and numerous other tea-related items. Marcia Baldwin, who opened the business in 2002, also offers a large selection of teas from award-winning tea companies, and delicious gourmet goodies to go with them. Marcia also offers both bulk teas and tea bags, and she carries around 200 varieties. Several of her teas are caffeine-free and decaffeinated, and there are a number of rare, hard-to-find teas.

Among their tea labels are Metropolitan, Harney & Sons, Market Spice, Barnes and Watson, Té, Golden Moon, Koala, Republic of Tea, Tao of Tea, Kinnell, and Bewley's. They are constantly adding new brands. Tea sampling is available.

The gift items include books on tea, a nice collection of tea-related Red Hat items, children's tea items, novelty items, and the shop features a nice selection of lighthouse memorabilia.

MC/V/AE/DEB/DIS/Checks
Wheelchair Accessible
On Street Parking

Store hours are Monday through Saturday, 10-5:30 and Sunday 12 to 4.

Proprietor's
*Autograph*_____*Date*_____

136

The Tea Cup

204 N. Tower Avenue
Centralia, Washington 98531
360-807-1717
kathisteacup@localaccess.com
Web site being developed.

Take I-5 to exit 82. Turn east on Harrison Avenue. Follow signs to city
center. Harrison turns to Main Street. Continue to Tower Avenue and turn
left. Go one block and the tea room is on the right side of the street.

This tea room, which was opened in 2003, is in a really great location in
the older part of Centralia, where it is surrounded by quaint shops and
antique stores. After a few hours of checking out the neighborhood, just
settle in for a delightful tea prepared by Kathy Rogers and her capable staff.
The extensive selection of teas is located on shelves where you can sniff
before choosing ... a fun way to make your decision. Labels include
Republic of Tea, Simpson and Vail, Numi, Burnes and Watson, and
Twining.

Tea is served at small tables in the main area behind a "white picket
fence." With the floral tablecloths, swags and flower arrangements, the
room has a garden feel to it. In the back of the store, there is a cheery
English Garden Room for special occasions or group gatherings.

Once settled in, it is time to make your selections for the High Tea. You
have a choice of sandwiches, soup, desserts and scone for $15. A 15%
gratuity is added for parties of 4 or more. The sandwich choices include
Salmon Loaf, Egg Salad, Cream Cheese Cucumber, Ham and Cheese,
Turkey Cranberry, Pecan Chicken and Apple Raisin.

If lunch is your meal of choice, you may select from a number of
specialty wraps, soup of the day, and organic green salads. The beverage

menu offers a variety of teas, coffees, pop,
juice and smoothies.

Allow time for browsing, as the gift
selection is large and varied. All are displayed
on interesting shelves, racks and other settings.

MC/V/DEB/Checks
Wheelchair Accessible
Free Street Parking

The tea room is open 10-5:30 Monday through Saturday. Tea is offered by
reservation Monday through Friday and 12-4:30 on Saturdays. Groups are
welcome.

Proprietor's
Autograph_____Date_____

The Tea Madame Tea Shoppe

at Windmill Gardens Café
16009 - 60th Street E Suite D
Sumner, Washington 98390
253-891-2900
monique@teamadame.com
www.teamadame.com

From Seattle, take I-5 to exit 154A onto Hwy 405. Take exit 2 onto Hwy 167. Exit onto 410 and travel 2.4 miles then take exit 166th Ave E. At the end of the ramp, turn left and go to 60th Avenue E. The café is .2 miles. From Tacoma, take I-5 to exit 135, go onto 167 to Meridian. Cross the bridge and turn right onto the ramp toward Sumner. Follow 1.2 miles and merge onto 410. Follow as above.

Monique Christian, owner of The Tea Madame, has 10-years experience in the restaurant business and has educated herself to become an expert on tea. She is on her way to becoming a tea master, and one visit to her shop will make you a believer. Her commitment to fresh food, service and exceptional dining is evident in the popularity of the Garden Café's Sunday High Tea gatherings.

Afternoon Tea, a weekly event priced at $20, offers an array of tea sandwiches, house-made scones, quiche tartlets, pastries and chocolates. A selection of teas is included and scones are served with Devonshire cream, butter and preserves.

Once a month Tea Madame holds a formal tea dinner at 5 p.m. and it is offered for $35. This elegant meal is hosted in a beautiful garden setting and is accompanied by a harpist. The menu changes to suit each month's theme and a sample menu is A Scent of Rose Tea - champagne toast, mini chive pancakes with goat cheese mousse and caramelized onions, cucumber tarts with radish butter, stuffed jumbo prawns over béchamel sauce, flower petal scones with Devonshire cream, chiffon cake with rose syrup, lemon curd fruit cups and chocolate-covered strawberries. Other themes are A Proper Southern Tea and A la Provence Tea.

Special events are held at Windmill Garden, including weddings and business meetings. Off-site catering is available.

V/MC/Checks   Wheelchair Accessible
Lot Parking

Tea time is every Sunday at 4. Seating is limited so reservations are required and pre-paid. They are not refundable.

Proprietor's
Autograph_____Date_____

Tea Time Garden

P.O. Box 34
North Lakewood, Washington 98259
360-652-8488
mail@teatimegarden.com
www.teatimegarden.com

Contact Bonnie to make arrangements to purchase tea..

Bonnie Rose describes her business as, "extraordinary loose tea blended with herbs and spices, fruit and flowers, for a naturally delicious brew." Her blending studio is Washington State Department of Agriculture and US Food and Drug Administration inspected and licensed. It is not open to the public.

Bonnie grew up in a British household where loose tea was part of every day life. Every time there was a joy, sorrow or achievement, tea marked the occasion. In her youth, she developed an interest in plants and began cultivating many tea "tisane" herbs and true tea-blends. She says, "happily every one has survived and is thriving today." After a friend suggested that she package and sell some of her teas, she worked out several recipes, created a brochure and started up her own company - Tea Time Garden!

Today, Bonnie goes by the unusual job description of Teaist - a tea artist or 'one who blends teas,' and she considers herself incredibly lucky to be able to create and sell something that has been so long a part of her life and one of her greatest pleasures. She is also an avid spinner, having learned to spin in 2003. She calls spinning sheer joy, moving meditation, and a place for her to ultimately relax, and she says that drinking a pot of fragrant loose tea while spinning is heaven on earth!

Bonnie sells an extensive line of teas including black, green, herbals and children's. Her teas come from India, Sri Lanka, China, Japan and Africa. The ingredients and directions are enclosed with every bag of tea. For more information, you can contact Bonnie by phone or email, or you can go to her website to find out more about her teas.

MC/V/DEB/Checks

Hours of operation are 9-5 on Monday through Friday.

Proprietor's
Autograph_____Date_____

The Teacup

2207 Queen Anne Avenue N.
Seattle, Washington 98109
206-283-5931 / 877-841-4890
www.seattleteacup.com

From I-5, take the Seattle Center exit and follow arterial around Lake
Union, under the underpass, and past the Space Needle. Go right on Denny
then right on 1st Street. From the north, go past Key Arena. Turn left on Roy
and go one block. Turn right on Queen Anne. They're between Boston and
McGrew Streets..

Owned by Elisabeth Knottingham, The Teacup was opened in 1991 and offers over 150 different loose teas, each hand-chosen by the staff and sold by the pound. Tea may be purchased by the cup or by the pot. They also offer an ever-changing menu of scones, cookies, tea breads and other treats.

There are shelves laden with tea accessories of every kind and tea may be purchased in bulk.

After a refreshing cup of tea and a sweet treat, a walk around this charming neighborhood is in order.

A world of world-class tea

Wheelchair Accessible
Street Parking

Open 10-6, seven days a week.

Proprietor's
*Autograph*_____*Date*_____

140

Tudor Inn

1108 South Oak Street
Port Angeles, Washington 98362
360-452-3138 / 866-286-2224
info@tudorinn.com
www.tudorinn.com

Tudor Inn is located in an established residential district on a bluff above the waterfront and historic downtown area. The inn is on the corner of 11th and Oak.

This beautiful three-story, half-timbered home was built in 1910 by an English gentleman, and the original woodwork and a fir stairwell still grace this comfortable inn. It has been tastefully restored to retain the rustic charm of the Tudor era, and is decorated with many fine antiques from Europe. The inn has been modernized to provide the comfort and ease of the present. It is now the home of Betsy Reed Schultz, who is also the tea hostess.

In the dining room, a large table with ladder-back chairs is set before a wall of windows which share a view of the porch and lovely front yard. A period chandelier hangs above the table, and crisp white linens, candles, china and silver set the tone for an elegant and memorable tea.

Adjacent to the dining room is the main parlor, which has a grand piano and wood-burning fireplace, and where additional tea guest may be seated.

The elaborate tea is served in courses and includes assorted juices, fruit compote, crumpets and scones with cream and jam, tea sandwiches, delicate cakes and cookies and tea or coffee. You are invited to "dress up" in your favorite hat and gloves, but should you not bring them, Betsy has extras of both!

Major Credit Card or Checks
Wheelchair Accessible
Free Street Parking

This Bed and Breakfast is open year-round and serves tea by reservations made at least one week in advance. Tea time is 12-3, October 15 through May 15, with one tea party per day. A non-refundable deposit is required.

Proprietor's
Autograph_____Date_____

Victorian Rose Tea Room

1130 Bethel Avenue
Port Orchard, Washington 98366
360-876-5695
admin@springhousegifts.com
www.springhousegifts.com

From SR16, take the Tremont exit. From the north, follow the exit. From the south, take a right. Go straight until you reach the stoplight at Bethel Road. Take a left and go straight, keeping to the left at the Y until you see Village Square, which is located across from the Post Office. The tea room is the pink and blue building on the left.

Victorian Rose Tea Room is in a charming "Painted Lady" style shop complete with a turret dining room. The beautiful pink building is something to behold and hard to miss. The interior is equally impressive.

High Tea is offered on specific days, but groups of 10 or more may reserve for tea on any day, usually at 3. The prices do not include tax and gratuity and pre-paid reservations are *required*. High Tea is $9.95 and it includes scones with whipped butter and jams, select fruit or veggies with dip, specialty desserts and tea or coffee. The Victorian Rose High Tea menu offers all of the above plus petite quiche and assorted tea sandwiches for $13.95. If you are hosting a party and would like your guests to leave with a special memento, a Fancy Floral Tea Cup may be added for $8.

The breakfast menu offers quiche, Eggs Benedict, crêpes, and other specialties for $5.95 to $8.95. Lunch items include salads, specialty sandwiches and soup priced from $3.95 to $9.95. Dinner is now offered and you can contact the tea room for details.

 A lovely gift shop, Springtime Dolls and Gifts, adjoins the tea room. It features many popular collectables as well as tea pots and tea sets.

MC/V/DIS/Checks
Wheelchair Accessible
Lot Parking

The shop is open Monday through Saturday 9-7 and Sunday 9-3. Breakfast, lunch and dinner are served everyday. Tea and desserts are also available daily. High teas are usually offered on the 4th Sunday at 3. Check their website for specifics.

Proprietor's
*Autograph*_____*Date*_____

Victorian Tea Connection

108 Vista Way
Kennewick, Washington 99336
509-783-3618
viconn@urx.com / www.victorianconnectiongifts.com

Hwy 395 north from Umatilla, take a right turn on Vista Way. From the south take a left on Vista Way. Clearwater joins Vista Way. The nearest cross street is 395 and Clearwater.

    Isolyn and Simon refer to their tea business as a "mom and pop kind of shop," where the needs of the customer are a priority to them. Teas are set up inside their gift store, in an area where the tea patrons will not be disturbed.

    There is one afternoon tea offered at a cost of $10, and it consists of scones, with Devonshire cream from England, curd and preserves, 3 or 4 different tea sandwiches, savories, fruit and pastries and tea. They continually fill your tea pot with boiling water to keep the tea hot! Each guest is given a choice of fine Ashby's Tea flavors, and they have many to choose from, including decaffeinated and herbal infusions.

    The gift shop, which encompasses 1800 square feet, carries a large line of Ashby's tea, as well as a variety of preserves and curds from England. They also carry fine china and crystal, lamps, linens and lace, framed artwork, collectables and much more. If there is something you are looking for but do not see in the gift shop, Isolyn will be more than happy to track it down for you. The emphasis is on service at Victorian Connection.

MV/V/AE/Checks
Credit cards accepted if reserved by phone
Not Wheelchair Accessible
Lot Parking

Hours of operation are 10-6, Monday through Saturday. Tea time is 3-5:30. Reservations are required; 2-6 people 3 days ahead and 7-12 people 1 week ahead. If you book for Saturday, they will stay open longer to accommodate you. No refund will be offered if reservation is cancelled.

Proprietor's
Autograph_____Date_____

The Victorian Tea Garden

614 The Parkway
Richland, Washington 99352
509-946-3606

The nearest cross streets are George Washington Way and Lee Boulevard.

Soft gold walls, hardwood floors and a large window set off by gold drapes welcome you to this lovely tea room. The tables, covered with purple and gold tablecloths topped with lace, add to the elegant ambiance you will enjoy while taking tea at The Victorian Tea Garden. Should you feel like "dressing up" a bit, a selection of hats is available for your use.

The owner, Lisa, describes her tea room as "Victorian with British food," and the menu certainly lives up to that description! Luncheon is served from 11 a.m., and includes English Meat Pie or Brocato Pie for $7.95, and sandwich choices such as egg/olive, cheese pimento or chicken salad, with fruit, cheese, crackers, a cup of soup and dessert, also for $7.95. A cup of Soup of the Day served with fruit, cheese and crackers is $3.95.

Four scones or a crumpet, with fruit and your choice of butter, Devon cream, jam or lemon curd is $5.95. High Tea is available for $9.95 and it includes a variety of teas with savories and sweets, delicate tea sandwiches, fruit, crackers and cheese.

Lisa asks that you "please take time to enjoy a leisurely afternoon tea, as it is never a hurry at The Victorian Tea Garden."

MC/V/AE/DIS/DC/Checks
Wheelchair Accessible
Street and Lot Parking

Open 11-4 Tuesday through Thursday and 11-7 Friday and Saturday. High Tea is from 1-4. Reservations are required for groups of 6 or more for High Tea.

Proprietor's
Autograph_____Date_____

Village Yarn & Tea Shop

19500 Ballinger Way N.E. #110
Shoreline, Washington 98155
206-361-7256
nancy@villageyarnandtea.com
www.villageyarnandtea.com

From I-5, take exit 177 east. Go approximately 1 mile to the corner of
Ballinger Way and 25th Avenue N.E. They are on the left hand side of the
street. The shop is 10 miles north of downtown Seattle.

Within a specialty yarn shop, which was opened in 2004, Nancy Small offers tea on Wednesdays and Sundays, with three sittings each day. Nancy calls her ambiance casual and happy ... perfect for a relaxing and friendly 'tea time' with friends. The Formal Tea, which is $18.95 per person, offers four courses of delicacies. The first course is a fruit sorbet, followed by croissants, scones, seasonal fruit and cheese. The next offering is sandwiches; cucumber and cream cheese, radish poppy seed and goat cheese with watercress. For the sweet finale, one will enjoy a lemon tart and brownies. The tea includes the house blend - Village Yarn and Tea Blend.

There are accommodations for 10 and groups may reserve the space. All teas require reservations.

Besides the house blend, 37 loose teas from around the world are available for purchase, and fresh baked goods are offered daily. You may want to complete your visit with a trip through the gift shop.

MC/V/DEB/Checks/Cash
Wheelchair Accessible
Lot Parking and Free Street Parking

The shop is open Monday, Tuesday, Wednesday and Friday 10-6, Thursday
10-8, Saturday from 10 to 5 and Sunday11-4. Tea is served on Wednesday
and Sunday at 11, 1 and 2:30. A two-day reservation is required, as is a
48-hour cancellation

Proprietor's
Autograph_____Date_____

Vintage Inn B & B
and Tea Parlor
310 W. 11th Street
Vancouver, Washington 98660
360-693-6635 or 888-693-6635
info@vintage-inn.com / www.vintage-inn.com

From I-5, take exit 1-C. Go west on 15th Street and
turn left at W. Columbia Street. Go four blocks to
11th Street and turn right. The Inn is on the left
hand side in the middle of the block.

Situated in the heart of the antique district, this 1903 Victorian inn has it all ... great hospitality, a wonderful place to stay and afternoon tea. What more could one ask for? Furnished in elegant antiques, seating for tea is in the formal dining room or the cozy garden room.

The table is set with antique china, crystal glasses and linen luncheon napkins. Fresh flowers from the garden adorn the table and the plates, and home-grown herbs are used in the recipes as well as to garnish the dishes. Menu selections may be tailored to each request and special dietary needs may be accommodated with prior arrangements. Afternoon Tea at the historic Vintage Inn includes a cup of homemade soup or seasonal fruit dish, scone with fruit preserves and imported clotted cream, a tray of tea sandwiches, fresh fruit and warm savory, sorbet, an assortment of decadent desserts, and a bottomless pot of tea for $21.95, not including sales tax and gratuity. Holiday teas in December are priced at $24.95 and special theme teas are priced individually, and vary according to the event.

The motto of the tea parlor is "Tea Urges Tranquility of the Soul," and it certainly will do that for you.

There is a small gift area of specialty tea items as you leave this most gracious home.

MC/V/Checks/Cash
Not Wheelchair accessible
Street Parking-Metered on Weekends,
and a Driveway

Tea is served Monday through Saturday by appointment. Reservations are
required at least one week in advance. Two-day cancellation policy. The
minimum reservation is 6 people and maximum is 24.

Proprietor's
Autograph_____Date_____

Wild Sage
World Teas, Tonics and Herbs
227 Adams Street
Port Townsend, Washington 98368
360-379-1222
www.wildsageteas.com

Just off the main street (Water Street) on Adams.

The world of tea is waiting to be discovered in this cozy, unique tea house in downtown Port Townsend. Featuring a wide assortment of more that 100 teas from around the world, the staff at Wild Sage is often quoted as saying, "so many teas, so little time." Specializing in fine black tea blends from England (Taylors of Harrogate), exquisite loose-leaf white, green and oolong teas (Tao of Tea), wonderful black and green blends (Harney & Sons) and exotic herbals from around the world, Wild Sage carries all types of fine teas in bulk, loose leaf tin, as well as tea bags. The tea house promotes and encourages the discovery of tea, its ancient culture, the life style and tea's many health benefits.

Wild Sage serves over 50 teas in bulk, either by the cup or by the ounce and encourages customers to "try before you buy." Staff delights in providing customers with tea information and answers to their personal tea questions.

This creative teahouse provides a serene retreat from the busy world. In addition to the teas, tonics and herbs served, Wild Sage serves delicious, local baked goodies, Belgian chocolates and Elixir Chinese health tonics. They specialize in 6 different types of masala chai's, fine high mountain oolongs, excellent China greens, robust breakfast blends, and Wild Sage's own organic herbal tea blends'.

Many customers are drawn to the store simply by its natural, enticing aroma. So, next time you are in Port Townsend, Washington's Victorian seaport, amble into Wild Sage teahouse and re-discover the wonderful world of teas, tonics and herbs waiting for you.

There is a gift shop featuring tea accessories, tea pots and gifts for your browsing pleasure.

MC/V/Cash
Wheelchair Accessible

Store hours are Monday through Saturday, 10-5:30 and Sunday, 11-5:30. Anytime is tea time!

Proprietor's
Autograph_____Date_____

147

Your Cup of Tea
Tea and Etiquette Programs
425-334-9751
fax 360-658-8887
ssspringer@att.net
www.yourcupoftea.biz

Location is determined at time of booking.

Susan Springer, a trained and certified Tea Etiquette Consultant, is the founder and director of Your Cup of Tea, a company which provides an opportunity for men, women and young people to learn proper etiquette for enjoying tea in social or business situations. Ms. Springer has a bachelor of arts degree in home economics, is certified in family and consumer sciences, is a member of and certified in Foundations of Tea - Level I and II by the Specialty Tea Institute, and is a graduate of the Protocol School of Washington, D.C., the leader in etiquette and protocol services. She is also a published author with works in *Tea A Magazine, Tea Time Gazette, Tea Bits,* and a columnist on tea-related topics for *The Country Register of Western Washington* newspaper.

With a delightful sense of humor, Ms. Springer presents the proper and correct protocols for tea and etiquette, and makes each presentation fun as well as educational for corporate workshops, retreats, tea rooms, clubs, churches and private events. The presentations are suitable for all genders and ages and are customized to meet your specific needs, budget and time requirements.

Susan is a consultant and is available by appointment.

Proprietor's
Autograph_____Date_____

Welcome

to

British

Columbia

Abkhazi Garden Tea Room

1964 Fairfield Road
Victoria, B.C., Canada V8S 1H4
250-598-8096 / fax: 250-598-8076
karen@conservancy.bc.ca
www.conservancy.bc.ca

Hwy17 becomes Blanchard Street. From Blanchard, turn east on Fairfield Road then right after Foul Bay Road. They are on the left side of the road.

Though not a traditional tea room, Abkhazi Garden is a wonderful place to take a cup of tea. Located in the former residence of Prince and Princess Nicholas Abkhazi, the tea room is in the living room of the modest home they built following their marriage in 1946. The unusual vaulted ceiling, finished with acoustic tile, enhanced the quality of sound in the room which often came from Peggy's grand piano. The walls are birch plywood which was a decorative finish that John Wade, the architect, pioneered in Victoria after World War II.

Following World War II, Peggy purchased the treed and rocky property where she started to build a sanctuary. After she and the prince married, they immediately embarked on a new, creative journey together, designing and building their home amidst an extraordinary garden. They first opened it to the public in 1949. Today, the gardens are under the care of The Land Conservancy of British Columbia, which acquired them in 2000. It is maintained by over 100 volunteers who help with everything from weeding to welcoming visitors to serving tea.

The room where tea is served features a large picture window which overlooks the gardens. There are numerous tables set about, and the piano

Peggy played sits in the corner of the room. Light permeates the room, making it warm and welcoming, much like the tea hostess, Karen Preston. Afternoon tea offers a homemade scone with strawberry jam and Devonshire cream with your choice of tea or coffee for $6.50. Other selections are lemon loaf or homemade shortbread with tea for $4.50. A pot of tea, coffee or juice may be purchased separately.

MC/V/DEB   Wheelchair Accessible   Street Parking
Prices are in Canadian Funds.

The Garden and tea room are open Wednesday through Sunday and Holidays 1-5. The last tea service is 4:30.

Proprietor's
*Autograph*_____*Date*_____

Adrienne's Tea Garden

5325 Cordova Bay Road
Victoria, B.C., Canada V8Y 2I3
250-658-1535/ fax 250-652-7797
t-tyme@shaw.ca
www.adriennesteagarden.

From downtown, take Blanchard and follow until it becomes Hwy17. Take Hwy 17 toward Cordoba Bay. At Sayward Street, take a right turn and go 1.1 miles. Mattick Farms Village is on your left.

What a pleasure it was to find this wonderful tea room, which was just a short and pleasant ride from Victoria. The village itself reminds one of the days when small shops and neighborly merchants were in vogue. The tea room is in the front row of village shops ... you can't miss it! As you enter, you are greeted by friendly servers and a display case of scrumptious desserts and pastries. That really sets the mood for tea time.

Seating is available in the main dining room, the sun room and outside (during good weather!). The abundance of windows, which are topped with a very cute 'Debbie Mumm' country print, make the room warm and welcoming. The print is carried out in the table tops and wall decor, and is set off by soft butter-yellow walls with a blue accent.

The owner, Fay Hextall, has been offering Afternoon Tea at the village for 17 years. The tea, which is offered daily, consists of tea sandwiches, savories, dainties, fruit and a raisin scone with Devon-style cream and jam for $15.95. Besides tea, Adrienne's features breakfast, and an extensive lunch menu. There is a quaint ice-cream counter where they also sell deli items and cappuccino, if you are on the run!

When planning to take tea at Adrienne's, allow yourself plenty of time, before or afterwards, to browse the shops in this charming collection of village shops. You will find wonderful gift items for friends and family, as well as fresh produce, household décor and so much more, for yourself.

INTER/MC/V
Wheelchair Accessible
Lot Parking
Prices are in Canadian Funds.

Hours of operation are 9-5 daily. Tea is offered from 11-5, seven days a week.

Proprietor's
Autograph_____Date_____

Applewood Country Gifts

Gifts, Tea Room, Bakery and Fudge
6345 - 120th Street, #112
North Delta, B.C., Canada V4E 2A6
604-596-9007

From Hwy 91, take the 64 Avenue exit. They are 8 blocks west of Hwy 10, on the S.W. corner of Scott and 64th in "Sunshine Village," tucked behind 7-11. Look for the Boston Pizza tower.

Sometimes we feel especially lucky in our search for tea rooms because it gives us the opportunity to meet people as nice as Carol Payne and Marianne Loades. If another tea room proprietor hadn't told us about Applewood, we would never have had the opportunity to meet these gracious and friendly "grandmas."

They have been in business for 12 years and have been offering tea for the last eight. The tea room area of the shop is fun and welcoming. The soft yellow wallpaper, with tea cups scattered all over it, just invites you to take tea. EVERYTHING is mismatched … the tablecloths, chairs, tables, china cups and saucers, cloth napkins, plates and creamers. Framed art covers the walls, vintage aprons enjoy a second life as window valances, and fresh flowers grace the tables. It is a charming and very interesting ambiance!

A Cream Tea is available for $4.50. Traditional High Tea is $18 and it offers finger sandwiches, mini savories, scones and assorted sweets. For $23, one may enjoy the High Tea Lunch, which adds a cup of soup and a salad to the previous tea. Both include a pot of their house label Metropolitan Tea. There is an extensive lunch menu priced at $7 and $8, and baked goods galore, such as their famous rhubarb upside-down cake. Two special "tea accompaniments" are homemade pie or crisp with ice cream or caramel sauce for $5.85, and cream cheese brownie with ice cream or whipped cream, crowned with Grandma's homemade berry sauce for $4.25. This is a bakery and fudge shop, and if you need to put your sweet tooth on hold, just purchase one of the delicious baked goodies of some of their signature fudge to take home. Don't forget to check out the large gift area with its vintage

and contemporary items. You may also purchase one of the 45 flavors of Metropolitan Tea that they retail.

MC/V/DEB   Wheelchair Accessible
Lot Parking
Prices are in Canadian Funds.

Open Monday through Saturday, 10-5:30. The last tea service is 5. Reservations are recommended, especially for large groups.

Proprietor's
*Autograph*_____*Date*_____

Bacchus Restaurant

at the Wedgewood Hotel
845 Hornby Street
Vancouver, B.C., Canada V6Z 1V1
604-608-5319
Bacchus@WedgewoodHotel.com
www.WedgewoodHotel.com

#1 Oak Street to 16th, left on 16th (west) to Hemlock, right on Hemlock onto Granville Bridge. Go to Smithe and turn left. Go to Hornby then take a right. The hotel is across from Lake Courts.

What could be a better setting for tea than a grand hotel? With its elegant old-world European décor, the lobby of the Wedgewood offers the perfect background for afternoon tea. The dark wood, heavy drapery, plush upholstery and abundance of fresh flowers bring back the feel of a time when Queen Victoria herself might have stopped in.

Owner Eleni offers a tea time that is rich with tradition yet suited to today's tastes. The Afternoon Tea at the Wedgewood consists of gourmet finger sandwiches, freshly baked scones with Devonshire cream and preserves, chocolate éclair, mini Bakewell tart, seasonal fruit tartlet, English fruit cake and lemon chiffon with white chocolate ganache, at a cost of $25. The Royal Afternoon Tea includes all of the above along with a Kir Royal or a glass of Blue Mountain Brut for $36. The tea list is lengthy and includes black, green, whole fruit tisanes and herbal infusions. Coffee is available and special dietary needs can be accommodated with advance request.

The award-winning restaurant also offers Sunday Brunch and romantic dinners, so if you are staying in town, you might want to put one of these meals on your agenda. It's just another reason to savor the atmosphere a little longer.

MC/V/AE/DC   Wheelchair Accessible
Metered Street Parking
Prices are in Canadian Funds.

The restaurant opens at 6:30 a.m. Monday through Friday and at 7 a.m. on Saturday and Sunday. Tea time is on Saturday and Sunday from 2 to 4. Reservations are recommended and there is a 24-hour cancellation policy. Groups are welcome but there is a minimum and maximum. Call for details.

Proprietor's
*Autograph*_____*Date*_____

The Blethering Place

2250 Oak Bay Avenue
Victoria, B.C., Canada V8R 1G5
250-598-1413
tearoom@theblethingplace.com
www.blethering.com

Hwy17 takes you into Oak Bay. The tea room is on the main thorough-fare, at the corner of Oak Bay and Monterey.

This was the first tea room we visited in Canada many years ago. Though we weren't doing tea tours until a few years ago, we always visited this special British tea room. Built in 1912 as a grocery store and post office, Blethering Place went through a few transitions before it finally became a tea room in 1975. Ken, the current owner, has built his business into a Victorian landmark enjoyed by locals and visitors alike. The emphasis is on friendly service and food that is baked in *their* ovens!

There are two tea sets, the first being Afternoon Tea, which is offered for $14.95. It consists of crust-less petite sandwiches, warm tea scones, Devonshire cream, fresh fruit, cakes, sausage roll, butter tart, tea or coffee and Blethering Place strawberry jam. The Full Afternoon Tea, which is priced at $16.95, is the same as the above but it includes English fruit Trifle (a weakness of mine!). Scones, tea biscuits, cinnamon buns, Nanaimo bars and lemon or butter tarts may be purchased à la carte. Numerous beverages are also available.

If you are interested in heavier fare, other meals are available. For breakfast, interesting items that may tempt you are, Bacon Butty, Eggs Benny and Boiled Eggs and Soldiers, as well as traditional favorites such as Belgium waffles, pancake and omelets. There is a lunch menu which includes soup, sandwiches, salads and quiche. An extensive dinner menu offers roast beef, salmon, turkey dinner, leg of lamb, fruit and vegetable curry, bangers 'n' mash, Shepherds Pie, crêpes and so much more! Many choices ... delicious food!

MC/V/DEB/Travelers Checks
Wheelchair Accessible
Lot and 2-hour Street Parking
Prices are in Canadian Funds.

The shop is open Monday through Friday 8 a.m.-9 p.m. Tea time is 11 a.m. to 7 p.m. Reservations are not required but are recommended.

Proprietor's
*Autograph*_____*Date*_____

Butchart Gardens

800 Benvenuto Avenue
Brentwood Bay, B.C., Canada V8M 1J8
250-652-4422 / 800-652-4422
email@butchartgardens.com / www.butchartgardens.com

From Hwy 1, take Hwy 17 north to Benvenuto Avenue.

I don't think anyone goes to Victoria without visiting the gardens. They are the result of the very industrious Jennie Butchart, who transformed her husband's lime quarry into a living work of art. The gardens remain in the family to this day and we are blessed that they choose to share them with us.

Tea is served in the original family residence, which is located on the grounds, and which everyone probably takes the time to see from the outside. The ponds and plants that surround the house are spectacular but the view from inside is just as breathtaking. Just knowing that this was the home of the founders of Butchart Gardens is magic in itself. As the original residents surely did, take a few moments to enjoy afternoon tea in one of the beautifully appointed rooms with a view of the gardens.

Afternoon Tea in the dining room consists of a fruit cup with yogurt citrus dressing, shrimp and Gruyere quiche, a savory homemade sausage roll with imported mustard and green tomato relish, savory tea sandwiches which include: egg salad with watercress, smoked salmon with maple Dijon cream cheese, cucumber with fresh ginger cream cheese, mango-curry chicken salad with toasted cashews, smoked ham with sweet grainy mustard, and a selection of sweets which include their own chocolate Grand Marnier truffle, orange apricot loaf, chocolate brandy Napoleon slice, shortbread cookie, a fresh fruit tart, their signature candied-ginger scone and a traditional black currant scone accompanied by strawberry jam and whipped Devon-style cream. The tea is presented on tiered servers and include coffee or tea for $23.75.

MC/V/AE/DC   Wheelchair Accessible   Lot Parking   RV's
Prices are in Canadian Funds.

The Gardens are open every day, though closing time varies depending on the season. Tea is offered from 12 to 4 and reservations are recommended during the summer. Admission to the Gardens is required for restaurant access. Special dietary needs can be accommodated.

Proprietor's
*Autograph*_____*Date*_____

Camellia Tea Room
At Milner Gardens and Woodlands
2179 West Island Highway
Qualicum Beach. B.C., Canada V9K 1G1
250-752-7514 / fax 250-752-3826
milnergardens@shaw.ca
www.milnergardens.org/index.htm

The Gardens are located 40 minutes north of Nanaimo. Take Hwy 19 north to the Qualicum Beach exit, drive straight through Qualicum Beach on Memorial Avenue to the water, turn right on West Island Hwy and the gardens are 1.2 miles on your left.

The Milner House was designed and constructed by Alex Fraser in 1931 for General Noel Money. It was designed to include features of a Ceylonese tea plantation house including the many screened doors leading out to the garden. Ray Milner, a founding director of Canadian Utilities, purchased the home in 1937 and began work on the Gardens with his first wife, Rina. Sadly, she passed away in 1952. He began more extensive work on the Gardens in 1954 after he married his second wife, Veronica. Renovations and additions to the house started that same year. Many rooms in the house are available for viewing during regular Garden hours.

The Camellia Tea Room is located in the Milner House and offers views of the Gardens, ocean and mountains beyond. Fresh scones are served with preserves made with berries and fruit grown in their Food Garden. Tea is $2.75 per person (GST included), and tea and pastries are offered for $7.50 per person. A variety of teas, hot and cold beverages and other sweets are also available.

The dining room seats 40 people and is on a first come/first served basis. During warm weather, the veranda can seat up to 14 more. Reservations may be made for tour groups. The house is available for rental, and large group luncheons may be arranged.

Wheelchair Accessible
Parking at the Entrance

Garden hours are based on the season so please call for specifics. They are closed mid-October to the end of March. Garden entry is $10 adults, $6 students and free under 12. The tea room is open from 1 to 4 during regular Garden hours.

Proprietor's
*Autograph*_____*Date*_____

Clancy's Tea Cosy

15223 Pacific Avenue
White Rock, B.C., Canada V4B 1P8
604-541-9010

From the south take 99 to White Rock exit (Marine Drive / 8th Avenue). Proceed to Stayte Road. and turn right then turn left on Pacific. From the north, take Hwy 10 and turn right on Johnson. Follow Johnson to Pacific and turn left.

It was such a treat to find this pleasant tea room in the heart of this charming ocean-side town. After driving down to the Promenade and doing a walk-about, we were ready to sit a while and enjoy a leisurely tea. The atmosphere is quite relaxing with its almost garden-like feel and Celtic music in the background. Burnt orange walls, with a deep green accent, are off-set with lots of lush plants, lace-topped tables and interesting wall décor. Besides the large main room, which has a bank of windows facing the street, there is a cozy nook off to one side for a more intimate setting. Wherever you choose to sit, the service is friendly and prompt.

Afternoon tea, which is served on the tallest servers we have ever seen, is $13.95 for 1, $21.95 for 2 or $34.95 for 3. Each person enjoys salmon, cucumber and sliced egg with tomato sandwiches, buttermilk scones with Devon cream and jam, a tart, a piece of cake and tea.

For lunch you may choose a sandwich, soup, salad or one of their other specialties. Scones and tarts are sold à la carte and sticky toffee pudding is offered for $3.95.

There are tea cups and saucer sets, tea pots, cozies, loose tea and other tea-related items for sale in the gift area.

CM/V/DEB
Handicapped Accessible
Free Street Parking
Prices are in Canadian Funds.

Hours are 11-4 Monday through Saturday. Closed Sundays and some holidays. Reservations are preferred, especially for groups.

*Proprietor's Autograph*_____*Date*_____

Cottage Tea Room

100 - 12220 Second Avenue
Richmond, B.C., Canada V7E 3L8
604-241-1853

From Hwy 99, take exit 32 (Steveston Highway) west into Steveston Village.
Take a left at 2nd Avenue.

We had the pleasure of spending Canada Day in Richmond, and while there took time to stop in for afternoon tea at Cottage Tea Room. It is a small shop located in the heart of the village, surrounded by other interesting shops and across the street from the boat docks. Though not fancy, it was very comfortable. Since it was a very busy time in town and there was so much going on, we were glad to take a break from all the activity for tea time. What we found were very friendly owners who really made an effort to make us feel welcome, as well as a tasty afternoon tea.

There are two tea sets to choose from: a Cream Tea for $4.25 and an Afternoon Tea which is $8.99. The latter, which is served on a tiered tray, consists of finger sandwiches, scone with Devon cream and jam, a chocolate dessert and a cookie. Coffee or tea is included. If you prefer, you may choose one of the following for $5.25: sausage roll or meat pie with chicken noodle soup or green pear soup or four tea sandwiches with one of the soups. Soup or a sandwich may also be ordered à la carte and they are priced from $2.75 to $5.50, and there is a nice selection of ice cream flavors to satisfy your sweet tooth. Besides the usual English teas, Chinese and Japanese teas are available.

Cash Only   Wheelchair Accessible   Free Lot and Street Parking
Prices are in Canadian Funds.

We know that this tea room is still in business,
but we were unable to get an update.

They are open 7 days a week and any time is tea time! Reservations not
required. Hours are 10:30-6 except for summer when they stay open until 9.

Proprietor's
Autograph_____Date_____

Crown Plaza Hotel Georgia

801 West Georgia Street
Vancouver, B.C., Canada V6C 1P7
604-682-5566 ext 3011
fb@hotelgeorgia.bc.ca
www.hotelgeorgia.bc.ca

The hotel is located between Howe Street and Burrard
Street in Downtown Vancouver.

Built in 1927 in the heart of Downtown Vancouver, the hotel is a social center for Vancouverites and a home-away-from-home for celebrities from around the world. The architecture captures the Georgian revival and the Hotel is one of the last buildings in Vancouver to be in the classical Beau-Arts tradition. It features a modern facility with unique character and traditional charm.

Afternoon Tea is served in the Casablanca Lounge which is nestled over the lobby and Howe Street. With its dark walls, animal print chairs and framed black and white portraits of classic film stars who have stayed at the hotel, it is the perfect place to take tea.

The generous Afternoon Tea, which is $19.95 per person, offers a selection of tea sandwiches - West coast smoked salmon, dill, capers, and cream cheese on baguette, honey ham, brie cheese and jalapeno jelly on potato chive scone, curried chicken, apple and watercress on banana bread and grilled vegetables and hummus in mini pita. This tea also includes a fresh baked scone with Devonshire cream and strawberry preserves, an assortment of elegant pastries and tea cakes with fresh fruit garnish and a freshly brewed pot of Mighty Leaf Tea. The Hotel Georgia Sparkling Wine Tea includes all the above and is served with Piccolo of Freixenet Cordon Negro for $29.90. For those looking for lighter fare, a pot of tea and two scones with Devonshire cream and strawberry preserves is $10.95 per person. There is also an extensive list of ports, sherrys and dessert wines to compliment your afternoon tea.

As the Crown Plaza Tea Menu says, "afternoon tea is life's finest pleasure." Treat yourself to a pleasurable experience in the Casablanca Lounge.

MC/V/AE/DEB   Not Wheelchair Accessible
Lot and Metered Street Parking
Prices are in Canadian Funds.

Tea is served Monday through Sunday from 2:30 to 5:30. Reservations are suggested.

Proprietor's
Autograph_____Date_____

The Fairmont Empress

721 Government Street
Victoria, B.C., Canada V8W 1W5
250-384-8111/ fax 250-389-2727
theempress@fairmont.com
www.fairmont.com/empress

Located in the Fairmont Empress Hotel in downtown Victoria, opposite the Inner Harbor and Tourist Info Center.

For almost a century, the majestic lobby of this landmark hotel has played host to England's most beloved ritual - the taking of afternoon tea.

Today, guests are seated at period tables and chairs or wing-backed chairs. Some tables are placed near the grand fireplace while others are set by the large picture windows that overlook the inner harbor. Regardless of where you sit, taking in the splendor of the room is an experience in itself. One last addition to the atmosphere is the pianist playing a baby grand piano during Afternoon Tea.

The Empress tea china was originally presented to King George V in 1914 and was first used by the hotel in 1939 for the royal visit of King George VI and Queen Elizabeth. The pattern is now produced by Royal Doulton exclusively for the Empress, and is available for purchase in the Fairmont Store adjacent to the tea lobby. Setting off the china are silver teapots, flatware, creamers and sugar bowls.

The tea menu offerings are seasonal fruit topped with Chantilly cream, tea sandwiches filled with cucumber, smoked BC salmon and cream cheese, carrot and ginger with cream cheese, open-faced shrimp mousse with fresh papaya garnish and curry mango chicken salad, traditional raisin scones with Devonshire double Jersey cream from a local BC farm and strawberry preserves, delicate bite-sized pastries, including French Valrhona Manjari chocolate truffles, fresh fruit and lemon curd tarts, miniature chocolate éclairs filled with milk chocolate mousse, and cardamom shortbread cookies. Everything is attractively arranged on tiered china and silver servers. At the end of the tea, a gift tin of Empress Blend tea is presented to each guest. The cost for this unforgettable experience is $36 to $55 depending on the season.

MC/V/AE/DC/Checks   Wheelchair Access   Lot and Metered Parking
Prices are in Canadian Funds

There are 5 seatings daily from 12:15 to 5. Reservations are required and should be made 1-2 weeks in advance. Tables will be held for 10 minutes after reservation time. The dress code is smart casual - no torn jeans, short-shorts, jogging pants or tank tops. Nice jeans or walking shorts permitted.

Proprietor's
*Autograph*_____*Date*_____

Fleuri Restaurant

At Sutton Place Hotel
845 Burrrard Street
Vancouver. B.C., Canada V6Z 2K6
604-642-2900 / 800-961-7555
fleuri@suttonplace.com / www.suttonplace.com

From Hwy 1, take the Grandview Hwy exit and follow as it becomes 12th Avenue. Follow 12th to Burrard Street and turn right. Follow to Burrard Street Bridge. Cross the bridge and continue for 6 blocks. The hotel is on the left just past Smithe Street and before Robson Street.

Just entering this beautiful hotel makes one feel special, and taking tea in the Fleuri dining room magnifies that feeling. This five-diamond rated hotel is elegant, charming and hospitable … the epitome of opulence. Lovely white-linen clad tables, gleaming silver, delicate china and fresh flowers await you in the elegant dining room, where you are treated to the delicious and artfully presented afternoon tea.

In the European tradition, the tea set offers fragrant teas from around the world, traditional sandwiches and French pastries, at a cost of $22 per person. The tea includes a cucumber and watercress sandwich, smoked salmon pinwheel with capers, Black Forest ham and Camembert croissant, raspberry chicken salad brioche, financier, Madeleine, éclair, scone, chocolate-dipped strawberry, Devonshire cream, preserves and of course, a pot of tea. Special dietary needs can be met with prior arrangements.

In addition to the Fleuri dining room, two private dining rooms are available for groups. The Pol Rogers I Room seats up to 14 guests and the Pol Rogers II Room accommodates up to 50 guests. They also offer outside catering.

Our afternoon spent taking tea at Sutton Place is a fond memory and we anxiously look forward to our next visit.

MC/V/AE/DIS/JCB/DEB
Wheelchair Accessible
Street and Valet Parking
Prices are in Canadian Funds.

The restaurant is open from 6:30 a.m. to 11 p.m., 7 days a week. Tea is offered from 2:30 p.m. to 5 p.m. daily. Reservations are required 1 week ahead.

Proprietor's
Autograph_____Date_____

Four Mile Roadhouse

199 Island Highway
Victoria, B.C., Canada V9B 1G1
250-479-2514

Take Hwy 17 from ferries in Sidney or Victoria to Mackenzie Avenue heading to Sooke. Stay on Mackenzie (it becomes Admirals Road), cross Hwy 1 and follow to Island Highway. Turn right and they are up the hill on the left.

One of the fun things about going on a Tea Room Tour is finding new and interesting places to take afternoon tea. This establishment, which opened in 1984, is just such a place. The large, Tudor-style restaurant and pub, with its shiny plank floors and numerous stained-glass windows, has the distinction of being the oldest building in Victoria. It was built circa 1858. The dining room where we took tea is decorated in a striking, jungle-like motif. The rafters are stained black. The table linens, ceiling fans, wrought-iron chandeliers and tulip oil-lamps that adorn each table are black. Even the rattan chairs have black-striped upholstery. The 20-foot corner couch where we were seated was upholstered in black with striped backs that match the chairs. Accents in red and beige are used in the large pillows on the couch and in other areas of the room. It is a really lovely room.

In another area of the restaurant, a room specifically set up for tea invites you to a more private environment. It is small and cozy, with numerous tables covered in gold-colored, crushed-velvet cloths. Memorabilia adorns the walls, a fireplace adds a warm atmosphere and stained glass windows lighten the room. This is where Afternoon Tea is presented, and what a tea it is! We were presented with an over-sized, tiered server rich with an abundance of tea foods - 4 large sandwiches, a basket of scones, a selection of 3 dessert bars and 5 types of fruit, plus an apple cut into the shape of a

swan. All of the tea, which we shared , was priced at only $12.95! The addition of real Devonshire cream is $1.95, and port or sherry is offered. Scones with strawberry jam and Devonshire cream are available from $3.95 to $7.95 and the dessert menu looks luscious!

Major Credit Cards   Wheelchair Accessible
Lot Parking
Prices are in Canadian Funds.

They are open 7 days-a-week from 11 a.m. to 10 p.m. Afternoon Tea is served daily from 2 to 5. Reservations are recommended, especially during the summer, but walk-ins are welcome.

Proprietor's
Autograph_____Date_____

The Gatsby Mansion

309 Belleville Street
Victoria, B.C., Canada V8V 1X2
250-388-8191 / 800-563-9656 / fax 250-920-5651
gatsby@bellevillepark.com
www.bellevillepark.com

Take Hwy 1 (Douglas Street at Inner Harbor) or Hwy 17 (Pat Bay Hwy coming from Swartz Bay Ferry Terminal). Gatsby Mansion is on the same street as the Parliament Building.

This beautiful heritage mansion, with its romantic history and lovely grounds, was the perfect place to take tea on a sunny Sunday afternoon. In good weather you can sit on the porch and watch all the activity in the neighboring market place, while enjoying a view of the Inner Harbor. Just a short walk from the harbor we took a break in our activities to enjoy tea and conversation at a corner table inside.

The tea set was delicious and consisted of sandwiches (we had fresh salmon, chicken and cucumber), fresh fruit, scones, cakes and tarts followed by a Pernod mousse. Loved the mousse!! The tea is served in three courses and is $21.95. The tea labels that they offer are Sir Thomas Lipton and Stash, though coffee is available for those who prefer. Everything was served at a leisurely pace which allowed us to enjoy our surroundings and each other.

The dining area is elegant and pleasantly appointed, with soft green walls, rather like sea-foam, and pale pink tablecloths offset with white napkins and a smaller white tablecloth. The chairs inside are pink and the large windows have floor-to-ceiling drapery in a pink and green floral pattern! Fresh flowers, chandeliers overhead, silver and crystal give the tables the perfect finishing touch. The next time we go, we will try outside seating, as it is set up just as nicely.

While there, do take time to tour the house. There are no official tours but most of the ground floor is public space. The gardens are also worth viewing and they were the pride and joy of the original owner, William Pendray.

MC/V/AE/DC/DIS
Not Wheelchair Accessible
Street and Lot Parking
Prices are in Canadian Funds.

The mansion is open year round, 24-hours a day. Tea time is 2-4 daily. Reservations are not required but are advised.

Proprietor's
*Autograph*_____*Date*_____

James Bay Tea Room & Restaurant

332 Menzies Street
Victoria, B.C., Canada V8V 2G9
250-382-8282
jamesbaytearoom@shaw.com
www.jamesbaytearoomandrestaurant.com

The tea room is located 3 blocks south of the Inner Harbor and directly
behind the Parliament Buildings at the corner of Menzies and Superior.

Owned by Yvonne and Bernd Woerpel, this charming tea room opened in 1983, and it continues to thrive as a gathering place. It is immediately evident that this is the place to come for afternoon tea. The room is filled with customers enjoying a break from work, travelers stopping in for the tea experience and locals taking time to sit a while with friends and neighbors. We felt like the latter!

The wonderful collection of Royal Family memorabilia is the first thing you see upon entering. Then, as you settle in, you notice the many lace-covered cottage windows that filter sunlight into the room. It is a most welcoming place!

Full menu selections for breakfast and lunch are available all day, as is tea service. Breakfasts are $5.90 to $10.40 and lunches are $3.75 for a cup of soup to $12.95. The choices for both are quite numerous.

There is a daily tea service which consists of egg salad and tuna salad finger sandwiches, toasted crumpet, scones with whipped cream and jam, assorted tarts and your choice of tea or coffee for $10.75. On Saturday and Sunday, High Tea is served that includes all of the above with the addition of fruit and custard trifle and fan wafer cookies for $14.50. A piccolo of champagne may be added for $5.50. If there are children in your party, peanut butter and jam finger sandwiches are offered for either tea service as an alternate for those 12 and under.

MC/V/AE/DEB
Wheelchair Accessible
Metered Street Parking
Prices are in Canadian Funds.

Open Monday through Saturday 7-5 and Sundays 8-5. All day is tea time.
Reservations are suggested depending on day, time and number in your
group. Groups are asked to reserve 48-hours ahead.

Proprietor's
Autograph_____Date_____

Jardin Estate Jewelers & Antiques

5221 9th Avenue
Okanagan Falls, B.C., Canada V0H 1R0
250-497-6733 / 888-615-5553
jardinantiques@yahoo.com / www.jardinantiques.com

Located right on Hwy 97, 15 minutes north of Oliver and south of Penticton.

The building where Jardin Antiques houses its treasures is often mistaken for an original farm house. That is because Theresa and Jorry Norlet worked hard to create such a look for their very special business. The outside is painted grey with two shades of deep burgundy trim, and that color scheme is continued inside where the walls are a pale pink and the wood floors are well worn. Most of the display cases are old oak and glass, adding to the feel of antiquity, lace tablecloths and French doors add to the feeling of warmth. Collectables such as older silver tea sets and china tea pots are set among some newer gift ware, though most of their inventory is vintage.

The garden area now boasts an extended patio where customers can take a break during their visit. This might be the perfect place to take a cup of tea, served in a real china cup along with one of their home-made scones with jam and whipped cream for $3.95, or perhaps a dessert of assorted squares or quiche and salad or chicken Kiev and salad for $5.50 would suit your fancy. Other choices are chicken cordon bleu and salad, broccoli chicken and salad, or homemade meatloaf with corn muffin and salad for $6.99. There are over 25 types of tea to choose from and coffee or cold drinks are available as well.

After your break, continue browsing through the antiques, gifts and estate jewelry that Jardin specializes in. They offer "old-fashioned service with modern convenience" so enjoy your visit and take time for tea.

V/MC/DEB
Wheelchair Accessible
Ample Lot Parking
Prices are in Canadian Funds.

May long weekend to December 24th, Monday through Saturday 10-5 and Sunday 12-4. Tea is available during business hours.

Proprietor's
*Autograph*_____*Date*_____

London Heritage Farm

6511 Dyke Road
Richmond, B.C., Canada V7E 3R3
604-271-5220 / fax same number
londonhf@telus.net
www.londonheritagefarm.com

Go west on Steveston to Gilbert Road, then south on Gilbert to Dyke Road. Go West on Dyke Road to London Farm. The nearest attraction is Steveston Village.

The farm, which is owned by the City of Richmond and the London Heritage Farm Society, is a fully furnished and restored 1880s farmhouse, situated on four acres, overlooking the Fraser River. The property was opened to the public in 1980. Around the house are herb and flower gardens which are open to the public for strolling, picnics, or just enjoying the peace and quiet of the area.

Other attractions on the site include the restored Spragg family barn, a heritage hand tool museum, an outdoor tool display, large farm equipment and buggies, bee hives and bee houses, chickens, allotment garden plots, a pond under restoration, a gazebo, walking paths, picnic tables, benches and a rose arbor.

An old-fashioned tea in their heritage-style tea room offers their exclusive blend of London Lady tea, freshly baked scones with home-made jam, cookies and other desserts for $6 per person. They use bone china tea cups and tea pots, lovely floral tablecloths and have "friendly service with a smile." Special theme teas, as well as group teas during the week, may be arranged.

You are invited to visit their gift shop where they feature their tea, scone mix and home-made jams as well as other items exclusive to London Farm. Call them and they will work with you in arranging tours and can give assistance to include other heritage sites in the historic Steveston Village area during your visit. The contact person is Trudean Fraser and she may be reached at the above phone number.

MC/V/DEB
Wheelchair Accessible
Free Parking
Prices are in Canadian Funds.

The house is open 7 days a week during June, July and August. Call regarding reservations and cancellation policy. There are special theme teas throughout the year.

*Proprietor's
Autograph_____Date_____*

Murchie's

825 West Pender Street
Vancouver, B.C., Canada
604-669-0783

From Burrard Street (heading for the waterfront), go to W. Pender Street and turn right. Go 1½ blocks and the tea room is between Howe and Hornby.

For over a hundred years, Murchie's has been importing and blending teas. It all began in 1894 when John Murchie and his sons began selecting, importing and blending the choicest Arabica coffees and the most flavorful teas. The business remains in the family to this day, and they promise to uphold this "tradition of excellence."

The new Vancouver store is completely different from the Victoria store. It is more modern, making it blend nicely with the downtown core. The one thing that remains the same is the traditional afternoon tea.

High Tea, which is $24.95, consists of Scotch currant scones with berry preserves or blueberry orange marmalade and fresh Devon cream, rosettes of B.C.'s wild smoked salmon presented on their own toasted baguettes with caper cream cheese, mini mille fueilles filled with Mediterranean tapenade and fresh cream cheese, delicate squares of their fresh baked bread garnished with mint butter and sliced cucumbers, tiny choux puffs filled to the brim with lemon chicken, elegant rolls of shaved Black Forest ham and their own peach chutney, rosemary scented shortbread, fresh fruit tartlets, lemon curd meringues, petite chocolate éclairs filled with orange pastry cream, Murchie's chocolate café squares and a selection of their own unique teas.

One of the true pleasures associated with taking tea at Murchie's is knowing that all the pastries, cakes and breads are made fresh daily in their own kitchen. And, of course, you can purchase some goodies to enjoy later!

MC/V/DEB   Wheelchair Accessible
Parking at Pacific Centre Mall
Prices are in Canadian Funds.

High Tea is offered on Saturday and Sunday at 1, 2:30 and 4, and Monday through Friday at 2:30.

Proprietor's
Autograph_____Date_____

Murchie's

1110 Government Street
Victoria, B.C., Canada V8W 1Y2
250-381-5451 / fax 250-383-3255
info@murchies.com
www.murchies.com

From the inner harbor, go north on Government Street. Murchie's is up the street on the left hand side.

It is hard to miss this Victoria landmark. Even before we started our quest to visit every tea room in North America, we were aware of Murchie's. The exterior of the building is beautiful and elegant. The wall of windows invites you to peek inside, but that is never enough. Once inside, you will find an extensive selection of teas from around the world, as well as every tea accessory you can imagine.

Upon entering, you will see a bakery to your right that has extensive glass display cases with every imaginable pastry available. Small tables are set about to enable you to take a cuppa with your favorite goodie.

Should you be seeking high tea, this establishment has a wonderful room set aside just for you. You step through large glass doors into the most interesting and exotic atmosphere ... lime-green walls, leopard-covered wrought iron chairs (which are very comfortable!), and framed relief pictures made from blocks of tea. The walls are stark white, the small round tables are covered with white floor-length cloths and a peach topper, and there are Neanthabella Palms placed about the room. The centerpiece is a black wrought- iron gazebo, where we enjoyed our afternoon tea.

The High Tea, which arrives on a tiered server, consists of a selection of their own unique teas, Scotch currant scones with berry preserves or blueberry-orange marmalade and Devon cream, rosettes of B.C.'s wild smoked salmon on a baguette, mini mille feuilles filled with tapenade, cucumber and mint sandwich, tiny choux puffs with lemon chicken, finger brioches with Black Forest ham and peach chutney, rosemary-scented shortbread, fruit tartlet, lemon curd meringues, petite chocolate éclair with orange pastry cream and Murchie's chocolate café square. All of the pastries, cakes and breads are made daily in their own kitchen. The cost of this wonderful tea is $24.

MC/V/DEB   Wheelchair Accessible   Street Parking
Prices are in Canadian Funds.

High Tea is offered at 2 p.m. and 4 p.m. daily. Reservations are required for High Tea, but lighter fare may be purchased in the bakery.

Proprietor's
*Autograph*_____*Date*_____

Oliver's Tearoom at Dickens Sweets

46945 Alexander Avenue
Chilliwack, B.C., Canada V2P 1L7
604-703-1981 / 604-793-1981
ahails@shaw.ca
www.dickenssweets.com

East from Vancouver, take exit 119B. Head north to Railway overpass. Take Slip Road to McDonald's. Dickens is on the east end. West from the Interior, take exit 120. Go north on Young Road. Cross railway tracks, Take the 2nd left and Dickens is on the right.

Oliver's Tearoom, owned by Fred and Anne Hails, is part of a very interesting complex which they opened in 2004. It contains a bakery, sweet shop, British grocery store, Dickens Museum and more. There is a library where you may relax and read British books and newspapers or watch one of their large variety of English comedy shows or dramas. Should the desire strike you, there is a piano where you can entertain other guests. If a little competition is what you seek, board games, chess and cards are available for your entertainment in the "copper room," or you can wear our hunting best and sit in the Garden Court. All of this and tea time, too!

Oliver's Tearoom is fashioned in true English style. Period pictures line the walls and linen cloths grace the tables. China tea cups and saucers are provided for your tea service. For cream teas, Ann offers Oliver Twist's "More Please" - dainty scones from $3.95 to $6.95 and large ones for $4.50 to $8.95. All include Devon Cream and strawberry preserves and a pot of Yorkshire Gold tea. Bob Cratchet's Savoury Tray contains an assortment of miniature savoury pastries and sandwiches for $7.95. The afternoon tea, A Taste of Britain, includes a selection of petite sandwiches, savoury pastries and sweet treats, all from their bakery, for $8.95. There is a Tiny Tim's Children's Tray for $3.95, and soup-of-the-day for $3.25 to $5.75.

There are also numerous other menu choice - from baked beans on toast and a Ploughman's Plate to luscious desserts and assorted beverages. Whatever your choice, a visit here is bound to be an event!

MC/V/DEB/Checks
Wheelchair Accessible
Lot and Street Parking

Shop hours are Monday through Saturday 10-5. Tea time is 11-4 and the last tea is served at 3:30. They are closed on state holidays. Reservations are recommended. Group reservations required 48-hours ahead.

Proprietor's
Autograph_____Date_____

Otter Point Bakery & Tea Room

#7 - 6717 West Coast Road
Sooke, B.C., Canada V0S 1N0
250-642-1825 / fax 250-642-7155

Take Hwy 14 north from Victoria toward Sooke. As you come into the center of town, the tea room is in a small strip mall on the right hand side of the street.

This is just another one of those tea rooms that we stumbled upon while heading to an appointed tea. Actually, we missed our turn and went about 100 yards too far ... right to Otter Point Bakery. Of course, we stopped to check it out and ended up having a cup of tea with the owner, Ruth Miller. Ruth has been offering tea in the small room adjacent to the bakery for 8 years, and it is obvious that she loves what she does. The décor is a bit different, as she has gone from a Victorian look to a more Oriental theme. Small, square, glass-topped tables are covered with cream-colored tablecloths with burgundy toppers and flowers grace each table. A lovely wisteria and hummingbird stained glass window can be enjoyed from the inside as well as the outside. During the summer, tables as set out on the front patio so one can enjoy the pleasant weather.

Almost all of the tea sets remains very Victorian. The Classic High Tea, which is $15.95, offers a platter of dainty sandwiches, savories, fruit and sweets. This is finished with a truly exquisite dessert of English trifle or parfait and a pot of tea or tisane. Victorian Afternoon Tea offers a delicious hot scone with Chantilly cream and home-made jam for $5.99 and the Truly Asian Experience includes your choice of an Asian tea for one accompanied by a delicious poppy seed, lemon, honey cake or a ginger scone for $6.95.

A Saturday Buffet Brunch is offered from 9:30 to 3 and is priced at $12.95 for adults, $4.99 for children 4 - 8-years old and free for under 3.

A variety of 25 teas is available for bulk purchase and, of course, baked goods in the glass case will tempt you any time you visit.

Wheelchair Accessible
Lot Parking
Prices are in Canadian Funds

The bakery is open Tuesday through Saturday 7-6. Any time is tea time! The Classic High Tea is only available by reservation and is offered from 1-4:30 daily. Saturday brunch is offered 9:30-3.

Proprietor's
Autograph_____Date_____

Point Ellice House

2616 Pleasant Street
Victoria, B.C., Canada V8T 4V3
250-389-1211 / 250-380-6506
cmha@mentalillnessrecovery.com
www.heritage.gov.bc.ca

From the north, go south on Hwy 17, turn right on Bay Street. Turn right on Pleasant Street and drive to the end of the street. From the harbor, get on the harbor ferry across from the Empress and ride to their dock.

This lovely home is a *must see* when visiting Victoria! It offers the best tour of a historical home that we have ever been to - original furnishings and décor, all the family's belongings, and a self-guided tour via head cassette that is very informative and entertaining. We get a sense that this was a happy home for the O'Reilly family and taking tea on their lawn, which overlooks the gorge and upper harbor, was a privilege. Today, surrounded by heritage plants and seated on wicker furniture under a pavilion tent, we are able to re-live those days, even if only for a short time.

Tea on the lawn has been offered for about 10 years, according to the executive director, Gail Simpson. The tea plate consists of 3-layer sandwiches, fruit, scone with Devon cream and homemade jam, dessert square, cake, cookie and Murchie's "Point Ellice Tea." If you prefer a cold beverage, lavender or rose petal lemonade is available. The cost is $16.95 and includes a tour of the home. There is a Fairy Tale Tea for children under 10. Special teas are offered at Christmas, and special event teas can be arranged. Dietary needs can sometimes be accommodated and some outside catering is offered.

Take your time when visiting Point Ellice House because there is so much to take in. Oh, yes, allow time for a quick game of croquet. The game is always set up on the lawn for anyone who wishes to play! Before your final departure, stop and browse the charming gift shop. There you will find tea- time items, original works of art by local artists and that special treasure you must have.

MC/V/AE/Checks
Wheelchair Accessible
Free Parking Lot
Prices are in Canadian Funds.

Tea is offered on weekends in May 10-4, and daily <u>by reservation</u> June to September. Tea time is 11-3.

Proprietor's
*Autograph*_____*Date*_____

Roedde House Museum

1415 Barclay Avenue
Vancouver, B.C., Canada V6G 1J6
604-684-7040
roeddehs@roeddehouse.org
www.roeddehouse.org

The museum is located at the corner of Barclay and Brougham, 2 blocks off Robson Street.

    Roedde House Museum was the home of Gustav and Matilda Roedde from 1893 until 1925. This beautiful heritage home has been lovingly restored and redecorated to reflect the family's life during those years. One can surely envision Mrs. Roedde serving tea in the parlour to her many friends and acquaintances. The work has been done under the direction of the Roedde House Preservation Society, which continues to maintain the home.

    Though this is not a tea room, Lady Grey tea and cookies are offered at the end of the Sunday afternoon tours in the den of this fine home. They are included in the price of admission which is $5 for adults and $4 for seniors. This is a wonderful opportunity to experience what it must have been like at the turn of the century to "take time for afternoon tea" in the parlour!

    After the tour, you are invited to visit the gift shop, where you can purchase items relating to the house and its history.

V/Checks
Wheelchair Accessible
Free Street and Lot Parking
Prices are in Canadian Funds.

The Museum is open for tours Wednesday through Friday 2-4. Tea is offered with the tour on Sundays 2-4. Groups are welcome. Reservations are not required, except for large groups.

Proprietor's
*Autograph*_____*Date*_____

The Rosewood Victoria Inn

595 Michigan Street
Victoria, B.C., Canada V8V 1S7
250-384-6644
rvi@aviawest.com / www.rosewoodvictoria.com

If traveling on Trans Canada Hwy (Hwy 1), also known as Douglas Street in Victoria, turn off at Michigan, which only goes one direction. They are on the corner of Michigan and Government, two blocks south of Victoria's famous Inner Harbor.

We were told about this lovely inn while on a tea room tour of Victoria, and were so pleased to hear about it. We spent a sizeable amount of time enjoying the ambiance and being treated to some delicious tea time treats. Jay Smith, the manager, was delightful to talk to and he shared much of the inn with us. The dining area is located off a comfortable sitting area, in a room with high-peaked ceilings from which massive, candle-filled wrought iron chandeliers hang. The olive green marble-look floors are set off with pale sage green walls, and crisp white French doors surround the room on three sides. Warm light permeates the area. On the one solid wall stands a massive hutch with colorful plates and glassware. The chairs have cushions in a deep red color, and plants abound for a garden room feel. On both sides of the room, through the French doors, one enters a cozy patio where an intimate tea may be enjoyed.

Beautiful dishes, with the "Victorian Garden" pattern, are set at each place. The Afternoon Tea set, which is $18.69, is served on a tiered server laden with fresh fruit, finger sandwiches, baked scones with jellies, marmalade and clotted cream, a lovely selection of sweets, tea , coffee and lemonade.

Special dietary needs can be accommodated with advance notice. Groups of up to 16 may reserve.

MC/V/AE/DEB
Wheelchair Accessible
1 Hour Street Parking
Prices are in Canadian Funds.

Tea is offered May 1st through September 31st, 11-5 daily. The last tea service is at 4:30 and reservations are recommended.

*Proprietor's
Autograph_____Date_____*

Secret Garden Tea Company

5559 West Boulevard
Vancouver, B.C., Canada V6M 3W6
604-261-3075 / fax 604-261-3075
kathy@secretgardentea.com
www.secretgardentea.com

The nearest major cross street is 41st and West Boulevard. The tea room is actually between 39th and 40th.

You can find this tea room, which is owned by Kathy Wyder and Erin Wyder, in a village-like community in the heart of Kerrisdale. Inside this not so secret place, patrons are seated at small tables which are set about the room, or in overstuffed chairs and couches in front of the fireplace. Flowers and plants decorated the room, as do tea-related gift items. Shelves near the middle of the room house the extensive selection of Secret Garden loose-leaf teas.

The tea menu offers four choices: The Mini High Tea, which consists of three miniature sweets, one miniature scone, raspberry jam and Devon cream for $9.95; the Demi High Tea, a sampling of the High tea for $11.95; the High Tea for $22.95 which is served on an elegant tiered server and includes tea sandwiches, mini scones served with Devon cream and jam, sweets and tea cake; and the Sharing High Tea, an assortment of sweets and scones served with raspberry jam and Devon cream. All teas include a pot of Secret Garden Tea.

Gourmet sandwiches, which are served with crisp organic greens, are priced at $9.95, and there are a number of salad choices for $8.95 and $9.95. Specialty items such as chicken pot pie, torte and garden omelette are also $9.95. For the lighter appetite, there are two soup choices priced at $4.25.

Breakfast has also been added to the menu.

MC/V/Debit
Wheelchair Accessible
Metered Street Parking
Prices are in Canadian Funds.

Open Monday through Saturday 8-7 and Sundays 9-6. Reservations required for High Tea service which is served at 12, 2 and 4 every day. There is a maximum of 20 people for group reservation. Parties of 8 or more must reserve with a credit card and a 15% gratuity is added.

Proprietor's
*Autograph*_____*Date*_____

Silk Road Aromatherapy and Tea Co.

1624 Government Street
Victoria, B.C., Canada V8W 1Z3
250-704-2688
silkroad@silkroadtea.com
www.silkroadtea.com

If you are driving south on Blanshard Street, towards downtown, turn right on Fisgard, then left on Government Street. They are on the west side of Government Street, two doors down from the Gate to Chinatown.

Though Silk Road is primarily a mail-order tea business, they offer the opportunity for customers to stop by for one of their daily Tea Samplings. This is the perfect way to try new teas and perhaps find your new favorite. Their selection is extensive so you will surely find something that suits your taste.

They have recently launched a new spa menu with some new services. Some of the new techniques will enhance your old favorites. The spa products are all natural and are made on site. A copy of the new menu may be picked up at the store or may be accessed through their website.

They have also added private tea tastings and aromatherapy workshops which may be booked year round by appointment. Seasonal workshops are scheduled monthly and more information is available on-line.

The tea tastings are a delightful and entertaining exploration of tea. You will find out more about flavours, history, cultural aspects and health benefits of tea. In every tea tasting, you will learn some delicious recipe ideas and get valuable tips on brewing methods to ensure that you get the best flavour and nutrient value each time you make a pot of tea.

Seasonal events are planned and some examples are: Japanese Tea Ceremonies, Chinese New Year tea party and their annual birthday party in March.

The tea selection includes green, herbals, semi-green, black, shaped and limited editions. Silk Road offers something for everyone who appreciates a good cup of tea.

MC/V/DEB   Wheelchair Accessible
Metered Street Parking
They offer 1-Hour Validation at City Parkades
Prices are in Canadian Funds.

The shop is open Monday through Saturday 10-6 and Sunday 11-5. Tea tasting and workshops by appointment.

*Proprietor's
Autograph_____Date_____*

Sweet Revenge Patisserie

4160 Main Street
Vancouver, B.C., Canada V5V 3P7
604-879-7933
info@sweet-revenge.ca
www.sweet-revenge.ca

From Hwy 99, turn east onto East King Edward Avenue. Turn right on
Main. They are at E. 26th Avenue.

The unique Edwardian décor with an Asian influence makes Sweet Revenge an interesting and rather glamorous place to take afternoon tea. You are surrounded by lush red wallpaper, oil lamps, antique-style furniture, soft wood floors and faux-tin ceiling. The surroundings, as well as the background music by such artists as Billie Holiday or Benny Goodman, invite you to make yourself at home and stay a while.

Everything is made-fresh daily in their bakery and is guaranteed to be up to your expectations. Some of the choices are so decadent that you must enjoy them in a leisurely manner, much like a pot of your favorite tea. Some of the home-made desserts include pear bread pudding, apple custard crisp, zuccotto, tiramisu and Crème Bruleé. Fresh fruit and assorted cheeses may also be ordered and be sure to ask your server for seasonal specials.

Sunday Afternoon Tea, which is $21.50 per person, includes focaccia bread with prosciutto, corn pie with ham, curry and sun-dried tomato bread with chutney chicken salad, croissant, cheese scone, zucchini muffin, honey-pecan tartlet, fruit tartlet, lemon loaf with lemon curd, season Crème Bruleé and your choice of tea. The tea selection includes black, green, rooibos, herbal and chi, and coffee, espresso drinks, soft drinks, milk, juices and alcoholic drinks are also available.

Before leaving, stop by the bakery and select something to take home. Wouldn't it be great to enjoy one of their special desserts the next day? Don't forget to pick up some bulk Metropolitan Tea while you are at it.

V/DEB   Wheelchair Accessible
Metered Street Parking
Prices are in Canadian Funds.

Hours of business are Monday through Thursday from 7 p.m. to midnight,
Friday and Saturday from 7 p.m. to 1 a.m., and Sunday from 2 p.m. to
midnight. Sunday Afternoon Tea is served from 2 p.m. to 6 p.m.

Proprietor's
*Autograph*_____*Date*_____

White Heather Tea Room

1885 Oak Bay Avenue
Victoria, B.C., Canada V8R 1C6
250-595-8020
www.whiteheathertearoom.com

From downtown Victoria, take Fort Street east to Oak Bay Avenue. Continue east on Oak Bay Avenue to Davie Street, which is the nearest cross street.

Soft pastel walls, fresh flowers and beautiful white-linen table clothes set the tone for this special Scottish-themed tea room. Though there isn't a tartan to be seen, Agnes Campbell has given her room a unique feel with large Tea Clipper Ship prints as well as botanical art work by Charles Dool. White china and glassware as well as floral draperies on the expansive windows complete the bright and cheery décor.

There are three tea selections to chose from. The Wee Tea at $9.75 consists of 2 tea sandwiches, mini cheese scone with chicken-apple filling, slice of tea loaf, and a piece of delicious Scottish shortbread. The Not So Wee Tea offers a selection of tea sandwiches, freshly baked scone with delicious preserves and Devon cream, mini cheese scone with chicken apple filling, savoury tart and a selection of fresh baking for $14.25. The Big Muckle Giant Tea For Two includes a selection of tea sandwiches, freshly baked scones with delicious preserves and Devon cream, mini smoked salmon and cream cheese sconewich with pepper jelly, savoury tart, cheese krispie with cream cheese and apple jelly, savoury surprise, and a wonderful selection of fresh baking for $34.95 for two people. A special seasonal tea menu is offered throughout the year.

Besides the tea menu, light breakfast items are offered from 9:30 to 11 and luncheon items such as soup, salads and sandwiches are available as well. Fresh baking changes daily, as they are constantly making new creations "to make you more cuddly."

Tea cozies as well as 22 different loose-leaf teas may be purchased from the small gift area.

MC/V/DEB   Wheelchair Accessible
1-Hour Street Parking and Lot
Prices are in Canadian Funds.

Hours of operation are Tuesday through Saturday from10-5. Tea is served 1:30-5. Reservations are required with a one-day advance notice. Available to groups from 15 to 30 people.

Proprietor's
Autograph_____Date_____

Windsor House Tea Room

and Restaurant

2340 Windsor Road
Victoria, B.C., Canada V8S 3E9
250-595-3135
lbrens@telus.net

Take Hwy 17 South. Turn left on Johnson-Oak/Bay Avenue. Continue onto Newport then turn left on Windsor Road. The Oak Bay Marina is one block west.

The tea room and restaurant, which were opened by Alison and Sally Ann in 2004, are located in an old Tudor-style townhouse, which has been converted into a charming and tranquil setting for afternoon tea. Private rooms are set up in a manner that allows you to feel that the space is all your own. Cute and quaint décor abounds with floral wallpaper, cottage windows and beautiful aging wood. They all add to the soothing feeling that envelops you as you sit and enjoy a cup of piping hot tea with friends or family.

Traditional High Tea is offered all day for $39.95 for two, and it includes finger sandwiches, sausage rolls, hot buttered crumpets, cream scones, assorted treats and sherry trifle. The Queen Victoria's Tea is $12.95 and offers tea sandwiches and cookies. King Edward's Tea, which is $17.95, has a seasonal green salad, cheese or raisin scone, tea sandwiches and a cookie. You may also select the Cheese and Fruit Platter for $9.95, if lighter fare is your desire. All include a pot of orange pekoe tea, and the scones are served with clotted cream and preserves.

Other menu offerings include many traditional English dishes such as Shepherd's Pie, Steak Pie, Welsh Rarebit, Bangers 'n' Mash, Crêpes and Ploughman's Plate. There are other items also, and all are priced between $4.95 and $12.95. Special dietary needs may be accommodated with prior arrangements, and outside catering is offered. A nice selection of delicious desserts are priced at $3.25 to $6.95, as well as a large assortment of beverages.

For your shopping pleasure, take time to check out the gift area which features many tea related items, including Metropolitan Tea - their house label.

MV/V/AE/DEB
Not Wheelchair Accessible
Street Parking
Prices are in Canadian Funds.

Open Tuesday through Saturday 10-4 and Sunday 11-4. Any time is teatime! Please call for large group reservations.

Proprietor's
*Autograph*_____*Date*_____

Welcome
To
Northern
California

An Afternoon to Remember

Tea Parlor and Gifts
452 Main Street
Newcastle, California 95658
916-663-6358
info@afternoontoremember.com
www.afternoontoremember.com

From Sacramento, take I-80 toward Reno. Take exit 115. Turn left, go over freeway. Stay on road, past post office on right. Curve around Post Office, turn right on Main. They are in the left side of the street next to Place Sierra Bank.

We had the pleasure of sharing a taxi with the owner, Amy Lawrence, when we were in Las Vegas for a Tea Expo in 2004. What a delight she was to talk to, and our ride was over way too soon! Her enthusiasm for tea time is definitely reflected in her tea room.

The décor is European, with two rooms – the parlor and the garden room. Amy calls her tea room, "an elegant retreat where you can reminisce with friends, enjoy homemade food and sip a great cup of tea." Their mission is to pamper each guest and make them feel relaxed and special, while educating them about tea.

There are three tea sets to choose from, starting with a Cream Tea for $6.95. This is followed by the Light Afternoon Tea which includes 2 scones, 3 tea sandwiches and 3 tea desserts. Finally, there is a Full Afternoon Tea with a slice of quiche, soup/salad, 2 scones, 3 tea sandwiches and 3 tea desserts. All include a pot of tea, Devonshire cream and lemon curd. A vegetarian tea is available with advance notice. Their house tea is Crème Brule and they offer it for sale in bulk.

After tea, take time to browse the gift shop for that something special to take home.

MC/V/AE/DEB/DIS/Checks
Wheelchair accessible
On-street Parking

Lots of pictures on their web site

They are open Wednesday through Saturday 11-5. Tea times are 11, 1 and 3. Reservations are preferred, with one week's notice for Saturday and same-day call for weekdays. Groups of up to 40 can be accommodated.

*Proprietor's
Autograph_____Date_____*

Keeping Still Mountain Tea Shop

405 Commercial Street
Nevada City, California 95959
530-265-2367
jicki@saber.net
www.keepingstillmountain.com

From I-80, take the Auburn Exit (Hwy 49) to Grass Valley. Take the Broad
Street exit at Nevada City. Stay on Broad until you see the Nevada Theatre
on your right. Turn left at N.Y. Hotel.

Jick Icasiano opened her tea establishment in 2004 in a most interesting
venue, the New York Hotel. Since Nevada City is such an interesting walk-
about town, stopping to take a cup of tea is the perfect respite.

This is an Asian-style tea shop with a tea room upstairs. They carry over
70 varieties of tea, as well as a wide variety of tea accessories for purchase.
Their premium gold-label selections are rare, limited productions and high-
quality grade teas which you might brew for special occasions and serve to
important guests. You may also indulge yourself and loved ones to a pot of
tea as a sign of appreciation.

A 32 oz. pot of tea may be purchased for $7 and a 16 oz. pot for $3.74.
Other beverage choices are iced tea and sparkling juice.

Afternoon Tea is offered by reservation for parties of 8 or more, and it
includes 2 sandwiches, quiche, fruit salad, pastry and choice of tea for $20.
Tea with cookies and pastries is available anytime during shop hours.

Bulk teas from all over the world, tea wares, books and gifts are available
in the ground-floor gift shop. Teas may also be ordered on-line.

V/MC/Checks
Wheelchair Accessible
Metered Public Parking Lot

Winter hours are Tuesday through Saturday 11-3 and Sunday and Monday
11-4. Tea is served during open hours. Call for other hours of operation.

Proprietor's
Autograph_____Date_____

Lisa's Tea Treasures

Tea Room and Gift Parlour
1145 Olsen Avenue
San Jose, California 95128
408-247-3613
www.lisasteatreasures.com

Call for directions. They are located near the Winchester Mystery House.

Having opened in 1993, Lisa's Tea Treasure is a well-established tea room in Santana Row. With its high ceilings, decorative border, and yellow-gold and mauve color scheme, the tea room has an elegant European feeling. Imported light fixtures and beautiful antiques set off the lovely tea tables which are finished with linen tablecloths, delicate fine china, tea cozies and silver strainers. The crowning touch - servers dressed in traditional 19th century costumes!

There are seven teas, priced at $19.95, to choose from: The Duchess Delight (English) has Decaf Boysenberry Tea served with ham and cheese quiche, cucumber tea sandwiches, scone and lemon tart; My Lady's Respite offers Earl Grey Tea, tea sandwiches, Portobello puff, scone, petít four, mini cream puff and mini tart; The Summer Regatta includes Peach-Strawberry Tea, chicken Waldorf salad over greens, toasted crumpets, pear almond savory and key lime cheesecake; Rajah's Prize (vegetarian) includes Strawberry Darjeeling Tea served with fruit, a slice of Brie, mini croissants, asparagus couscous savories and carrot cake; The Kings Ransom (Italy) has a Vanilla Floral Tea, mini pizza puffs, Caprese salad, pesto and nut sandwiches and hazelnut torte; Louis XIVs Favourite Tea (French) includes Blackberry Jasmine Tea, green salad in Raspberry Vinaigrette, fruit and almonds, Brie en Croute, toasted crumpets and Marquis au Chocolat; and the Marquis Light Delight Tea (fat free) has Lemon-Mint Green Tea, fresh fruit and cottage cheese, cucumber and yogurt sandwiches and sorbet in a frozen fruit shell. Scones are served with Devonshire cream and preserves. For

children, The Court Jesters Tea includes a festive decaf Watermelon Berry Tea, Pigs in a blanket, jam and peanut butter sandwiches, applesauce sundae, mini cupcake and petít four critter, all for $13.95. Some side dishes are available.

Gift Shop   Wheelchair Accessible   Lot Parking

Hours of operation are Monday through Saturday 10-6 and Sunday 11-5:30. Tea is served 1-4 with the last tea service at 4. Reservations for groups with a credit card guarantee and 2-day cancellation policy. Special teas are offered in conjunction with monthly holidays.

Proprietor's
*Autograph*_____*Date*_____

Lovejoy's Tea Room

1351 Church Street
San Francisco, California 94114
415-648-5895
www.lovejoystearoom.com

Take Lombard to Divisadero. Turn right and follow until Divisadero becomes Castro. Follow Castro to Clipper and make a left turn. Take Clipper to Church. They are located on the corner of Church and Clipper.

This interesting and fun tea room first opened in the early 1990s, moving to its current location in Noe Valley in 2000. It was originally an antique store that served a good cup of tea. The customers become more interested in the tea and scones, and the rest, as they say, is history.

Warmed by light from the windows and shades of pink, the tea room is a welcoming place. Muna Nash, co-owner with Gillian Britley, likens it to "your eccentric great aunt's living room ... cozy and cluttered." The tables, chairs, linens and china are all mismatched, and the result is a place that the owners feel reflects the diversity of San Francisco. It blends together the traditions of tea service with an eclectic, quirky and playful spirit.

Tea services are numerous and begin with a Sweet Tea for $7.95 and a Cream Tea for $8.95. They are followed by a Light Tea of one sandwich, scone, fresh fruit and shortbread tea biscuit for $11.95 and the High Tea featuring two sandwiches, coleslaw, greens, scone, fruit and tea biscuit for $14.95. The High Tea may be purchased for two with the addition of two sandwiches, a scone and one tea selection for $27.95. The Queen's Tea includes two sandwiches, coleslaw, greens, scone, crumpet with lemon curd, fresh fruit, a petít four and a shortbread tea biscuit for $18.95. For children the Wee Tea is $8.95 and has a sandwich, scone, fresh fruit and tea or hot chocolate. All teas include a pot of tea, and double Devon cream and preserves for the scones.

A gift shop is located across the street, so be sure to take time to browse.

MC/V
Limited Wheelchair Access
2-Hour Metered Street Parking

Open Wednesday, Thursday, Saturday and Sunday 11-6, and Fridays until 7. Reservations are recommended, especially on weekends.

Proprietor's
*Autograph*_____*Date*_____

Mistletoe and Roses

121 W. Main Street
Turlock, California 93580
209-632-2178
webe03@sbcglobal.net
www.mistletoeandroses.com

From Hwy 99, take Central Turlock / Main Street exit. Stay on Main Street to Historic Downtown Turlock. Mistletoe and Roses is in the Main Street Plaza.

Sisters Lorna and Elaine Weber had a dream of some day owning a unique gift cottage, followed by the idea of offering tea. They realized that dream when, in 1998, they opened Mistletoe and Roses in Atwater. Then in 2001, they opened at their present location in Turlock's Main Street Plaza.

One has lunch or takes tea in the English Tea Garden which features a gazebo, dining room and outside courtyard. The tearoom has lovely print yellow wallpaper, lace-covered tables, eclectic chairs and tables, and large cottage windows. All add to the charm of this English cottage tea room.

The Afternoon Tea, which requires reservations, includes soup in a teacup, fruit medley, scones with curd and cream, tea sandwiches, cheese and fruit, tea cookies and cake with berry sauce for $19.99 per person (includes tax and gratuity).

For lighter fare, there is a Cottage Tea Sampler which has tea sandwiches, fruit, cheese, scone and curd for $8. Luncheon items include croissant sandwiches, specialty salads and a fruit and cheese platter, and a daily special priced at $6.50 and $7 each. Desserts, scones and soup may be purchased à la carte and there are a number of beverages to choose from. Special dietary needs can be accommodated with prior arrangements.

Remember to take time to check out the gift shop which offers home accessories, English tea items, garden items and a charming baby section. Wendy Lawton Dolls are sold exclusively at Mistletoe and Roses, as well.

MC/V/AE/DIS/Checks
Wheelchair Accessible
Street and Lot Parking

The gift cottage is open Monday through Saturday 10-6. The tea garden is open Monday through Saturday 11-3, with the Queen Anne Tea being offered by reservation at 2.

Proprietor's
*Autograph*_____*Date*_____

Over Tea

755 Petaluma Avenue
Sepastopol, California 95472
707-823-1966
overtea@comcast.net
www.geocities.com/overteasonomacounty

From Santa Rosa, Take Hwy 12 to Sebastopol. Turn left onto North Main Street, remain in left lane. Cross over Petaluma Avenue and drive directly into the Sebastopol Antiques Mall's driveway. Go left at the far end of the building.

While visiting family in California, we had the opportunity to meet Cynthia Wong, who opened her tearoom in 2003. It was easy to see how much she enjoyed hosting guests, and how much she strived to make everyone's visit as enjoyable as possible.

Cindy has turned the area, which is set at the end of an antique mall, into an oasis where one can escape the cares of the day. White linen-clad tables dotted with pastel napkins welcome you, and a generous array of tea accoutrements complete the look. Many gift items for sale are set about the area.

The tea services are numerous starting with a Cream Tea for $8.95, and A Spot of Tea, with scone and finger sandwiches for $12.95. Stopped for Tea offers scone, garden salad and quiche for $13.95. The Simplic-a-tea includes scone, choice of sandwich and simple dessert for $15. Assorted sandwiches may be substituted for $2. Tea for Two is offered at $34.95 and it includes scones, assorted sandwiches, and simple desserts. For $19.95 per person, Your Majest-tea offers scone, mini muffin, assorted sandwiches with

savories and assorted desserts. All the above teas include a pot of tea, lemon curd, "heavenshire" cream and strawberry preserves. Children may enjoy a tea for $9.95 that includes scone, assorted sandwiches and child's dessert. Light lunches are also available, coffee is offered, and outside catering may be arranged.

MC/V/Cash
Wheelchair Accessible
Lot and Street Parking

The tea room is open Wednesday and Thursday 12-3; Friday and Saturday 11-4. Reservations or cancellations are required at least two weeks in advance. Any time is tea time except for special occasions. Occasionally, theme or holiday teas are offered.

Proprietor's
Autograph_____Date_____

Partea Time Tea House & Gift Shop

727 Sutter Street
Folsom, California 95630
916-351-5844
parteatime@comcast.net
www.parteatimeteahouse.com

Take Hwy 50 to Folsom Boulevard. exit (exit 23) and proceed north to Sutter Street.

In the words of the owners, Kathy Freeman and Tom Field, "our goal at Partea Time is to provide a sanctuary, a place that provides a soothing atmosphere that, when accompanied by a pot of tea, is especially welcome in this hectic world." That is the essence of tea time!

This tearoom, located in Historic Folsom, has a large dining room and two smaller upstairs rooms which are decorated in the English style, definitely with a Victorian touch. Pastel tablecloths, soft-yellow walls and dark-wood shelves laden with gifts greet you upon entering the tea room. There are hats set about for dress up fun, too!

The tea selections start with Cream Tea for $6.95 and Dessert Tea for $8.95. They are followed by Light Afternoon Tea which includes a scone, salad and assorted finger sandwiches for $15.95, and Full Afternoon Tea which offers a scone, salad, assorted finger sandwiches and an individual plate of assorted desserts for $17.95. All include a pot of tea selected from their extensive list of Metropolitan Teas. Scones are accompanied by Devonshire cream and English preserves. Vegetarian and diabetic diets can be accommodated with prior arrangements.

For children, there are four tea choices from the Cream Tea priced at $3.95 to the Full Afternoon Tea offering a scone, assorted finger

sandwiches, salad, individual plate of assorted desserts and a pot of tea or punch for $14.95. Tea Parties are a specialty, especially Young Ladies Dress-up Tea.

MC/V/DEB/Checks
Wheelchair Accessible
Parking at Both Ends of the Block

The shop is open Monday through Sunday 10-4. Any time is tea time and the last tea service is 4. p.m. Groups are welcome with large groups requiring 3-weeks reservation notice. There is a $50 deposit for groups of 8 or more, up to 48-hours before reservation time.

Proprietor's
Autograph_____Date_____

Secret Garden Tea House

721 Lincoln Way
San Francisco, California 94122
415-566-8834
sgtea@comcast.net
www.secretgardenteahouse.net

Traveling south on 19th Avenue, turn right on Lincoln Way. Go 10 blocks and the tea room is on the left hand side of the street between 8th and 9th.

After an afternoon of wandering through Golden Gate Park, what better way to relax than to take tea at this wonderful tea house. Just across from the park, Annie has created a warm and welcoming oasis. The décor offers intimate tables covered in pink floral clothes and white ladder-back chairs. White chandeliers, white shelves and matching rose floral china complete the charming ambiance.

The numerous tea sets are served on white-plated tiered servers and include your choice of tea, cocoa, milk or lemonade. Scones are served with Double Devon Cream and preserves. For $10.95, the Lady's Cream Tea offers two scones. Oscar's Surprise includes two scones, two tea cookies and a selection from the dessert tray for $13.95 and the Garden Escape has a tasty assortment of mini savories and an assortment of tea cookies and mini sweets for $14.95. There are two teas offered at $18.95. The first is Earl's Favorite: a scone, 6 tea sandwiches (your choice from the list below), a savory, and an assortment of tea pastries and sweets; and The Bedford's Delight: a scone, 6 assorted tea sandwiches, a savory and dessert of the day. The sandwich choices are: cucumber mint, chicken curry, chutney and cheddar, egg salad, grill ham and Swiss, pesto tomato and turkey and cranberry. For children twelve and under, there is a Prince or Princess tea

which includes a scone, mini quiche, peanut butter and jelly tea sandwiches, a petít four and a mini sweet for $13.95. Annie also offers teas for special occasions such as birthdays and showers.

MC/V/AE/DIS/DEB
Wheelchair accessible
Enter Golden Gate Park at 9th Avenue
and go right to park on
Martin Luther King Blvd.

The tea room hours are Tuesday through Friday 12-6 , and Saturday and Sunday 11:30-5:30.

Proprietor's
Autograph_____Date_____

Tea Garden Springs

38 Miller Avenue
Mill Valley, California 94941
415-389-7123
www.teagardensprings.com

From Hwy101, take E. Blithedale/Tiburon exit. From north, take a left and from south, take a right. Continue straight through lights in residential-looking area. When you enter the "small town," go left on Sunnydale & Park. They are above Jenni Lows Chinese Restaurant. They are near the Mill Valley Train.

This beautiful Asian-themed teahouse, which is a tribute to the old days of China, is a special meeting place evoking ancient temples and natural springs. The décor is red, gold, green and neutrals and features plants, a stream and Buddha wall hangings. Autumn Light, the proprietor, tells us that the teahouse opened in 1994, and its longevity is a testament to its success.

You are invited to arrive early and sip a calming cup of tea or vitalizing herbal elixir in their serenely beautiful tea garden as you prepare to receive an experience of touch.

Tea Garden Springs is a holistic health spa, a Zen spa of vision, health and vitality. It is important to note that they do not replace medical services. Numerous spa body therapies are offered and each treatment ends with a Dosha - specific herbal tea elixir and chyawanprash, a rejuvenating health tonic.

You are offered specific Ayurvedic home care advice and products to incorporate into your life. Each week they offer an evening of group meditation followed by a discussion to help you - enquire into present experience, rediscover what you already know and deepen your practice through meditation.

Numerous Chinese green teas and blended herbals, as well as teapots and tea sets are available for purchase.

Credit card and address are required at the time of booking. 24-hour cancellation notice is required or your reservation will be subject to a minimum charge of $60 for each hour of service booked.

MC/ V/AE/DIS/Checks
Not Wheelchair Accessible
Lot and Metered Street Parking

The shop is open seven days a week from 9:30 a.m. to 7:30 p.m. All day is "Tea Time." The last tea is served at 7.

Proprietor's
Autograph_____Date_____

Teance / Celadon Fine Teas

1111 Solano Avenue
Albany, California 94706
510-524-1696
winnie@teance.com
www.teance.com

Take Hwy 80 to the Albany exit, which is after Berkeley. The landmark
Theater Albany is next door.

Winnie Yu calls Teance, which opened in 2002, "an oasis of calm aesthetic." The centerpiece, made of concrete, is a round tea bar which is used for tea tasting. Cheng Design of California, an award winning designer, created this oasis. Table service is available and it seats about 30 people. A running waterfall fountain also acts as another bar.

Winnie tells us that they specialize in premium whole-leaf teas from China, Taiwan, Japan and Korea, and that their tea service is strictly Asian style. The teas are imported directly from farms. Education is very important to them and customers visit Teance to learn about teas at the tea bar.

The tea selections include ultra-low caffeine whites, hand-picked greens, no-caffeine florals & medicinals, a large selection of oolongs, and 100%-oxidized red and black teas. There is also a selection of cold tea drinks.

Orders are per pot and there is a 10% discount for 2 orders shared in the same pot. Remember to ask your server for the pastry selection of the day.

If you wish to purchase one of these teas to enjoy at home, Teance sells them in bulk. They also offer beautiful, and some "one of a kind" tea wares for sale.

MC/V/Checks
Wheelchair Accessible
Lot and Street Parking

Business hours are Tuesday through Thursday and Sunday 11:30-7. Friday
and Saturday hours are 11:30-10.

Proprietor's
Autograph_____Date_____

Treasured Teatime

3214 Riverside Blvd.
Sacramento, California 95818
916-930-9401
treasuredteatime@netscape.net
www.treasuredteatime.net

Going north on I-5, take Sutterville Exit. Go right on Sutterville to immediate right on Riverside (going north again) approximately 1/2 mile. Going south on I-5 to Hwy 50 to Broadway Street exit, turn right to Broadway and left on Broadway to Riverside Blvd. Turn right, go 1 mile.

As you enter the tea room, which was opened by Cheryl and Larry Steuck in 2001, you are first struck by the bright-yellow walls and abundance of white furnishings and décor. White lace-covered shelves hold a wonderful selection of gifts and tea accoutrements. A white picket fence separates the gift area from the tea room. In the tea room, small round glass-topped white tables are covered with Battenberg lace cloths, white linen napkins, silverware, silver creamers and sugar bowls and white china plates.

Before being served, you select a tea cup and saucer from Cheryl's collection of over 100; and if you wish, you can choose one of her 60 hats to wear.

Victorian Afternoon Tea consists of finger sandwiches, savories, soup of the day, scones with lemon or lime curd and Devonshire cream, fruit, assorted desserts and hot or iced tea for $15.95. Tea and scones ($10), tea, scone and sandwich ($12) or Teddy Teas ($12) are reserved for weekdays but are sometimes available on weekends. The menu changes monthly and seasonal treats are included each month. The tea always includes the traditional English cucumber sandwich.

A catered Afternoon Tea, for a minimum of 15 people, is available for $20 per person. You provide the location and they provide almost everything else. There is an extensive list of items to choose from to make your tea complete and memorable.

Treasured Teatime carries a selection of 80 teas which may be purchased in bulk in the extensive gift area. Take time to look around!

MC/V/DIS/AE/DEB   Wheelchair Accessible   Lot Parking

The shop is open Tuesday through Saturday 10-6 and Sunday 1-5.
Tea services are Tuesday through Friday 12 and 2, Saturday 11, 1 and 3, and Sunday 2. Reservations are encouraged.

Proprietor's
Autograph_____Date_____

Windsor Tea Room
at the King George Hotel
334 Mason Street
San Francisco, California 94102
415-781-5050 ext. 158 / 800-288-6005
mat@kinggeorge.com
www.kinggeorge.com

They are located 7 blocks from Union Square on Mason Street between Geary and O'Farrell Streets.

Whenever I go "home" I seek out a tea room to visit. This was a destination for us some years ago, and we found it to have a very charming and warm English ambiance. You are surrounded by royal works of art, and are treated to classical music playing in the background. The manager is Mathieu Lalonchelle, and he states that the tea room re-opened in 2004.

The location of the Windsor Tea Room is in one of San Francisco's many classic boutique hotels, and it is close to the core of the city. You may easily reach it by bus or cab, or for the more ambitious it is walking distance from Union Square.

There are numerous teas to choose from, starting with the Devonshire Cream Tea at $10.50. More substantial teas are the Queen Mary Tea offering tea sandwiches and tea cookies for $15.95, or the King George Tea which starts with a scone with double Devonshire cream and preserves, followed by a selection of tea sandwiches and concluding with your choice of tea cookies or a fresh fruit tart for $19.95. All include a bottomless pot of Lindsay's Tea. For children under 10, the Teddy Bear Tea has a choice of tea or hot chocolate, scone and a selection of tea cookies. This tea also comes with a 5-inch plush teddy and a special surprise!

MC/V/AE/DEB/DIS/JCB
Wheelchair Accessible
Lot Parking

Tea is served from 1 to 4:30 and the last tea service is 4:30.

Proprietor's
*Autograph*_____*Date*_____

Welcome to Favorite Recipes

Beverages

Heaven Coins
"Silk Road"
Victoria, B.C., Canada

Mix brewed Golden Phoenix tea with equal parts
apple or pear juice. Pour over ice cream.

Lavender Tea
"The Pleasures of Tea, Recipes and Rituals"

3 fresh pesticide-free lavender flowers *or*
1/3 teaspoon dried
4 teaspoons orange pekoe tea
Lavender honey, to taste

Pour boiling water into the teapot and set aside for 5 minutes. Discard the water.

Gently crush the lavender leaves to release their flavor, put them into a tea ball, and add the tea. Cover the tea ball and place in the teapot. Cover with about 6 cups boiling water and let steep for 5 minutes. Remove the tea ball and serve the tea with lavender honey on the side.

Makes 4-6 servings.

Used with permission of Sterling Publishers Co, Inc., 387 Park Ave. S., NY, NY. 10016 from THE PLEASURES OF TEA, Recipes and Rituals by the Editors of Victoria Magazine, © 1999 by Hearst Communications, Inc., published by Hearst Books, a Division of Sterling Publishing Co., Inc.

Pearl Lantern
"Silk Road"
Victoria, B.C., Canada

Dissolve 1 tablespoon of white or dark hot
chocolate powder per cup of Lychee Fruit tea, or
mix brewed tea with equal parts hot cocoa. Top
with whipped cream.

Victorian Iced Tea
"Foxwood House"
Newport, Washington

4 individual tea bags
4 cups boiling water
1 can (11½ oz.) frozen cranberry-raspberry
juice concentrate, thawed
4 cups cold water

Place tea bags in a teapot, add boiling water.
Cover and steep for 5 minutes. Remove and discard
tea bags. Refrigerate tea in a covered container.
Just before serving, combine cranberry-raspberry
concentrate and cold water in a 2½ quart pitcher,
stir in tea.

Serve over ice. Garnish with mint.

Yield: 10 - 1 cup servings

Berry Punch
"A la Fontaine"
Albany, Oregon

2 quarts of Necterberry juice
1 frozen white grape juice
1 liter of ginger ale

This is rich, full bodied drink.
Blend and enjoy!

Lemon Ginger Tea Punch
"Deepwood Estate"
Salem, Oregon

8 tea bags
3 quarts boiling water
3/4 cups sugar
1 - 12 ounce can lemonade
1 - 32 ounce bottle ginger ale, chilled

Place the tea bags in boiling water and steep for 10 minutes. Remove the tea bags and add the sugar, stirring until completely dissolved. Add the lemonade and chill. Just before serving, add the ginger ale. Serve in a punch bowl or pitchers garnished with lemon slices.

Recipe is from Janice Palmquist's cookbook;
"Deepwood Delights – Secrets for Enjoyable Teas"

Iced Tea "Punch"
Sharron
Corvallis, Oregon

I want to share my favorite way to make the *best* iced tea!

Bring a kettle of water just to boiling point. In a strainer place 4 heaping teaspoons of assorted teas; one teaspoon fruit flavored, two teaspoons black and two teaspoons of flavored green tea. My favorites are Strawberries and Cream, Earl Grey de la Crème and Sweet Lemon Shake or Green Oasis.

Place a strainer in the teapot, pour water over it and steep for 5 minutes. Remove strainer. Cool and enjoy over lots of ice! I like sweet tea so add Splenda for flavor.

Iced Green Tea
"The Tea and Herb Shop"
Corvallis, Oregon

4 Tablespoons Dazhang Mountain Green Tea
1 Tablespoon peppermint leaves
1 Tablespoon lemon balm
1 teaspoon fresh grated ginger
Pinch of lavender flowers

Bring 4 cups of water to a boil. Put ingredients in boiling water and stir. Steep for 5 minutes. Strain. Add 3½ cups cold water. Refrigerate until cold then serve over ice.

Sandwiches

Savories

Salads

Soups

Parsley, Olives & Tuna Salad Rolls
"Red Hats, Purple Shoes & Afternoon Tea"
CQ Products
800-887-4445
Coupeville, Washington

2 (6 oz.) cans water packed tuna, well drained
1/2 cup mayonnaise
2 teaspoons fresh lemon juice
3 tablespoons fresh minced parsley
1/3 cup chopped green olives
1/4 cup grated parmesan cheese
1 head green leaf lettuce
2 (12 inch) tortillas

In medium bowl, mix drained tuna, mayonnaise, lemon juice, parsley, green olives, and parmesan cheese. Stir until well combined. Arrange leaf lettuce over tortilla to cover. Spread mixture over leaf lettuce then roll the tortilla tightly. Refrigerate until ready to serve. To serve, slice into 1 inch rounds.

Avocado Rolls
"All the Tea In China"
Yvonne Wrightman

1 very ripe avocado
1 tablespoon lime juice
1 tablespoon finely chopped walnuts
salt and pepper
10 slices whole-wheat, sandwich bread, buttered

Combine the first 4 ingredients and blend well. Spread bread lightly with butter then with the avocado mixture. Roll up and fasten with toothpicks. Wrap in plastic wrap and chill well. Remove picks and serve. Cut in thirds to serve.

Makes 30

Walnut - Date Cheese Balls
"Breakfast at Four, Tea at Nine"
Sue Carroll

2/3 cup chopped dates
8 ounces sharp Cheddar cheese, cut into
1-inch pieces
8 ounces softened cream cheese, cut into
1-inch pieces
2 tablespoons rum
2/3 cup coarsely chopped walnuts

In a food processor, combine the dates, Cheddar cheese, cream cheese, and rum and process for one minute. Form into balls and refrigerate for several hours. Press the walnuts onto the top and sides of the cheese ball. Serve with crackers, and apple and pear slices.

Note: This can be refrigerated, in a tightly sealed container, for up to 2 weeks.

Reprinted with permission of
Callawind Publications 1998

Toasted Pecan Tea Sandwiches

"Lynden's Cup of Tea"
Lynden, Washington

Preheat oven to 350°

4 teaspoons melted butter
4 cups pecan halves
6 tablespoons Worcestershire sauce
a little salt
16 oz. cream cheese

Combine the above ingredients. Stir to coat thoroughly and set aside to marinate for 5 minutes. Drain the pecans and spread on a cookie sheet. Toast for 15 minutes or until dry. Chop the pecans and set aside.

Blend cream cheese with the nuts. Taste and add seasonings as needed - Worcestershire, Tabasco, Cayenne and garlic salt. Spread on fresh bread of your choice and cut into tea sandwiches.

Date and Walnut Tea Sandwiches
"Lynden's Cup of Tea"
Lynden, Washington

2 cups dates
1½ cups walnuts
1/2 cup cream cheese
1/4 cup honey

Combine dates and walnuts in food processor. Don't grind to a powder - try to keep it "finely chunky." Put in a bowl and mix in cream cheese and honey. Add more cream cheese if it's not creamy. Spread on fresh raisin bread and cut into tea sandwich shapes.

Egg Savories
"An Olde World Charm"
Boring, Oregon

Boiled eggs
Salt
Pepper
Celery seeds

Boil eggs, cool, peel and cut in half. Place halves on a plate and sprinkle each half with salt and pepper. Pour celery seeds in a small bowl. Take pinches of the seeds and place on the yolk of each egg half. These can be made a day in advance.

Mandarin Salad
"Over Tea"
Sebastopol, California

3-4 packages of mixed greens
or
1 each of red leaf, green leaf and iceberg
2 large cans of Mandarin oranges
1/2 cup slivered almonds
1 tablespoon butter
2 teaspoons sugar

Melt butter, add sugar then almonds, until candied. Spread on foil, cool, break into small bits.

Dressing

2 tablespoons vinegar
2 tablespoons sugar
1/4 cup oil
Dash of white pepper
1/2 teaspoon Salt

Shake until sugar dissolves. Enjoy!

Frozen Strawberry Mousse
"Campbell House Inn"
Eugene, Oregon

1 (16-oz.) package of frozen strawberries
8 oz. Cream cheese (softened)
1/2 pint whipping cream (whipped)
1/4 cup sugar
1/4 cup frozen orange juice concentrate

Whip the whipping cream with the sugar and set aside. Whip the softened cream cheese separately. Mix the strawberries and orange juice concentrate into the cream cheese. Fold in the whipping cream. Pour in individual molds or small containers and freeze overnight. All to soften 10 minutes prior to serving.

Chicken Hazelnut Sandwiches

"Campbell House Inn"
Eugene, Oregon

1 loaf bread (they use Western Hazelnut)
4 cups shredded chicken breast
1/3 cup mayonnaise
1/2 teaspoon salt
1 teaspoon Cajun seasoning

In a large bowl, mix ingredients together. The amount of mayonnaise and seasoning can be adjusted to taste. Finely chopped hazelnuts may be added to the mixture if desired.

Spread mixture generously on a slice of bread. Top with another slice. Trim off crusts for a sophisticated sandwich, and cut into 3 fingers.

Elegant Avocado Soup
"Lets Do Tea:"
Nada Lou and Verna Marie

1 can condensed cream of chicken soup
1 soup can of water
1 large, peeled and pitted ripe avocado
(check for ripeness - you should be able to gently
make a slight impression with your thumb on the top
third of the fruit. If it is hard or too soft, run away!)
1 teaspoon good curry powder

Whirl all together in your blender and then pour into a sauce pan and heat gently … don't boil. Serve at once with a float of whipped cream.

Makes 6 dainty servings

The ladies share, "believe it or not, "avocado" is the soup. This is such a delicate and very easy soup to make and lovely for the tea table. You will have everyone guessing..."

Reprinted with permission

Fried Chicken Salad
"Delicate Pleasures, A Tea Room"
Sedro-Woolley, Washington

1 whole fried chicken, cold
1/3 cup mayonnaise
1/3 cup diced celery
2 tablespoons sun flower seeds

Skin, bone and dice cold fried chicken. Mix all ingredients together. Refrigerate

The above is served on a slice of high-quality white and wheat bread.

Carrot Cashew Soup
"Steeped in Comfort"
Lakewood, Washigton

3 lbs. carrots
2 large russet potatoes
3 cloves of garlic
Water (she uses chicken broth or stock)
Salt
2 oz. butter
1 large onion
1/3 cup cashews (she uses 2 lbs. of cashews
per 5 # carrots)
1 to 2 cups milk (can use cream or canned milk)
Pinch of nutmeg
1/2 teaspoon basil

Peel the carrots and cut them into chunks. Do the same with the potatoes. Peel the garlic and leave whole. Put all these ingredients and 1 tsp. salt into the soup pot with enough water or stock to cover. Bring to a boil and simmer until carrots are tender.

Chop the onions and sauté in butter. Add the cashews and cook until the onion is transparent and the cashews lightly toasted. Add to simmering soup pot.

When the vegetables are tender, remove from heat. Run the soup through a blender, adding milk as needed. Add enough milk so that you have desired consistency. Return the soup to the pot and heat gently. Season to taste with nutmeg, basil and salt. Do not boil. Enjoy!

Judy says that she always serves this as a "cup of comfort," their soup of the day with a small basil/black pepper biscuit and butter. People enjoy the nutty flavor and often ask if it is pumpkin/peanut soup.

Holiday Tea Sandwich
"Anna's Tea Room"
Coupeville, Washington

Bread of your choice
Cream cheese
Food coloring
White cheddar cheese
Tomato slices

Color the cream cheese appropriately for the holiday - green for Christmas, pink for Valentine's Day, blue for Fourth if July. Cut bread into rounds using a small biscuit cutter or cookie cutter. Spread each round with the colored cream cheese. Cut the white cheddar into thin slices and cut rounds out of slices. Place cheese on top of the cream cheese. Top with the tomato slices.

Reprinted from The Country Register Aug/Sep 2005 edition. Printed with permission from Kristin Schricker, owner/manager of Anna's Tea Room

Artichoke & Shrimp Tea Sandwiches
"Afternoon Tea Serenade"
Sharon O'Connor

One (8 ounce can) artichoke hearts, drained
1 cup cooked baby shrimp
1/4 cup mayonnaise
1/4 cup sour cream
Cumin oil to taste*
2 wheat bread slices

In a medium bowl, mash the artichoke hearts with a fork until smooth. Stir in the baby shrimp. In a small bowl, mix the mayonnaise, sour cream and cumin oil to taste until smooth. Fold the mayonnaise mixture into the artichoke mixture and blend. Spread the bread slices evenly with the topping. Slice the crust off the bread and cut the bread into 4 triangles.

Makes 8 sandwiches

*Cumin Oil
1½ cup vegetable or grape seed oil
1/2 teaspoon ground cumin

In a small saucepan, bring the oil and cumin to a simmer. Remove from heat, cover and let sit overnight.

Curry Chicken Rolls
"A Year of Teas at Elmwood Inn"
Shelley and Bruce Richardson

6 oz. cream cheese, room temperature
2 tablespoons orange marmalade
2 teaspoon curry powder
1/4 teaspoon pepper
1/4 teaspoon salt
3 cups finely chopped cooked chicken
3 tablespoons minced onion
3 tablespoons minced celery
1 cup finely chopped almonds, toasted

In a mixing bowl, combine first five ingredients. Beat until smooth. Stir in the chicken, onion and celery. Shape into 1-inch balls and roll in almonds. Chill for two days or freeze up to one month.

Makes 3½ dozen

Printed with permission from: Elmwood Inn Fine Teas & Benjamin Press, 205 East Fourth Street, Perryville, KY 40468, 859-332-2400, Freear@sm.com

This book can be ordered by calling
800-765-2139

Cream Cheese & Date Tea Sandwiches

"Tea Time"
Nancy and Roni Akmon

3 oz. dried pitted dates, chopped
6 oz. cream cheese, softened
8 slices of cinnamon and raisin sandwich bread
4 tablespoons unsalted butter, softened
Fresh sprigs of mint

Chop the dates fine. In a small bowl combine the dates and cream cheese. Mix well until combined.

Spread bread slices with the butter. Spread half of the bread slices with the cream cheese mixture. Press the other slices on top to form 4 sandwiches.

Trim off the crusts. Cut each sandwich into 3 fingers (make two parallel cuts to form 3 fingers). Place sandwiches on serving platter. Garnish each sandwich with a small sprig of mint. The tea sandwiches may be made up to 2-hours ahead, if they are covered tightly and refrigerated.

Bleu Cheese, Walnut & Pear Sandwich

"Tea CozyCooking"
Diane Lareau AmEnde

4 tablespoons cream cheese, softened
2 tablespoons bleu cheese
unsalted butter, softened
6 slices thin multi-grain, pumpernickel or rye bread
1/2 cup walnuts, chopped very fine and toasted
fresh pears, ripe and cut into 12 thin slices.

Mash both cheeses together in a small bowl with a fork until they are smooth and combined. Spread each slice of bread with a thin layer of butter. Spread equal amounts of cheese on 3 slices of bread. Sprinkle a heaping tablespoon of walnuts over cheese. Place four thin slices of pear on top of cheese and nuts. Cover with remaining bread slices. Press down firmly. Remove crusts and cut into 4 pieces. Serve immediately or place on holding plate and cover with damp paper towel and plastic wrap and chill until serving time.

Diane calls this, "a classic English tea sandwich of sophisticated tastes."

Printed with permission.
Contact - www.teacozycooking.com
860-646-7057

Smoked Salmon Pinwheels
"A Little English Book of Teas"
Rosa Mashiter

5 or 6 thin slices of soft brown bread, crusts removed
1 cup low-fat cream cheese
1½ tablespoons lemon juice
1 tablespoon very finely chopped fresh parsley
1 tablespoon very finely chopped watercress
Black pepper
Pinch of cayenne pepper
4 oz. smoked salmon slices
lemon twist and watercress to garnish

Using a rolling pin, slightly flatten and stretch the bread. Cream the cheese, lemon juice, parsley and watercress together, mixing in the seasonings. Spread the mixture evenly over the bread, cover with the slices of smoked salmon and very carefully roll up firmly.

New Potatoes Stuffed With Ham
"A Tea For All Seasons"
Bruce and Shelley Richardson
Elmwood Inn

15-20 small new potatoes, similar in size
1 cup finely chopped ham
1 tablespoon. Dijon mustard
1 cup Gruyere cheese
Green onion tops

Wash the potatoes. Place them in a large kettle with enough water to cover. Add 1 Tbsp. salt. Bring to a boil and cook just until done, 20-30 minutes. Drain and cool. Cut 1/3 off the top of each potato. With a melon scoop or tomato shark, scoop out each piece leaving enough potato to allow each section to stand on its own. In a food processor, mix ham and mustard. Spread the mixture in the bottom of each potato boat and top with cheese and a few julienne green onion strips. They can be made well ahead of your event.

Published with permission: Elmwood Inn Fine Teas & Benjamin Press, 205 East Fourth Street, Perryville, Ky. 40468, 859-332-2400. This book can be purchased by calling 800-765-1239.

Chicken Pineapple Finger Sandwich
"Cynthian Catering and Teas"
Dallas, Oregon

3 boneless skinless chicken breasts-baked and cubed
1 cup drained crushed pineapple
1/2 cup chopped almonds
1/8 teaspoon. cumin
1/8 teaspoon salt
1 cup whipped cream cheese

Blend all of the above together. Cut crusts from bread. Spread a thin layer of chicken mixture to make sandwich. Cut in quarters. Secure with frill picks.

Bacon Ranch Pinwheels
"Sister Act Catering"
Corvallis, Oregon

1 can Pillsbury crescent rolls
1/2 cup shredded Cheddar cheese
1/4 cup chopped green onions
2 tablespoons ranch dressing
1/4 cup bacon pieces (4 pieces)

Heat oven to 350 degrees. Lightly flour a
cutting board. Roll out 4 of the triangles to make a
4 x 11 inch rectangle. Repeat with the other
4 triangles. Pinch the edges together. Spread
dressing over the top, followed by the cheese,
onions and bacon. Roll tightly from the smaller end.
Cut into 8 slices. Place on un-greased baking sheet
and bake for 12-17 minutes, until lightly browned.

Makes 16 servings

My Sister's Chicken Salad
"The Healing Garden Tearoom & Flowers"
Tacoma, Washington

4 cups of cooked chicken, diced or shredded
1½ cups of celery, diced
4 hardboiled eggs, chopped
2 tablespoons lemon juice
1/2 cup sour cream
1/2 cup mayonnaise
2 teaspoons curry powder

Mix all ingredients together, add salt and pepper to taste, chill and use for chicken salad sandwiches.

Artichoke Bisque
"Country Cottage"
Jacksonville, Oregon

18 cups chicken broth
9 Tablespoons flour
3 sweet yellow onions, chopped fine
6 Tablespoons butter
#10 can of artichokes packed in water, drained
1½ teaspoons tarragon

Sauté butter and onions for 10 minutes until clear. Add flour to make rue. Add broth, artichokes and tarragon. Puree in food processor or with hand blender. Top with Gremolata and serve.

Gremolata

3 cups finely chopped parsley
9 Tablespoons olive oil
6 cloves garlic
Pepper to taste
1 teaspoon lemon zest to taste

Micro-plane lemon for zest then add to parsley and puree in food processor. Add the rest of the ingredients and continue to puree.

This is one of their favorite high tea soups!
It is light yet rich in flavor.

Cinnamon Butter & Mandarin Orange Spread Sandwich
"Country Cottage"
Jacksonville, Oregon

Cinnamon Butter

1 cup butter - softened not melted
1 cup brown sugar - loosely packed
1½ tablespoons cinnamon

Mix together until creamy (should have a balance of flavors). Refrigerate. When ready to use, take out 1-hour ahead so it is soft enough to spread.

Mandarin Orange Spread

6 oz. whipped cream cheese
1/2 small can of mandarin oranges drained and patted dry with a paper towel

Mix together until incorporated. Mandarin oranges will be broken up into small pieces.

Serve these two spreads on dark brown rye bread using the Cinnamon Butter on one slice and the Mandarin Orange Spread on the other slice. Trim off crust and cut into 4 triangles.

Scones, Desserts and Toppings

Christmas Clover Cookies
"The Twelve Teas of Christmas"
by Emilie Barnes

1 cup shortening
2 2/3 cups flour
1/2 cup white sugar
2 teaspoons cream of tartar
1/2 cup brown sugar
1 teaspoon baking soda
1 egg
food coloring
3 teaspoons milk
raisins or nuts
2 teaspoons vanilla

Mix shortening, sugars, egg, milk, and vanilla. Add sifted dry ingredients, divide dough into 3 parts and put in separate bowls. Add green food coloring to one bowl, red to another, and leave the third plain. Chill dough 1 hour. With each color, roll small amount of dough in hand and lay one of each color together on cookie sheet in the form of a cloverleaf. Put raisins or nuts in the center. Bake in preheated oven at 350° until done.

Taken from:
The Twelve Teas of Christmas by Emilie Barnes
Copyright 1999 by Harvest House Publishing,
Eugene, OR. Used by Permission

Whipped Shortbread Cookies

"Mrs. O'Reilly's Notebook of Recipes"
Point Ellice House, Victoria, B.C., Canada

2 cups soft butter
1 cup sifted icing sugar
1 teaspoon vanilla
1/2 cup cornstarch
3 cups all purpose flour

Preheat oven to 350°. Cream butter and sugar together.

Add remaining ingredients one at a time. Drop batter using a teaspoon or pipe onto a sheet of parchment. Bake 15-20 minutes.

Dip into melted semisweet chocolate if desired.

Makes 35 shortbread cookies.

Hot Fruit Salad
Janice Palmquist
"Deepwood Estate, Tea Hostess"
Salem, Oregon

1 can cherry pie filling
1 can pineapple chunks
1 can peaches, sliced
1 (15oz.) mandarin oranges
1 can apricots, sliced
1 small jar chunky applesauce
1 can pears, sliced
1/2 cup brown sugar
1 teaspoon cinnamon

Mix all ingredients (including the juice in canned fruits) in a crock pot. Cover and cook on low for 3-4 hours. Looks nice in a pretty dish topped with coconut or toasted nuts.

Enjoy!

French Strawberries
Barbara Burnett
"Red Hats with Hat-Attitude"

4 cups strawberries, hulled and halved
1 cup whipping cream
3 tablespoons frozen orange juice concentrate,
thawed
2 tablespoons sour cream
1/2 cup plus 2 tablespoons powdered sugar, divided
1/8 teaspoon vanilla extract
1/4 teaspoon cinnamon

Sprinkle strawberries with orange juice concentrate and 1/2 cup sugar; gently stir. Refrigerate for 1½ hours. In another bowl, whip cream until soft peaks form, then stir in remaining sugar, sour cream, vanilla, and cinnamon. Fold chilled strawberries into whipped cream mixture.

Makes 4 to 6 servings.

Recipe courtesy of:
Barbara Burnett
Design Originals
2425 Cullen Street
Fort Worth, TX 76107
ph 800-877-7820 Ext. 133
Web www.d-originals.com
E-mail bburnett@d-originals.com

No-Fail Butter Mints
"Afternoon Tea at Pittock Mansion"
The Pittock Mansion Society
Portland ,Oregon

1/2 cup butter or margarine
1 tablespoon water
1 pound powdered sugar
Few drops of peppermint flavoring or
flavoring you like

Mix softened butter or margarine, water, and sifted powder sugar in a sauce pan. Cook over low heat until smooth. Drop in little spots on wax paper or foil, or roll into little patties.

Serves lots! Makes about 1½ pounds of candy.

Testers Notes: Almond flavoring is also good. If you use real butter instead of margarine, you will have a more buttery taste. Also, for today's cooks, we have the option of using candy molds which are available now.

Almond Macaroons
"The Book of Afternoon Tea"
Lesley Mackley

2 egg whites
3/4 cup ground blanched almonds
1/2 cup sugar
2 teaspoons cornstarch
1/4 teaspoon almond extract
1/2 cup blanched almond halves

Preheat oven to 350°. Line 2 baking sheets with parchment or waxed paper. Reserve 2 teaspoons egg white. In a large bowl, put the remaining egg whites and beat until soft peaks.

Fold in ground almonds, sugar, cornstarch and almond extract until mixture is smooth. Put 6 spoonfuls of mixture onto each baking sheet and flatten slightly. Place an almond half in center of each macaroon. Brush lightly with reserved egg white.

Bake 20 minutes, until very lightly browned. Cool on baking sheet. When cold, remove macaroons from paper.

Makes 12

Walnut - Chocolate Cookies
by Pat Alburey
The book of "Cookies"

2 egg whites
3/4 cup superfine sugar
1¾ cups (6 oz.) walnuts, finely ground
3 oz. semi-sweet chocolate, finely grated
25 walnut halves, cut in half

Preheat oven to 350°. Line several baking sheets with rice paper. In a medium-sized bowl, beat egg whites until stiff peaks form.

Very carefully fold sugar, ground walnuts and chocolate into egg whites until mixture is smooth. Spoon into a piping bag fitted with a 3/4 inch plain tip. Pipe small circles, about 1½ inches in diameter, on prepared sheets, spacing well apart.

Place a walnut quarter in the center of each circle. Bake 20 minutes. Remove from oven; leave cookies on baking sheets until cool, remove cookies and peel paper off each.

Makes about 50 cookies

From "The book of *Cookies*", by HP Books.
Published by The Berkeley Publishing Group

Orange Shortbread
by Sue Carroll
"Breakfast at Nine, Tea at Four"

1 cup softened butter (1/2 pound)
3/4 cup confectioners' sugar
1 teaspoon grated orange zest
2 teaspoons frozen orange juice concentrate, thawed
1¾ cups all-purpose flour
Sliced almonds

Preheat the oven to 300°. Lightly grease a 15 x 10 x 1-inch jelly roll pan.

Beat the butter with an electric mixer at medium speed. Add the sugar gradually, beating well. Beat in the orange zest and orange juice concentrate. Stir in the flour.

Press the dough into the prepared pan and prick all over with a fork. Cut into 1½-inch diamonds and place an almond slice in the center of each.

Bake for 30 minutes or until lightly browned.

Re-cut the diamonds while warm. Cool in the pan on a wire rack.

Yield: 48 cookies

Reprinted with permission of
Callawind Publications 1998

Foxwood House Scones

Foxwood House
Newport, Washington

3 cups all-purpose flour
1/2 cup sugar
2½ teaspoons baking powder
1/2 teaspoons baking soda
6 tablespoons cold butter
(no substitutes)
1 cup (8 ounces) vanilla yogurt
1/4 cup plus 2 tablespoons milk, divided
1 1/3 cups dried fruit (cherries)
2/3 cup vanilla or white chips

In a large bowl, combine the flour, sugar, baking powder and baking soda. Cut in butter until the mixture resembles coarse crumbs. Combine yogurt and 1/4 cup milk; stir into crumb mixture just until moistened. Knead in the cherries and chips.

On a greased baking sheet, put the dough into a 9 inch circle. Cut into eight wedges; separate wedges. Brush with the remaining milk. Bake at 400° for 20-25 minutes or until golden brown.

Serve warm
Serves 8

Coconut Melts
"An Olde World Charm"
Boring, Oregon

3 egg whites
1/4 cup confectioners sugar
3 tablespoons flour
1 cup coconut

While your oven is preheating to 350°, lightly spray oil coating on a baking sheet. Beat egg whites until fluffy! Add confectioners sugar and stir well. Stir in flour. Stir in coconut. Dolop level teaspoons of coconut dough onto baking sheet, one inch apart (just leave a bit of room to spread out). Bake on center rack in oven until light brown on the edges. Let cool before removing from sheet. Place wax paper between layers of melts, so they don't stick together! Freezes well up to 4 weeks or keep in well sealed containers for up to 7 days.

Uses: can be served plain or chocolate dipped.

Earl Grey Chocolate Tarts
"Lynden's Cup of Tea"
Lynden, Washington

Pastry

5 tablespoon unsalted butter at room temperature
1/4 cup confectioner's sugar
2 tablespoon almond flour
(you can purchase this at some grocery stores. If you
can't find it, just grind whole blanched almonds in a
coffee grinder or food processor)
1 large egg yolk, at room temperature
pinch of salt
1 cup of cake flour

In a mixer, beat the butter, sugar, almond flour
and egg yolk on medium speed just until mixed.
Slowly add the flour, at low speed, until the dough
begins to clump together (you may need more or
less flour). Remove the dough from the mixing
bowl and press in a thick disk. Wrap in plastic and
refrigerate for at least 1-hour. Place the dough on a
lightly floured surface and begin to roll it out until it
is about 1/8 inch thick and cut small circles to fit
small tart pans. Press them into pans and pierce the
bottom with a fork several times. Cover with plastic
and refrigerate for at least 30 minutes. Preheat oven
to 350°. Remove plastic wrap and bake until lightly
browned, about 15 minutes. Cool completely.

Continued on next page -

Earl Grey Tarts
continued -

Filling

1½ cups heavy cream
1/4 cup Earl Grey tea leaves
12 oz. bittersweet chocolate, finely chopped
3 tablespoon honey
3 tablespoon unsalted butter

In a medium saucepan, over medium heat, bring the cream to a simmer. Remove the pan from the heat and add the tea. Let stand for 3 minutes. Strain the cream into a bowl. Try to allow time for as much cream as possible to drip through. Return the cream to the saucepan and reheat to a simmer. Place the finely chopped chocolate into a medium bowl. Pour the simmering cream over the chocolate and let stand for about 3 minutes. Whisk until smooth. Whisk in the honey and the butter. Pour the mixture into the tart shells and refrigerate until the filling sets, about 1 hour.

Serve with ice cream, or their favorite Devonshire cream.

Lavender Love Cookies
"Rose Tree Cottage Tea Room"
Sequim, Washington

1/2 cup butter
1/4 cup granulated sugar
1½ cup all purpose flour
1 tablespoon dried culinary lavender,
roughly chopped
2 tablespoons superfine sugar for sprinkling

Cream together the butter and sugar until fluffy. Stir in the flour and lavender, and bring the mixture together into a soft ball. Cover and chill for 15 minutes.

Preheat the oven to 400°. Roll out the dough on a lightly floured surface and cut out about 18 cookies using a 2 inch heart shaped cookie cutter. Place on baking sheet and bake for about 10 minutes until golden.

Sprinkle with sugar, then let stand 5 minutes to set. Using a metal spatula, transfer carefully from the baking sheet onto a wire rack to cool completely.

Marci says, "serve to your favorite friends with our favorite tea."

Makes about 18 cookies

Pavlova
"The ANZAC Tea Parlour"
The Dalles, Oregon

4 egg whites
1 scant cup (6oz.) castor sugar
1/2 teaspoon corn flour
1/2 teaspoon vinegar
1/2 teaspoon vanilla essence

Whisk the egg whites until they are quite stiff. Add the sugar a spoonful at a time., beating well to dissolve each quantity. Add the corn flour with the last amount of sugar, then fold in the vinegar and vanilla essence. Draw a 7-inch circle on greased, greaseproof paper placed on a greased baking tray. Sprinkle lightly with corn flour. Spread the mixture to cover the circle in a dome-like cake shape. Place in a cool or very slow oven (200-250°) for 1½ - 2-hours until crispy and dry. Open the oven door and let cool before removing, then peel away the paper. Serve Pavlova with whipped cream piled on top with fruit arranged over the cream.

Topping
1/2 pint whipping cream
2-3 teaspoon icing sugar
1/2 teaspoon vanilla essence
8 oz. strawberries
4 Chinese gooseberries
6 passion fruit

Whip the cream and sweeten slightly with icing sugar and vanilla. Hull and clean strawberries; peel and slice Chinese gooseberries; cut passion fruit into halves and scoop out the pulp with a teaspoon.

Serves 6-8

Cream Scones
"The ANZAC Tea Parlour"
The Dalles, Oregon

2 cups all purpose flour (pastry flour works great)
1/4 cup castor sugar (Bev uses baker's sugar)
1 tablespoon baking powder
1/4 teaspoon salt
1/3 cup cold butter, cut into pieces
1 cup heavy whipping cream
1 teaspoon orange zest
1/2 cup currants
2 tablespoon whipping cream or
one egg white, beaten

Preheat oven to 375°. Sift together flour, sugar, baking powder and salt. Use a pastry blender and add the cold butter until the consistency is coarse and crumbly. Add 1 cup of whipping cream, stirring just until moistened (you may add more cream, depending on your flour). Now add the currants and orange zest. Turn out on lightly floured surface, and cut with round biscuit cutter. Place each scone about 2 inches apart on a nonstick baking sheet. Brush the tops of the scones with the remaining 2 tablespoons of whipping cream or egg whites. Sprinkle with sugar. Bake at 375° for 15 minutes or until golden brown. Serve warm with Devonshire cream and jam.

Yield: 1 dozen

Sticky Toffee Pudding
"Lynden's Cup of Tea"
Lynden, Washington

Cake

1 cup chopped dates
1 cup water
1 teaspoon baking soda

Put dates in sauce pan with water and bring to a boil.
Reduce the heat to medium and simmer until softened -
5 minutes. Remove from heat, stir in the baking soda,
and set aside. The mixture will foam up and turn green -
don't be alarmed, this is normal!

1/4 cup butter softened to room temp
3/4 cup plus 2 tablespoons Golden superfine sugar
1 teaspoon vanilla extract
2 eggs
1¼ cup plus 1 tablespoon self-rising flour, sifted

Combine butter and sugar in a bowl. Beat on
medium speed for about 4 minutes, until well combined
and lighter in color. Beat in vanilla. Add the eggs, one
at a time, beating well after each addition. With a
wooden spoon, stir in the flour and then the date
mixture. Pour the batter into greased pans and bake for
about 15 minutes (they use muffin tins).

Carmel Sauce

1/2 cup packed brown sugar
1/4 cup honey
1/2 cup butter
1/4 cup heavy cream

Combine sauce ingredients *except cream*, heat to a
simmer. Cook until it thickens and gets bubbly. Add
cream. It will bubble. Remove from heat.

Pour a generous amount of sauce on cake and top it
off with your favorite Devonshire cream.

Toasted Almond Truffles
"The Tea Cup"
Centralia, Washington

1/2 cup evaporated milk
1/4 cup sugar
1 package milk chocolate morsels
1/2 teaspoon almond extract
1 cup fine chopped toasted almonds

Combine milk and sugar in a heavy saucepan. Bring mixture to a full rolling boil and boil for 3 minutes, stirring constantly. Remove from heat and stir in chocolate morsels and almond extract until morsels melt and mixture is smooth. Cover and refrigerate 45 minutes until firm. Shape into 1 inch balls and roll in almonds. Refrigerate until ready to serve.

Pumpkin Bars
"The Tea Cup"
Centralia, Washington

3/4 cups butter
2 cups of sugar
16 oz. of pumpkin
4 eggs
2 cups flour
2 teaspoons baking powder
1 teaspoon cinnamon
1/2 teaspoon baking soda
1/2 teaspoon salt
1/4 teaspoon nutmeg
1 cup walnuts

Mix the butter and sugar until creamy. Blend in all other ingredients until smooth. Bake at 350° for 30 to 35 minutes.

Frosting

3 oz. cream cheese
1/2 cup butter
1 teaspoon vanilla
3 cups powdered sugar

Blend until smooth. Frost cooled bars.

Brown Sugar Shortbread
"Village Yarn & Tea Shop"
Shoreline, Washington

1/2 lb. unsalted butter
1/2 cup brown sugar
2 cups unbleached flour
1 teaspoon vanilla
3/4 teaspoon salt

Preheat oven to 325°. Cream butter and sugar until well whipped. Mix in vanilla. Add flour and salt and mix just until combined. Press into a 9 x 13 pan. Use square cookie presses to imprint decorative designs into the dough and bake for 35 minutes or until edges are just browned. Cool completely and cut into squares.

Verna's Zesty Lemon Curd
"Let's Do Tea"
Nada Lou and Verna Marie

3 eggs
2 cups sugar
1/2 pound butter, cut into tablespoon-sized pieces
3/4 cup fresh lemon juice
Grated peel of 1 lemon

In the top of a double boiler, combine all ingredients. Cook and stir over boiling water until thickened like pudding. Remove from heat and cool. Chill until ready to serve. Spread on muffins or rolls, over waffles or scones. Keeps well in the refrigerator up to 2 weeks.

Yield: 3 cups

Reprinted with permission

Lazy Peach Pie
"An Afternoon to Remember"
Newcastle, California

1/2 cup butter
1 cup sugar
1 cup flour
2 teaspoons baking powder
3/4 cup milk
1 large can of sliced peaches

Preheat oven to 350°. Place butter in 9 x 13 pan and melt in oven while it is preheating. Take out when melted. Sift sugar, flour and baking powder. Mix the sifted ingredients with the milk. Pour the mixture over the melted butter in the pan.

Pour the can of peaches (not drained) over the batter. Do not mix.

Sprinkle cinnamon and sugar over the top.

Bake at 350° for 1 hour.

Lemon Curd
"Point Ellice House"
Victoria, B.C., Canada

2 cups sugar
4 eggs
Peel of 4 lemons
1 cup lemon juice
1/2 cup butter

Beat sugar and eggs smooth. Whisk in remaining ingredients, except butter. Set mixture over double boiler until thickened and smooth. Remove from heat and cut in butter. Pour into jar. Most suitable for filling tart shells.

This is from Caroline O'Reilly's recipes-circa 1910.
Point Ellice House still uses this recipe.
Reprinted with permission.

The Campbell House Scones
"Campbell House Inn"
Eugene, Oregon

3 cups all-purpose flour
1/3 cup sugar
2½ teaspoons baking powder
1/2 teaspoon baking powder
3/4 teaspoon salt
3/4 cups firm butter (1½ sticks) cut into small pieces
3/4 cup chopped dried fruit or nuts (optional)
1 cup buttermilk

In a large bowl, stir together the flour, sugar, baking powder, soda and salt until thoroughly blended. Using a pastry blender or knife, cut the butter into the flour mixture until it resembles coarse cornmeal. Stir in fruit and nuts if desired. Make a well in the center of the butter-flour mixture; add the buttermilk all at once. Stir the mixture with a fork until the dough pulls away from the sides of the bowl. With your hands, gather the dough into a ball; turn out onto a lightly floured board. Divide the dough into four parts and lightly pat each part into a circle. Cut each circle into four parts and place the wedges on a greased cookie sheet. Sprinkle the scones with cinnamon-sugar if desired.

Bake at 400° for 12 minutes.

Makes 16 scones
Serve warm with jam & butter.

Chilled Strawberry Soup
"Applewood Country Gifts"
North Delta, B.C., Canada

2 lbs. strawberries
2 cups orange juice
1 cup sugar

Cook the above and when soft puree. Add:

2 tablespoons lemon juice
1 tablespoons lemon zest
1/2 teaspoon cinnamon
1/2 teaspoon nutmeg
1/2 teaspoon cloves
2 cups buttermilk

Chill and serve in stemmed glasses with whipped cream swirl, slice of fresh berry and sprig of mint or lemon balm.

In Marianne's own words ... *"delish!"*

Aunt Rose's Pound Cake
"Applewood Country Gifts"
North Delta, B.C., Canada

1 cup butter
8 oz. cream cheese
2 cups sugar
2 teaspoons vanilla

Beat the above ingredients then add -
2¼ cups flour
1½ teaspoons baking powder

Stir in 6 eggs

Pour into a greased and floured bundt pan.
Bake 45 minutes to one hour until golden brown
and a tester comes out clean. Serve with raspberries,
whipped cream and a dusting of icing sugar.

Victoria Pudding
"Point Ellice House"
Victoria, B.C., Canada

4 eggs
1 pint of milk
3/4 oz. Isinglass flavoured with brandy
vanilla

Make a custard with the ingredients. Let custard become quite cold, it will be thick and lumpy. Dip a mould in water, with a spoon arrange the custard in the bottom carefully filling the holes. Slice some sponge cakes in halves, dip them in Sherry, place in layers in the centre with jam between, filling the space round with the custard. It should remain at least 12-hours to stiffen. Serve with strawberry jelly.

This is one of Caroline O'Reilly's recipe-circa 1910.
Reprinted with permission.

Lemon Curd
"Touch of Elegance"
St. John, Washington

3/4 stick unsalted butter (6 tablespoons)
1 tablespoon fresh lemon zest
1/2 cup fresh lemon juice
1/2 cup sugar
3 large eggs
2 egg yolks

Melt butter with zest, lemon juice and sugar. Stir over moderate heat, stirring until sugar is dissolved and mixture just comes to a simmer.

In a bowl, whisk together eggs then whisk in lemon mixture until combined. Transfer lemon curd to pan and heat over moderate heat, whisking constantly until it just begins to simmer. Pour through a fine sieve into a bowl and cool slightly. Chill with it's surface covered with plastic wrap at least 2-hours, or until cold. Keep refrigerated up to 3 days.

Enjoy!

Almond Macaroons
The Book of "Afternoon Tea"
by Lesley Mackley

2 egg whites
3/4 cups ground blanched almonds
1/2 cup sugar
2 teaspoons cornstarch
1/4 teaspoon almond extract
12 blanched almond halves

Preheat oven to 350°. Line 2 baking sheets with parchment paper or waxed paper. Reserve 2 teaspoons of egg white. In a large bowl, put remaining egg whites and beat until stiff peaks form.

Fold in ground almonds, sugar, cornstarch and almond extract until mixture is smooth. Put 6 teaspoons of mixture onto each baking sheet and flatten slightly. Place an almond half in center of each macaroon. Brush lightly with reserved egg white.

Bake 20 minutes, until very lightly browned. Cool on baking sheet. When cold, remove macaroons from paper.

Makes 12

From "The Book of *Afternoon Teas*" by HPBooks. Published by The Berkley Publishing Group

Orange Delights
"A Year of Teas at Elmwood Inn"
Shelley and Bruce Richardson

1 box vanilla wafers, finely crushed
1/2 cup frozen undiluted orange juice
3/4 cup sifted powdered sugar
3/4 cup flaked coconut
1/2 cup finely chopped pecans or walnuts
1/4 cup white corn syrup

Mix all ingredients together and shape into 1 inch balls. Store in a covered container in the refrigerator or freezer. When ready to serve, roll in powdered sugar.

Makes 4 dozen

Cheese Scones
"Simply Scones"
Leslie Weiner and Barbara Albright

2 cups all-purpose flour
2 teaspoons baking powder
1/4 teaspoons salt
Generous dash ground red pepper
1½ cups shredded Cheddar cheese
3 tablespoons grated Parmesan cheese
1/3 cup unsalted butter, chilled
1/3 cup milk
2 large eggs
1 egg yolk mixed with 1 teaspoon water for glaze
(optional)

Preheat oven to 400°. Lightly butter a 10 inch diameter circle in the center of a baking sheet. In a large bowl, stir together the flour, baking powder, salt and red pepper. Stir in the cheese. Cut the butter into 1/2 inch cubes and distribute them over the flour mixture. With a pastry blender or two knives used scissors fashion, cut in the butter until the mixture resembles coarse crumbs. In a small bowl, stir together the milk and 2 eggs. Add the milk mixture to the flour mixture and stir until combined.

Spread the dough into an 8 inch diameter circle in the center of the prepared baking sheet. If desired, brush with egg mixture over the top of the dough. With a serrated knife, cut into 8 wedges. Bake for 15 to 17 minutes, or until the top is lightly browned and a cake tester or toothpick inserted in the center of a scone comes out clean.

Rose Manor Crumpets
"Tea Time at the Inn'
Gail Greco

1/2 oz. dry yeast (2 packages)
1 teaspoon sugar
3½ cups warm water
4 cups all-purpose flour
2 tablespoons baking powder
1½ teaspoons salt

Dissolve yeast and sugar in warm water. Add flour, baking powder and salt. Whisk until frothy. Heat griddle to 450°. Grease inside of crumpet rings and place them on heated griddle. Pour 3/4 cup batter into each ring. Cook until bubbles form and become dry on top. Remove ring and turn crumpets to brown lightly. Toast crumpet and serve with butter.

Yield:24

Almond Tea Cake

"Scones, Muffins and Tea Cakes"
Collins Publishers San Francisco, CA.

1 cup unsalted butter
3/4 cup granulated sugar
1 egg, separated
3½ oz. almond paste
1 teaspoon almond extract
2 cups, sifted all-purpose flour
1/2 cup sliced almonds

Preheat oven to 350°. In a bowl with an electric mixer, cream the butter and sugar. Add the egg yolks, almond paste and almond extract. Then add the flour and mix until just blended.

Press the cake batter into a round 8 inch ungreased cake pan (it will seem crumbly, so spread the batter with your fingertips until level).

In a small bowl, beat the egg white until foamy. With the back of a metal spoon, spread the beaten egg white over the cake. Sprinkle evenly with the sliced almonds. Bake for 30 minutes or until golden brown. Let cool for 15 minutes, then cut into 8 wedges.

Serves 8

Lavender Fresh Fruit

"Celebrate Lavender Festival Cookbook"
Sequim Lavender Growers Association"

1 cup cantaloupe, cut bite-size
1 cup strawberries, cleaned and cut
1 cup green grapes
1 cup dairy sour cream
2 tablespoons brown sugar
1 teaspoon ground lavender

Prepare fruit. Mix sour cream, brown sugar and lavender. Serve fruit with sour cream mixture as a topping.

Lemon - Herb Tea Sherbet
"Totally Teatime Cookbook"
Helene Siegel and Karen Gillingham

2½ cups water
6 lemon herb tea bags
1/2 cup sugar
1/4 cup light corn syrup

Bring 1½ cups water to boil. Add tea bags and steep 5 minutes. Remove bags and press out as much liquid as possible. Add remaining water, sugar and corn syrup. Bring to simmer, stirring to dissolve sugar. Simmer 2 minutes.

Cool then chill. Freeze in ice cream maker according to manufacturer's instructions.

Serves 4

Toasted Walnut Fudge Bread
"Chocolate for Breakfast and Tea"
Down to Earth Publications

1 cup coarsely chopped walnuts
3 oz. semisweet chocolate, melted and cooled
1 cup butter
1 cup sugar
5 eggs
2¼ cups flour
1 teaspoon baking soda
1 teaspoon salt
1 cup buttermilk
1 teaspoon vanilla extract

Preheat oven to 350°. Grease two 9 x 5 loaf pans. Spread walnuts on a baking sheet. Toast at 350° for 3 to 5 minutes or until fragrant. Cool. Melt chocolate in a microwave-proof dish by microwaving on medium high for 25 second intervals, stirring in between, until smooth. Cool. With an electric mixer, cream butter and sugar. Beat in eggs one at a time. Mix in cooled chocolate. In a separate bowl, mix flour, baking soda and salt. Stir buttermilk and vanilla together. Add flour and buttermilk alternately to chocolate mixture. Stir in walnuts. Divide batter between the two prepared pans. Bake for 55 to 60 minutes, or until knife or toothpick comes out clean. Cool bread in pan for 10 minutes, then remove form pan and cool on a wire rack. Serve warm or toasted with butter.

Makes 2 loaves

Blueberry Curd
"The Tea Table"
Bruce and Shelly Richardson
Elmwood Inn

4 cups fresh blueberries, slightly crushed
1/2 cup fresh lemon juice
1 cup sugar
4 eggs (beaten)
1/2 cup unsalted butter
1 tablespoon lemon zest

In a heavy pan, combine berries, lemon juice, sugar and eggs. Stir constantly over medium heat until blue berries are very soft. Next, add pieces of butter and the zest slowly, stirring constantly over medium heat until mixture just starts to boil. Immediately remove from heat. Cool. Pour into a covered container and place in refrigeration until ready to use. Stir before serving.

Printed with permission: Elmwood Inn Fine Teas & Benjamin Press. 205 East Fourth Street, Perryville, KY. 40468, 859-332-2400, freear@msn.com
This book may be purchased by calling 800-765-2139

Earl Grey Crème Bruleé
"The Great Tea Rooms of America"
Bruce and Shelley Richardson
Elmwood Inn

1½ quarts heavy cream
5 whole large eggs, slightly beaten
5 large egg yolks, slightly beaten
1½ cups brown sugar
1 cup white sugar
1 cup Earl Grey tea, strongly brewed

Preheat oven to 350°. Place heavy cream, slightly beaten eggs, egg yolks and sugars in the top of double boiler. Cook over medium heat, stirring frequently until slightly thickened. Add tea and pour into small ramekins. Bake until set, approximately 50-60 minutes. Custard is done when knife stuck in center comes out clean. Cool to room temperature and refrigerate overnight.

Mix a small amount of brown sugar and white sugar together. Pat lightly on top of custard and then torch until sugar melts. Serve immediately.

Printed with permission; Elmwood Inn Fine Teas & Benjamin Press, 205 East Fourth Street, Perryville, KY 40468, 859-332-2400, freear@msn.com

This book may be ordered by calling
800-765-2139

Maids of Honour
"The Great Tea Rooms of Britain"
Bruce and Shelley Richardson
Elmwood Inn

1/2 pound rich shortcrust pastry
4 oz. curd cheese or cottage cheese
3 oz. butter, room temperature
2 eggs, beaten
1½ oz. brandy
1/2 cup sugar
3 oz. cold baked potato
1/4 cup ground almonds
1/2 teaspoon grated nutmeg
grated rind of two lemons
3 tablespoons lemon juice

Preheat the oven to 350°. Grease 16 patty tins. Roll out the chilled pastry on a lightly floured board. Use a 3 inch cookie cutter to cut out the rounds of thin pastry. Line the tins with the pastry. Beat together the curd cheese and butter. Add the beaten eggs, brandy and sugar. Beat once again. In a separate bowl, beat together the potatoes, almonds, nutmeg, lemon rind and juice. Gradually blend in the cheese mixture. Beat thoroughly. Spoon the filling into the pastry shells and bake for 35 to 40 minutes or until set. Remove from the oven and leave to cool in the tins for 10 minutes before lifting carefully on to a wire rack for finish cooling.

Printed with permission: Elmwood Inn Fine Teas & Benjamin Press, 205 East Fourth Street, Perryville, KY 40468, 859-332-2400, freear@msn.com

This book may be ordered by calling
800-765-2139

Doris' Lemon Icebox Tarts
"Savoure"
Eugene, Oregon

Shortbread Crust

2½ cups flour
2/3 cups sugar
1/2 teaspoon salt
1 cup (2 sticks) butter, cubed
2 large egg yolks

Blend in food processor until dough forms a ball. Divide in half, wrap and refrigerate for 30 minutes. Divide each dough disk into 6 equal balls (total 12) and roll out each and fit into well-greased mini-tart pan. If, by the time you are finished putting the crust in the 12 tart pans, the dough has become too soft, place tart pans on cookie sheet un the freezer for 15 minutes. Before cooking, prick crusts thoroughly with a fork. Cook at 400° for 10 minutes or until crusts become slightly golden. Remove from oven and brush crusts with egg yolk and return to the oven for 2 minutes more.

Continued on next page -

Lemon Icebox Tarts
Continued -

<u>Lemon filling</u>

6-8 lemons (for 2 tablespoon zest and 1½ cups juice)
4 cans condensed milk
3 egg yolks, whisked until creamy NOT Frothy

Stir together lemon zest, juice, condensed milk and yolks. Fill pre-baked shortbread shells. Cook at 350° for 15 minutes. Allow to cool and then refrigerate for at least 1½ hours. Must be served cold.

Cindy's mother-in-law is *thrilled* to share this recipe with you.

Index

Tea Rooms Index - Oregon
Alphabetical Listing
(City Listing on page 284)

Tea Rooms Index - Oregon
Alphabetical Listing
(City Listing on page 284)

Tea Rooms Index - Washington
Alphabetical Listing
(City Listing on page 287)

Tea Rooms Index - Washington
Alphabetical Listing
(City Listing on page 287)

Tea Rooms Index - British Columbia

Alphabetical Listing

(City Listing on page 290)

Tea Rooms Index - Northern California

Alphabetical Listing

(City Listing on page 291)

Tea Rooms Index - Oregon
City Listing
(Alphabetical Listing on page 278)

Tea Rooms Index - Oregon
City Listing
(Alphabetical Listing on page 278)

Tea Rooms Index - Oregon
City Listing
(Alphabetical Listing on page 278)

Tea Rooms Index - Washington
City Listing
(Alphabetical Listing on page 280)

Tea Rooms Index - Washington
City Listing
(Alphabetical Listing on page 280)

Tea Rooms Index - Washington
City Listing
(Alphabetical Listing on page 280)

Tea Rooms Index - British Columbia

City Listing
(Alphabetical Listing on page 282)

Tea Rooms Index - Northern California

City Listing
(Alphabetical Listing on page 283)

Recipes Index

Beverages

Sandwiches, Savories, Salads and Soups

Recipes Index

Scones, Desserts & Toppings

Tea in the Right Company
So Whom to Invite

How imperfect are we
That we cannot find time for tea!

How we rush to be better,
To be sharper, to be more fine.
And yet we fail to fully live
In the wisdom of our time.

Perfection can be found most simply
By having the right company at tea.

Whether it is with those we love or,
With an angel stranger,
From that which is in front of us,
To that which eventually could be
Discovered by having the right company at tea.

Earlene Grey ©   *01-04*
Oregon City, Oregon

Earlene Grey is a published
author and her tea poetry is a
welcome addition to her work.
Her desire is to provide the
reader with a moment of peace
and a vision of tranquility.

www.earlenegrey.com

I believe that everyone who visits tea rooms and craft stores is familiar with the *Country Register*. It is usually set in a prominent place near the entrance, to insure that no one leaves without a copy. It works for us, and we look forward to each issue, anxious to see if any new tea rooms are listed

Barbara Floyd, the founder and publisher of the newspaper, is an entrepreneur at heart. When her children were young, she started an arts and crafts fundraiser for their school. When the school phased out that event, Barbara started one of the first "home" arts and crafts shows. It eventually became a gift shop close to her home. Along with her daughter, Barbra-Jean, she also created the first tea room and gift shop in Arizona. Under new ownership, "Gooseberries" is still operating in Phoenix, Arizona.

Needing an affordable means of advertising, Barbara started the *Arizona Country Register* in 1988. The paper has helped bond gift shop and tea room owners, crafters, quilters and customers together state wide. Eventually, people asked to start *Country Registers* in their own states and a licensing agreement was formed. There are now over 40 *Country Registers* in the United States and Canada. When traveling, we have found the *Country Register* to be a wonderful resource for finding Tea Rooms. We also enjoy all of the tea related articles.

You can contact The Country Register at www.countryregister.com

Thanks, Barbara, for your promotion of tea!

295

About TeaTimeAdventures.Com

Teatimeadventures.com is your link to current information about the Tea Rooms listed in this guide and beyond. It will keep you posted on new tea purveyors as well as seasonal or permanent closures. When traveling you can preview the best tea offerings for your destination.

This web site provides a list of upcoming tea events, updated news, current happenings, a newsletter, recipes and much more. Please visit and enjoy this resource designed with tea lovers in mind, and use our comments page to let us know what else may be of interest to you.

teatimeadventures.com

Be a TEA ROOM Spotter

When you're out-and-about and discover a new tea spot, please let us know. Many of our best new "finds" come from tea spotters like you. *Thank you for sharing.*

How to Report a New Tea Room

You can email the information to us at: *demontigny@proaxis.com* or use our web sites new tea room page at *teatimeadventures.com.* If you prefer to mail it in, send the information requested below with the tea rooms business card, and a flyer, if possible, to:

> Tea Rooms Northwest Staff
> 2397 NW Kings Blvd. # 148
> Corvallis, Oregon 97330

Tea Room Name:_____

Contact Person:_____

Address:_____

City:_____

State/Province/Zip:_____

Phone:_____

Referred by:_____

Address:_____

City:_____

State/Province/Zip:_____

Is Journaling for You?

Journaling is a wonderful, lasting keepsake of your time spent with family and friends enjoying a tea-time experience. Keeping a journal can nurture your sentimental side and feed the desire to capture special moments in your life.

If you are smitten by the tea experience as we are, or you have "Tea Room" memories you would like to save, then journaling is for you. Our mission is to promote your tea room experience as much as possible!

The *TEA TIME JOURNAL* is a unique journal and measures 8½" x 5½". The 80 page book features space to journal 30 tea room visits. You can record your observations on the menus, presentations, service, with room for pictures. The *TEATIME JOURNAL* includes a tea glossary, trivia, tea facts, our favorite scone recipe, tea quiz, and plenty of room for your thoughts and inspirations. The *TEA TIME JOURNAL* is the perfect gift for all tea lovers.

For ordering information see next page or visit our web site at *teatimeadventures.com* and click on "journaling".

A Tea Time Journal
is the perfect gift for
tea lovers everywhere

To order copies of the
TEA TIME JOURNAL, please
provide us with the information listed
below or make a photocopy of this page.
Send your order along with a
check or money order
in the amount of $11.95 USD
($9.95 + $2 S&H for the first book)
and .25 for each additional book
going to the same address
(for foreign shipments, please inquire)

J&S Publishing
2397 N.W. Kings Blvd. # 148
Corvallis, Oregon 97330 USA

If you prefer to pay by credit card,
you may do so on the web at:
www.paypal.com

Name: _____

Address: _____

City: _____

State/Providence/Zip: _____

You may also contact us at:
demontigny@proaxis.com

Tea Rooms Northwest
Your Guide to Tea Rooms, Tea Events and Tea Time Recipes

This book takes you on a journey through Northwest tea rooms with a vivid description of the atmosphere and foods at tea rooms in Oregon, Washington, British Columbia and Northern California.

We invite you to take this book in hand and visit the many outstanding tearooms the Pacific Northwest has to offer.

For more information go to
teatimeadventures.com

$19.95 plus $4.25 S&H for the first book
and .25 for each additional book
going to the same address

J&S Publishing
2397 N.W. Kings Blvd. # 148
Corvallis, Oregon 97330 USA

If you prefer to pay by credit card,
you may do so on the web at:
www.paypal.com

Name: _____

Address: _____

City: _____

State/Providence/Zip: _____

For wholesale information contact us at:
demontigny@proaxis.com

New Tea Room Discoveries

New Tea Room Discoveries